THE PRESENCE OF

# Whales

# THE PRESENCE OF

# Whales

## Contemporary Writings on the Whale

EDITED BY

## FRANK STEWART

Alaska Northwest Books™
Anchorage • Seattle • Portland

Library of Congress Cataloging-in-Publication Data
The presence of whales : contemporary writings on the whale / edited
    by Frank Stewart.
      p.    cm.
    Includes bibliographical references (p. 305) and index.
    ISBN 0-88240-464-4 (acid-free paper)
    1. Whales.    I. Stewart, Frank, 1946–    .
QL737.C4P74   1995
599.5—dc20                         95–2745
                                             CIP

Managing Editor: Ellen Harkins Wheat
Editor: Linda Gunnarson
Production Editor: Kris Fulsaas
Designer: Lynne Faulk

**Photo Credits**: Cover: *Humpback whale, Southeast Alaska.* Michio Hoshino, courtesy of Minden Pictures. Page 21: *Killer whales, Blackfish Sound, British Columbia.* David E. Myers. Page 85: *Female humpback whale and calf, South Kona Coast on the island of Hawai`i.* Wayne Levin. Page 129: *Pilot whales, South Kona Coast on the island of Hawai`i.* Wayne Levin. Page 203: *Humpback whale, North Kohala Coast on the island of Hawai`i.* Wayne Levin. Page 247: *Killer whale, Blackfish Sound, British Columbia.* David E. Myers.

Alaska Northwest Books™
An imprint of Graphic Arts Center Publishing Company
2208 NW Market Street, Suite 300, Seattle, WA 98107
Catalog and order dept.: P.O. Box 10306, Portland, OR 97210
800-452-3032

Printed on acid-free paper in the United States of America

*The story of the whale is so remarkable, that were there not so many witnesses, I would not venture to tell it, lest I be accused of exaggeration.*

—J. D. B. Stillman,
aboard the ship *Plymouth*,
November 1850

# Contents

## DEATH AT SEA AND ON SHORE

## A SPLENDID BUT UNCERTAIN COMPANY

# Acknowledgments

Thanks foremost to Marlene Blessing, whose enthusiasm for whales, nature study, and good writing about nature in general made this book possible. I also wish to thank Ellen Harkins Wheat for consistently invaluable editorial guidance, criticism, and good cheer throughout the project. Linda Gunnarson gave the book keen professional editing. And Kathy Matsueda supported the book by typing the manuscript and organizing the files.

Not least of all, I wish to acknowledge the generous spirit of the scientists and writers whose work is reprinted here.

FRANK STEWART

INTRODUCTION

# To Keep Warm
# All the Great World

Not far from my small farm on the lower slopes of Hawaii's Mauna Kea volcano is a stony, volcanic hill that inclines due west into the deep mid–Pacific Ocean. Located at the terminus of the road from the upland plains to the coastal highway, the hill is nearly bare except for sun-bleached amber grasses, mesquite, and occasional stands of kukui nut trees. Dry and windswept, this is, in many ways, a sacred place. At the base of the hill, a white-sand cove known as Pelekane conceals a submerged stone temple dedicated by the old Hawaiians to the shark gods. Black tips and grays breed here in the shadowy, azure waters. Along the protected shoreline endangered green sea turtles rest and feed.

But the hill itself, called Pu'ukoholā, Hill of the Whale, is even more sacred than the sheltered cove. In 1790, following the divine augury of his priests, King Kamehameha the Great chose the summit as the site for one of his most important temples. The structure's stone platform overlooks an immense oceanic horizon, lapis blue in the luminous sunlight. The ancient Polynesians must have given the hill its name long before the temple was raised and watched in amazement from its crest as the enormous mammals they called koholā breached and spouted in seasonal migrations along the fertile coast.

Koholā's population would have been impressive before the nineteenth century. In his essay in this book, Charles Bergman recalls for us the coastline of Cape Cod as it was recorded by Richard Mather in 1635: "multitudes of great whales . . . spewing up water in the air like the smoke of chimneys and making the sea about them white and hoary . . . which [sight] now has grown ordinary and usual to behold." In the Gulf of St. Lawrence in the seventeenth century, French missionaries complained that there were so many whales—principally northern right whales—they "hindered our rest by their continuous movement and the noise of their spoutings." In 1705, one missionary wrote that whales near the shores of New Brunswick and Nova Scotia were "in such abundance [and] came so close to the land they could be harpooned from the rocks."

Although the Hawaiian and North Pacific waters during the same period probably did not contain the large numbers of right whales found in the Gulf of St. Lawrence, we can only guess at how many cetaceans grazed in the bright subtropical seas. Unlike Native Americans along the New England coast and in the Arctic, and unlike Europeans who hunted the once-plentiful northern right whales to near extinction, the ancient Hawaiians for all their ocean skills were never whalers. They considered the sperm whale a manifestation of one of their gods, and they watched in reverence as it and the many species of this huge, glorious mammal passed through their bays and beyond their reefs.

From the Hill of the Whale today, onlookers can witness lines of humpbacks traveling north each spring along the coast, heading for their feeding grounds off western Canada and Alaska. My fascination with whales began along this same coast many years ago, while motoring in a small fishing boat south of Pu`ukoholā, anxiously scanning the horizon for a distinctive spout or a supple dorsal fin. Young students and friends, we skimmed the hooked point of Kealakekua Bay and worked north again toward Kailua-Kona, dreaming in the salty wind, the motor thrumming, our eyes straining into the blue glare. In those days, in the early 1960s, sighting a humpback was not common in local waters. That you can now observe a plenitude of whales here is a testament to the change of attitude, behavior, and laws occurring within just a generation.

Until 1964, when perhaps fewer than 1,000 humpbacks were left alive in the entire North Pacific, whales were still being commercially pursued off Hawai`i. Today, in contrast, the U.S. Marine Mammal Protection Act makes it a crime to approach within 100 yards of the islands' humpbacks. The act protects the whales not only from relentless hunters with harpoon guns, but also from those armed with cameras, eager to get close enough to caress these great beasts, pat their heads, and scratch their chins. Except for Japan and Norway, which, despite the condemnation of the world community, still insist on slaughtering whales for "research," nations no longer regard these creatures as so many tons of steak, machine oil, or pet food; ingredients for cosmetics, pharmaceuticals, and fertilizer; or the raw materials for umbrellas, corsets, whip handles, buttons, and piano keys. We now feel much as Henry Thoreau did about such killing: "These are petty and accidental uses" for whales, he wrote in *The Maine Woods*, "just as if a strange race were to kill us in order to make buttons and flageolets [flutes] of our bones."

In recent years, numerous books have been written for general audiences about the smaller members of the order Cetacea. Dolphins and porpoises star on television, in movies, and in aquarium shows where they leap through hoops and squeak into microphones. But relatively little has been available to general audiences about the largest species in the order. While scientific knowledge has bounded ahead, few of us—including our popular writers and our poets of the outdoors—ever meet up with great whales. Their world is too remote from our own. And so the leviathan has remained unfamiliar, wrapped in folklore and imagined principally as a shadowy, underwater behemoth, something so large we have to simplify it to comprehend it.

*The Presence of Whales* brings together some of the best contemporary writings on the great whales, creatures such as blues and fins, which are the most immense animals ever to have lived; sleek and massive killer whales, once thought to be the sea's most vicious predators; and the mysterious belugas and narwhals. Led by the voices of particularly eloquent marine scientists, poets, and nature writers, we are brought face to face, in a literary way, with these wild and elusive marine creatures. Here we learn fascinating new facts about whales, gathered through firsthand fieldwork and observations, and hear personal stories of some of the men and women who study cetaceans. At the same time, through informed meditations on the presence of whales, we come to realize why their survival is ethically, spiritually, and ecologically important to us and to the rest of the living world.

The book's opening section, "Sharing the World with Giants," contains essays of an introductory nature, inspired by the writers' close proximity to whales in the open ocean. Next, "Songs from the Deep" explores one of the most fascinating aspects of whale behavior, their calls, so beautiful and cadenced they are referred to as "songs." "Sightings of the Leviathan" presents compelling accounts of tireless fieldwork with whales and includes discussions of the myths that we have spun to account for them. "Death at Sea and on Shore" examines the enigma of whale strandings and the violent deaths that visit whales, reminding us that, for all the sentiment we may have for them, they live in a wild and harsh environment. "A Splendid but Uncertain Company" describes the remarkable privilege humans feel when near whales, and the consequences, both good and bad, of our contact with these grand and in many ways fragile beasts. The book concludes with a list of organizations concerned with whale protection and a list of further readings to guide readers to other works about whales.

In the book's various selections we get to know the kinds of authors who are writing most eloquently about whales today. The majority are scientists whose work demonstrates that deeply felt experience—including the sense of awe and delight that most people feel in the presence of great whales—is not contrary to science and science writing. They are as moved by wonder as the poets, novelists, and nature essayists whose perspectives—based always on firsthand encounters and careful attention to fact—are also included here. Indeed, as environmental writer Bruce Obee observed in his book *Guardians of the Whales,* for all their care to be objective as researchers, cetologists frequently feel "an inconcealable devotion to the animals, a commitment to the whales' unfettered existence in the wild . . . More often than not, it is these scientific 'purists' who are at the forefront of battles over the rights and protection of wild whales."

The scientific study of cetaceans is fairly recent and has come into its own in just the last four decades. The advances in oceanography and marine ecology brought about by defense and weapons research during World War II made possible the dramatic breakthroughs in cetology that occurred in the 1970s and 1980s. As marine biologists in these years documented the widespread destruction of oceanic and coastal zone habitats, they also noted the decline in whale populations, which were falling to their lowest recorded levels—to near zero for some species.

Commercial whaling had much to do with the decline. At its peak in the 1960s, the harvesting of whales reached 66,000 per year, decimating populations that had been pursued for more than 200 years. Once whaling began in earnest in this century, the seven most heavily hunted species were reduced to 20 percent of their estimated pre-exploitation populations, and in some cases to far lower percentages. The southern population of blue whales, for example, is thought to be less than 1 percent of its original level, and humpbacks are estimated to be no more than 3 percent of theirs. Whale killing was not only excessive—and it may yet result in complete extinction of some species that hang on the brink of vanishing—it was also barbaric in its killing methods and in the suffering it caused the animals. On a limited scale, unfortunately it still goes on.

But much has also changed for the good in the past fifteen years. Some species of whales, under international protection—albeit belated—are rebounding. In June 1994, for example, the U.S. Fish and Wildlife Service officially removed the California gray whale from the Endangered Species list. This by no means assures that gray whale populations have completely recovered. Like all whales, they still must cope with polluted waters, tainted food sources, and toxic seabeds. In their case, they are also threatened by the potential ills of inbreeding—the result of having too small a pool of mating individuals. Humpback whales, too, seem to be increasing in number, as do certain species of right whales. Even blue whales, whose imminent extinction was predicted as recently as 1989, seem to be recovering, particularly off the southern coast of California. All is not lost, not yet, thanks to the work of scientists, writers, artists, activists, and ordinary citizens who, as they have increased our knowledge about the marine environment, have changed the world's understanding of the great whales.

In fact, whales have become a popular symbol of the catastrophic effect human activities are having on global biodiversity. If we can destroy such remarkable marine mammals—beasts who do not compete with us for living space, who are not predators on our domestic livestock, who are not physical threats to us in any way, and whose complexity and beauty are impressive and enriching—then nothing is safe from our destructive impulse. That we have such a symbol, and that it has the power to change our hearts and compel us to do better, should encourage us to hope that we can undo some of the damage of the past. Once whales have enthralled a person's imagination, the effect is long-lasting. "It has been absolutely fascinating for me to watch it happen," cetologist Roger Payne has written. Whales "tend to lodge in the breasts of people —sometimes they lodge crosswise where they stick for life."

Today, no matter how accustomed the populace around Pu'ukoholā has become to seeing whales, motorists still stop their cars at the height of the season to view the spectacle of the powerful, wild creatures in the waters below. On the best mornings they can glimpse not only the mottled backs and silver vapor plumes of graceful, forty-ton mammals and their calves cruising north, but also one or more of these grand creatures breaching in a half-turn, their dark shapes flashing within a cascade of jewels, propelled aloft, or so it seems, on huge, scalloped wings, all white below, poised above the waves as though on the verge of flight.

For centuries, people knew whales only in those brief moments when they broke the surface of the sea. The majority of their lives was invisible to humans not only because they roam across vast, uninhabited areas of the earth's surface, but also because they frequent such astonishing depths: nearly 400 feet down for humpbacks like the ones seen gamboling below the Hill of the Whale; and for sperm whales more than 10,000 feet down—a depth at which the pressure in the lightless, frigid water is more than two tons per square inch. For most of human history, then, encountering one of these mammals alive was an experience few people ever had. Not until whales were captured by photography and their images televised did they begin to seem real, their movements in the water graceful, and their habits curiously gentle and unthreatening. Our long-sleeping sympathy for these creatures had suddenly been aroused.

Perhaps zoologist Victor B. Scheffer, author of *The Year of the Whale,* best explains why this affection, once awakened, has become so strong: "Our fascination with whales is compounded by their mystery, their wildness, and their behavior traits resembling those of humans. Many whales live in families, play in the moonlight, talk to one another and care for one another in distress. We are drawn to them because we sense that the bloodlines of the whale and the human long ago were one."

Some 60 million to 100 million years ago, the order Cetacea evolved from four-legged, milk-producing land mammals that gave birth to live young and breathed air through lungs very like our own. But once these creatures entered the ancient seas and gave up shore life, they took on forms and developed behaviors amazingly diverse. The earliest cetaceans included seventy-foot-long monsters that, save for their blade-shaped forelimbs, must have looked like nightmarish serpents cruising the shallow coastal waters for prey. Modern-day whales and dolphins, although they vary markedly in shape, have bodies more like torpedoes than snakes, with horizontal flukes, paddles or flippers, and a nostril opening, or blowhole, at the top of the head. Their kin are found from pole to pole: some flourish in warm, freshwater rivers and lakes, while others prefer frigid polar ice floes; some graze the continental shelves and muddy ocean shallows; and some migrate seasonally farther than any other mammal. About ten species of whales live exclusively in the deep ocean, where virtually nothing of their migratory and social patterns has been uncovered.

Even the number of species in each of the two suborders of living Cetacea (there is a third suborder comprising ancient species identified only through their fossils) is difficult to know for certain. Not only is whale taxonomy controversial and vexing, there is no reason to believe that all cetaceans living on the planet have been discovered. The very largest species—baleen whales such as blues and humpbacks—were thoroughly described as early as 1878. But new species of toothed whales continue to appear: eleven have been distinguished since 1908, including five since 1956. And the latest, the pygmy beaked whale (*Mesoplodon peruvianus* Reyes, Mead, and Van Waerbeek) was discovered in only 1991. At least one other new species of beaked whale has been sighted in the eastern Pacific but has yet to be captured.

Discoveries of new species have not radically altered whale taxonomy, however. Of the two suborders of living cetaceans, the one containing the most species is called Odontoceti, the toothed whales. Approximately sixty-five species belong to this group. They are generally small—under thirty feet in length—and the smallest of them are commonly called porpoises or dolphins.

Not every toothed whale is small, however. Sperm whales, the largest, are massive, reaching sixty feet in length and weighing nearly sixty tons. They often seek their prey thousands of feet below the surface, in the total darkness of the ocean depths, where they easily outmaneuver and overpower squid thirty feet long. Other large toothed whales include Baird's beaked whale, which may reach forty feet in length.

But probably the most striking of all the toothed cetaceans is the so-called killer whale, or orca, which can grow to about thirty-two feet in length, weigh ten tons, and reach speeds of thirty miles per hour. For centuries orcas were regarded as—to use the words of the nineteenth-century whaler and naturalist Charles Scammon—vicious "wolves of the ocean." In her essay "Whale Watcher," reprinted in this book, Paula Bock recounts how their reputations were altered as a result of the first orcas being captured by public aquariums in the mid-1960s. Bock's essay also notes the way orca confinement quickly gave rise to ethical questions concerning the rights of whales to remain in the wild, questions explored further in Jonathan White's interview with Roger Payne.

The other suborder of living whales is called Mysticeti, or baleen whales. This grouping contains at least eleven known species, comprising some of the largest creatures ever to have lived. Feeding primarily on plankton and tiny crustaceans, baleen whales filter their food through rows of bristles, or baleen, hanging from the roofs of their mouths. The palates of some baleen whales may sprout parallel rows of as many as 400 fibrous plates, fringed like hairy sieves. Their methods of feeding include drawing in great gulps of water that massively distend their throats, then expelling the water through the baleen filters with tremendous force, trapping within them the small krill, zooplankton, and other creatures that make up their diet. Other feeding methods include skimming the surface, mouth ajar, for copepod crustaceans, as the right whale frequently does; plowing the bottom for benthic amphipods, as is the habit of gray whales; and weaving a "bubble net" around a school of fish in order to trap them, as humpbacks have been known to do.

The largest Mysticeti are in the family collectively called rorquals, and the largest of these are the blue whales. Almost unbelievably gigantic, blue whales grow to more than 100 feet in length and can weigh more than 180 tons—the equivalent mass of 2,000 human beings. Blue whales fast during much of the winter, but in summer they sustain their powerful bodies by consuming about three million calories each day in the form of forty million small, shrimplike krill less then two inches long. Rolling onto their sides in relatively shallow water and puffing out their massive throats, blue whales charge into thick clouds of the tiny crustaceans, gulp in the krill along with fifty to seventy tons of water, filter this living soup through their baleen, and consume about a ton of food with each swallow.

But as wondrous as these mammoth creatures are, they are only slighty more impressive than the fin whale, which is similar in shape to the blue and is the second largest earth creature: about seventy feet long and weighing more than 100 tons. Unlike their blue cousins, fin whales are dark gray to brownish black, and their heads are colored asymmetrically: pale yellowish to pure white on the right side only. On the darker left side, two lighter stripes called chevrons run along their backs. Some scientists speculate that this lopsided coloration helps the fin whale corral its prey by frightening schools of fish into a tight bunch as it circles them in a clockwise direction.

Besides blue and fin whales, the other rorquals are the sei, Bryde's, minke, and humpback whales. All rorquals are fast swimmers, but their speed, size, and beauty have not protected them from humankind. The giant blue whales, for example, were among the first to be slaughtered nearly to extinction by modern whalers. And their plight has been shared by the members of the two additional families of baleen whales: the various right whales and the bowhead, and the gray whale.

Although we have given these animals names and categorized them in various groups, we actually know little about whale anatomy and all the subtle physical characteristics that distinguish them. And we know even less of their natural history: their feeding methods, reproduction, communication, intelligence, and social dynamics. In fact, as biologist Kenneth Balcomb tells us, "we literally know more about the solar system than we know about the social dynamics of whales."

I remember walking in the warm dawn light on Maui's shoreline several summers ago. The waves were unusually quiet and released a sweet briny odor because it was so early, and the last morning stars still shone. The rocky shore where I stood fell away into the deep channel between Makena and the island of Kaho'olawe close by. Abruptly, out of the placid waves rose a pair of arched, dusky forms so close to me it seemed as if I could touch them. Like silent black wheels, a humpback mother and calf rose and fell effortlessly, rhythmically, through the cool water. The entire dawn seemed to ride on their backs. Beyond them I could see the running lights and brawny iron bulk of a low-lying freighter plying the interisland seas. I couldn't help but remember the impression whales and ships made on John Muir when he reached Alaska in 1879. "Our ship," Muir wrote in a letter home, "with its great iron heart beating on through calm and storm, is a burly, noble spectacle. But think of the hearts of these whales beating warm against the sea, through darkness and night. On and on for centuries. How the red life-blood must rush and gurgle in and out of the huge ventricles, bucketfuls, barrelfuls at a beat. One might well wish to come near these stupendous lives, but no close contact is allowed. We on land, they in the sea to fill and keep warm all the great world."

Muir could not have known how devastating the next hundred years would be for those creatures he reckoned "neighbors in the unexplored wilderness of the sea . . . friends and fellow-citizens in the one harmonious commonwealth of the world." He could only have guessed how, in unhealthy and destructive ways, we would soon crowd these creatures with hearts as mighty as ships' engines. Only in the last half of this century have we come to know how highly specialized whales are, and therefore how vulnerable when confronted with relatively small changes in their environments. The huge frames of many are dependent on tiny prey species, and their oversized organs are susceptible to minute traces of poisons we've dumped into their environments: PCBs, DDT, mirex and its degradation products such as kepone, and other carcinogens.

Charles Mayo, of the Center for Coastal Studies in Provincetown, Massachusetts, summarized recently the plight of the seas in which whales must swim. "Largely for avarice and ignorance we treat the richest eco-system on our earth not as our garden but as our dumping ground," Mayo told a meeting of the American Cetacean Society in 1990. "Clearly there can be no hope for the ocean or for its great whales . . . if we do not learn about the ocean what we are coming to realize too late about the land: that toxic wastes come back to poison us from the places where we dispose of them, that their destructive power is too great to be managed, and that their noxious and far-reaching influence lasts longer than we ever thought . . . To the degree that we can personalize the richness of the ocean system and the delicate balances on which it depends, we may hope to succeed in ultimately saving the whales."

This book is intended to help personalize whales, and to urge readers —with both reason and emotion—to the next step: understanding that we cannot save the whales unless we protect the great oceans and water-ways of the earth. If we fail to preserve their diverse and intricate habitats, we risk "catapulting ourselves into an alien environment," as biologist E. O. Wilson predicts in *The Diversity of Life:* "we will have become like the pilot whales that inexplicably beach themselves on New England shores." Wilson's words recall those attributed to another great naturalist, the Indian chief Seattle: "What happens to beasts can happen to man. All things are connected. If the great beasts are gone, men would surely die of a great loneliness of spirit." *The Presence of Whales* is meant to make us all witnesses, to show us the privilege of being among whales and why their disappearance from our lives would be a tragedy for the human spirit.

Frank Stewart
Kalopā, Hawai`i
December 1994

# Sharing
the World
with Giants

DIANE ACKERMAN

# The Moon by Whale Light

In mid-October 1990, I flew to meet Roger Payne, one of the foremost whale scientists, on the wind-scoured slice of Argentina known as Patagonia, a land renowned for its blustery deserts, unusual wildlife, and rugged, self-reliant people. From the airport at Trelew (named after one of the many Welshmen who settled the region), we drove three hours northeast, to the Valdés Peninsula, a bludgeon-shaped piece of land separating two bays. Because both bays have a small mouth, their waters are much calmer than those of the galloping Atlantic, and migrating right whales stop there every year to raise their babies and engage in courtship, before continuing on south to the krill-rich feeding grounds of Antarctica. Twenty years before, when Roger had realized that the highly endangered right whales were pausing in the bays, he established a study site on the inside curve of the northern bay—on a somewhat hilly, scimitar-shaped beach below two cliffs—and the New York Zoological Society built a field station there. Technically, its address is Lot 39. But Campamento Ballenas

DIANE ACKERMAN's nonfiction books include *The Rarest of the Rare; A Natural History of Love; On Extended Wings*, a memoir about learning to fly; and *A Natural History of the Senses*. She is also an acclaimed poet, whose books include *Jaguar of Sweet Laughter: New and Selected Poems*. The essay printed here, which originally appeared in a slightly different form in *The New Yorker*, was published in *The Moon by Whale Light*. Copyright © 1991 by Diane Ackerman. Reprinted by permission of Random House, Inc.

is what most people call it, pronouncing the double *l* as a "zh," as Patagonians do, filling even their language with the sounds of the wind.

A drive north through flat scrub desert on a road dusty as a mine-shaft led us past a shrine of Coca-Cola bottles. Many years earlier, a woman had died of thirst in this desert, but her infant miraculously survived. Legend had it that the Virgin Mary appeared at the spot where the baby was found. Now Argentinians stopped to leave a tribute of old bottles. Finally, we reached a gate in a wire fence. Roger opened it by fiddling with a lever system made of pipes and wires, and we proceeded down a bumpy, wind-gutted, water-eroded road. On a rise overlooking the camp, we paused a moment. Below us, dwarfed by ancient, fossil-peppered cliffs on the rim of the ocean, surrounded by thorn bushes and ice plants, sat a small, one-story house of white stucco, plus two Quonset huts and an assortment of tents. On the two cliffs—one right behind the main house, the other about a mile away—were small corrugated-metal huts. Night was falling fast, and the ocean had begun to darken, but here and there a small burst of white floated over the water, as if shot from an atomizer, where a whale was surfacing to breathe.

Continuing down to camp, we pulled up to the house. On its cement porch, tripods, cameras, and telescopes were roped to the roof beams to keep them from hitting the ground when they blew over, as they inevitably did. A whale's large weathered jawbone, attached to the wall by chains, made a cozy bench. A wooden swing, hanging from one rafter, rocked gently back and forth as if occupied by a ghost. A handmade birdhouse tucked up against the porch roof held a brown wren-sized bird, a nesting plain-mantled tit spine-tail. Lying next to the front door, part of a whale's skull—four feet across and about three feet wide—served as a table, on which someone had left a windbreaker. The house's windows were made to open and tilt down, to balance binoculars.

Tents were tucked in among the thorn bushes, either near the ocean or on a rise near the main house. Mine was a khaki tent billowing at the edge of the beach. After I zipped the tent closed, horizontally and vertically, I crawled into my down sleeping bag and tried to sleep. The wind, swiveling smartly through the thorn bushes and gulleys, sounded like wet sheets blowing on a line. A snuffling, gargling noise seemed to be right outside the tent. Then a loud snort startled me, and I unzipped the flaps and looked out. There was no wild animal lurking beside my tent or on the beach. A huge moon floated low in the sky. The night was drenched with stars. It was like looking up at a planetarium. Two large cottony blurs hovered overhead, and to my delight I realized they were the Magellanic Clouds—neighboring galaxies of countless stars visible only from the Southern Hemisphere—which I had never seen before. In the moonlight, the ocean poured its black satin, and then a small white cloud appeared, like a corsage just above the water. A loud snuffle followed, and I realized: I have been listening to the night sounds of whales.

In the morning, I woke to loud soughings and raspings, and I looked out and saw four whales lolling close to shore. Rolling and blowing, they waved their flippers in the air, turned lazily, peaked their flukes. I could see, farther out, three more whales blow as they surfaced. Farther still, a lone whale breached, hurling itself high into the air, shattering the water when it hit, sending up great columns of spray; then it breached seven times more. The bay was full of whales. It is as wonderful as discovering dinosaurs in your garden. Petrels, sooty shearwaters, and black-brown albatrosses soared along the beach. Oystercatchers triple-chimed like a doorbell as they patrolled the waves. The air was cold and damp, and I dressed quickly and walked down to the dining hall, just in time to see a hairy armadillo (which Argentinians call a *peludo*) scurrying away from the front door with a crust of bread in its mouth. PELUDO PALACE, a plaque said at the front door. In front of the building, a wooden bench was held up by two perforated cans used to ship snakes. All the antivenin for the local species of pit viper came from snakes captured in camp. Next to the bench, the vertebra of a right whale lay in the sun beside several old anchors.

After breakfast, we packed sandwiches for lunch, put on exposure suits and fishermen's oilskins, and climbed into the Zodiacs. There were many experiments to conduct, and the blustery day was just calm enough to launch the boats. My Zodiac included Tom Ford, a doctor from Massachusetts studying the bacteria in the exhalation of whales; Juan, a university student; Roger's wife, Kate; and Roger, who was at the helm. When we saw whale tails and a lot of spray and movement in the distance, we headed straight for them, slowing down after fifteen minutes as we spiraled close. A confusion of flippers and tails slid across the surface of the water, where a number of whales were rolling. One whale in the middle of the group suddenly rolled upside-down.

"How many whales are we looking at?" I asked.

"That female," Roger said, outlining her body in the air, "is belly-up at the surface, trying to avoid mating. There's a male on the near side of her"—he pointed out a long, dark shape—"and also one on the far side of her." Now I saw the two males surfacing and blowing. "But if you look down, you'll see that there's a third male holding his breath underneath her, waiting for her to turn from the belly-up position, in which her blowhole is underwater and she can't breathe, to a belly-down position. She has to roll in order to breathe. Sooner or later, she's got to roll toward one of the two males flanking her. But when she's on enough of an even keel to be breathing air, she's accessible to the male who's underneath her. A mating group often includes this many males. If one of them leaves the group after he's mated with the female, then she can easily avoid the other two, and that means they won't get a chance to mate with her. If there are four males, though, and if two mate with her and leave, the other two won't necessarily get a chance to. So you get into very complicated situations, in which some males have no opportunity to mate with a particular female."

"This doesn't sound very cheery from the female's point of view," I said. Rolling over to breathe, the female whale gave out an aggressive growl as a male put a flipper across her back. With a twist, she pulled a few yards away and the three males followed her. She rolled onto her back again.

"Okay. Let's look at it from her point of view," Roger said. "If you are a female coming into this area, you don't have any means of choosing a mate, and chances are you're going to be raped repeatedly by males in a group. But there is one way you can favor a particular male. You can wait until you're mated with by the male you wish to be mated with and then just leave the area. You get the hell out as fast as you can. I think that's what's happening here."

As we watched the melee of mating, it was tough to tell which parts belonged to which whale. A shadow climbed the female's belly, and she flailed and swerved. Being upside-down did not protect her from mating, because a male whale's erect penis, which is tapered, can be as much as nine feet long. And it is controllable. A human male cannot voluntarily move his penis by more than a few millimeters, but a right whale can move his all around like a long finger. It's stored inside the whale, and when he's swimming around, it is invisible. He also has internal testes. Human males have external testes, because the testes must stay cool or the male won't be fertile. Nobody really understands how whales can have their testes inside, for streamlining, and not have their fertility affected. When a whale dies, the penis is extruded. All European woodcuts depicting dead sperm whales on a beach show a whale with an extended penis. Every sperm whale north of forty degrees north latitude is male; so every sperm whale stranded in Europe was a male.

Half a mile away, a whale's tail hovered in the air, splashed down, then hovered again, this time for quite a while. He was only indulging a favorite whale pastime; they entertain themselves by balancing their tails in the air. It is like someone holding a stick on the tip of his finger.

Hours had quickly passed, and Kate broke out a sack of ham-and-cheese sandwiches and small, sweet Argentine tangerines and passed them around. Roger unwrapped a camera with a telephoto lens, stood up, and photographed the fine display of mating and balancing whales. Then he carefully wrapped the camera and stowed it in a watertight trunk.

"In right whales, you have a very curious thing," he said, sitting down. "The testes of a male blue whale, the largest whale in the world, weigh about seventy kilos—a hundred and fifty-four pounds—combined. You might ask: 'What do the testes of a male right whale weigh, since it's a much smaller animal?' The answer is one metric ton—twenty-two hundred pounds! These are the largest testes ever recorded in any animal."

"Why should there be such a difference?"

"For a very interesting reason, which has been most clearly demonstrated among the primates," Roger said. "Thirty-three species of primates have been studied in which something is known about both the weight of the testes in the male and their techniques of mating—whether a given female mates with one male or with several males. If you plot a graph of testes weight versus body size, you discover that those primate species in which several males mate with the same female have testes that are much larger than those in which only one male mates with a female. The classic example is the difference between a chimpanzee and a gorilla. The chimp, a species that has multiple matings, has testes much larger than a human being's, and they're very visible. Now consider the great, big, brutish gorilla male, which has total dominion over a group of females. Someone may eventually challenge him for his position, but until then when he mates with a female, he has no doubt that he is the father of her offspring. He therefore has to produce only enough sperm to fertilize an egg in each of his females. The result is that he has such small testes that when you dissect a male gorilla, you can hardly find them. The reason a chimpanzee has such large testes is that when he mates with a female, she has probably just mated with another male, and if he is to have any hope of success, he must produce enough sperm to wash out the contribution of sperm from the previous male and replace it with his own."

"And in the case of human beings?" I asked.

Roger laughed. "Yes, that's the tantalizing question. If you look at the chart, everything with outsized testes is several males mating with a female, and everything with small testes is a monogamous species in which females and males are faithful to each other. Human beings lie right on the borderline, and it's hard to predict which side they're going to fall toward. That may partly explain our marital ambiguities and the problems we cause ourselves socially. Consider whales and their mating systems. Right whales are the supreme example of incredible sperm competition. A male who is going to mate with a female is competing with a whole series of males. When you watch the mating groups here, for instance, you see that a single female mates with several males in the course of an afternoon. If you are a male, probably your best strategy for any given mating session is to be the last, not the first. The male that mates last is the one that has the most sperm of his left in the female. He is presumably producing colossal quantities of sperm and flooding it into the female's reproductive tract, trying to fill it as much as possible with his sperm and, again, trying to wash out the sperm of the previous males."

"*Ballenas!*" Juan called, pointing a few hundred yards behind us to where three whales were swimming in tandem. A mother and baby were being followed at a short distance by an adolescent whale.

"That's probably her calf from the previous year," Roger said, and went on: "One of the things I've noticed over the years is often when several males are trying to mate with a female, one of the males will try to push the female under the water so that he can mate with her, and it's always a failure. And I thought, what a bozo this whale is, until I finally realized that I was the one who was a bozo. What I was watching was one male pushing a female under for the purpose of letting another male mate with her. That's not a bad strategy if what you want to do in a few hours' session is be the last to mate. But it's the kind of strategy that would also invite cheating. The best way to get around cheating would be to be in a group of males that include male relatives of yours. Then even if it's another male who gets in the successful last mating—the mating that will result in fertilization of the egg—the sperm that won would at least have most of your genes in it. But now you've got a problem. You can't identify your father, nor can he identify you. You haven't got a clue who he is. So you can't go join your father's mating group. But there is a male relative that you *can* identify, and that's your brother. You know who your mother is—you lived with her for a year or fourteen months before you were weaned—and if she comes back with a young calf and if it's a male, it's your brother and you know that.

"Well, here's where a truly fascinating thing comes up. The females with calves in Argentina are spread out along the same section of coast. They move together as a group, but their interactions at very close range are fairly infrequent. For the most part, they're strung out like beads on a string. They seem to be aware of where the others are, and they avoid one another in some ways but stick together very strongly. A female with one calf might swim up to another female with a calf, and everything is fine until the calves begin to play. The second the calves begin to play, the mothers break it up, working hard if necessary. They will swim assiduously between the two calves until each one gets her calf to swim off with her. Why? Because at this time of the year, the mother is starving. She has swum up from the feeding grounds, which are maybe a couple thousand miles away, without eating; she has given birth to a calf without eating, and has pumped a blubber coat onto it and increased its size enormously without eating; and she must return to the feeding grounds without eating. She has been starving for several months. Every single motion that her calf makes she pays for, so what she does is lead it away from any kind of play—except the one kind she tolerates—she appears to tolerate play with an adolescent.

"Now, here comes our big frustration. We can identify whales best when we're looking directly down on top of them from a plane, because of their callosities [the bumps on their heads], whose pattern, placement, size, and form are different on every whale—we can easily tell them apart. But to follow the whales that way means paying two hundred dollars an hour to fly, and that's ruinously expensive. We can't afford to hang around long enough to watch much behavior, so we really don't know who these adolescents are that the females allow to play with their young. My suspicion is that they are older brothers and that what the mothers are doing is allowing brothers to get to know each other, so that later on they can become a more effective mating group, which in turn will ensure that her genes have a better chance of being passed on. We have one example of a mating group that stayed together for almost six weeks and traveled together for 185 miles. That means that there would be a chance for reciprocal altruism to go into effect. One male could help another today, and the other returns the favor tomorrow."

The adolescent whale drifted away from the mother and calf

and began swimming slowly toward us, curious, no doubt, about a black rubber fish with many moving animals inside it. Then, blowing and tossing its tail, it dove directly under the boat. A long shadow, spotted with white at one end where the head's callosities glowed, floated underneath us for what seemed like minutes. It surfaced with a blow, rolled onto one side, and curved back toward us. Its tail had a slightly ragged line of notches, probably orca bites.

"Watch the tail," Roger warned. "If you ever see the tail coming down on you, leap fast into the water. Don't even think about it. Just jump. You don't want to get crushed between the boat and the tail." But the whale dove back underneath the boat, rolling onto one side, apparently so it could look at us, then surfaced on the other side and blew a fine mist, which poured over us, smelling sweet, like wet fur. The whale circled back again and this time swam right alongside the boat. Its huge head, floating on the surface, came so close I could look into the blowholes, opening and closing like two hands held palms-together and pressing wide apart like a bellows at fingers and thumbs. A few hairs sprouted around the blowholes. Still quite young, the whale was only about thirty-five feet long. It had thick callosities, with whale lice clinging all over them, and the black skin was streaked with fine lines of the sort one sees on a window after rain. Males tend to have more callosities, as well as scrapes along their backs from fighting; and we thought this was a male. It brought its mouth toward the boat and nudged it. Stretching over the gunwale, I touched its head delicately with one finger. Its whole body flinched. How can it be so sensitive that it can feel a human's slightest touch? I wondered. And its skin was startlingly soft, like oiled chamois.

The sound of light artillery in the distance drew our gaze to two breaching whales, hurling themselves into the air, half-twisting, like a top running out of momentum, and splashing onto their sides in thick geysers of spume. By then, the adolescent had returned to the other side of the boat and was languidly rubbing one whole flank along the gunwale, as a cat might twine between someone's legs. After several passes, it swam away, leaving "footprints" behind it—large pools of smooth, calm, glassy water. The afternoon had already dwindled into the short hours of twilight. The falling sun had lost a lot of its heat, and we were all starting to feel chilly, so we headed back to camp. Near shore, we watched a whale roll over and over; there were many shells and pebbles in the shallows, and it could have been scratching the way a dog enjoys rolling in the dirt. It waved a flipper in the air, followed with the semaphore of its flukes. At last we landed on the beach and dragged the Zodiac into the boathouse.

At sunset, an orange fur lay along the horizon and the sea grew blue-gray. Areas of wet sand, exposed by the withdrawing tide, shone like an array of hand mirrors. Venus appeared overhead, bright as a whistle blow, with the small pinprick light of Mercury at its side. As night fell, the shallows shimmered like ice and the frantic winds began to sound like freight trains. The wind has a large vocabulary in Patagonia. It shushes through the thorn bushes, it rattles the corrugated-metal walls; it flutes through the arroyos; it makes the cliffs sound as if they are being scoured by a wire whisk. A night heron cried *owow*. A whale sneezing loudly sounded as if an iron patio chair were being dragged across a cement floor. In the distance, three whales blew bushes of mist. Over the apricot horizon, the sky billowed upward, pale green to thick teal to a translucent wafer of azure blue.

After dinner, I hunted my way back to the tent, behind a sheep fence and among a clutch of thorn bushes, on the ledge of the beach; zipped my tent shut; and crawled into my sleeping bag.

Fifteen minutes later, I heard footsteps outside. "Asleep yet?" Kate said. "I think there's an orca calling. Come on down to the beach."

At the shoreline, Tom was holding a tape recorder attached to a hydrophone line running out into the bay. Over the years, Roger had produced a library of right-whale recordings. Right whales make many different sounds: funny, serious, strange, underwater, in the air. Probably, they mean a variety of things; it's more mystery that remains to be solved. Despite the full moon, the sea and sky blurred in a creamy fog both eerie and radiant. Small green bioluminescent creatures flashed from the shallows. Whales glittered as they surfaced, and the moon seemed only their reflection. Close to shore, a right whale blew loudly. Another whale sneezed. The hydrophone picked up a stretched meow. No orcas were calling, but many right whales sighed and bleated through the pallid fog under the brilliant moon. Shivering, we decided to call it a night and returned to our tents and huts for a chilly sleep.

Over the next few days, camp life continued on its routine of hard work by day and antic bilingual meals at night. The ocean was too cold to bathe in, and people took turns driving an old pickup truck into Puerto Madryn to fill up the drinking-water jugs and buy fresh food. Inflation had skyrocketed in Argentina, and a truck bought for $2,000 ten years before was now worth several times that. But no one could afford to sell his truck, since new ones were much more expensive, whereas repairs were relatively cheap. All machinery—cars, generators, pumps—was in a perpetual state of mended dereliction. The camp's generator wasn't working, and the water tanks behind the house were also broken. Sometimes, dead rats were found floating in them, and we joked about passing out drinking water *con rata* or *sin rata*, as if they were just hairy ice cubes. Luckily, a workman was putting things back in order.

Although a core group of researchers remained in the camp, dozens of new people arrived and others departed. Doug Allen, an underwater photographer, who had curly red hair, a sunburn, and a thick Scottish accent, dropped by regularly and charmed us with his stark independence and gentle gregariousness, a combination very Patagonian. We adopted his word *suss*, which means to spy out something. One day, he casually reported that when he was in the water that morning, filming, he got too close to a calf and was walloped on the back of the head hard enough "to see stars." He believed that it was an accident, but he was clearly shaken; nevertheless, he would go out filming close to whales again the next day. A British filmmaker, John Waters, and his wife and their six-week-old baby, who had been born in a nearby town, came to live in camp for a while. A Japanese film crew stopped by for two days of filming. Whale researchers from Puerto Madryn came and went, as well as two game wardens. The New York Zoological Society, which ran and supported the camp, in part, had arranged for members on a guided tour of Patagonia to drop in for an hour or so. Another, similar group, we were delighted to discover, included John Emlen, the now-retired field biologist who had inspired Roger, George Schaller, and many other scientists to go out and study the ways of animals in the wild.

What drew researchers, film crews, and tourists alike was not just the abundance of whales in the bays but the continuity of Roger's work. Just as the callosities on right whales' heads made individuals easy to identify, so did the markings on the tails of humpbacks. But humpbacks are difficult to study. They have never been observed mating, for example. At the whale camp, researchers could live and work very close to right whales and watch their social behavior and record their sounds. Roger felt lucky to have found a species of whale that could be conveniently observed from shore. The camp was conducting the world's longest whale study based on known individuals. Each year researchers flew over in a plane, took photographs, and compared them to a file of known individuals. As of the most recent count, 960 whales had been identified. There were some right whales near South Africa, some off Australia, but only a total of about 3,500 left in the world. In the bays we explored, there were said to be about 1,200. Roger studied humpbacks in many areas, but right whales only in Patagonia, from this remarkable site.

One day, after the Japanese film crew packed up their gear and disappeared down the road in a tornado of dust, Roger and I sat on the porch steps and talked about Japanese whaling. If Roger had been especially generous with the film crew, who were making a two-hour documentary to be shown on Japanese television, it was because Japan desperately needs to change its attitude toward whales.

"The world has whales that appear to be intelligent, that can sing songs, change those songs, and use rhyme and human laws of composition," Roger said. "They form bubble nets of great intricacy and complexity and cooperatively feed together in clever ways. This is not the sort of animal you should turn into fat and oil and lipstick and margarine and cat food and corset stays. Whaling isn't something that has ever improved people very much. I'm going to Japan later in the year to talk with the Japanese people about whales. Once the people learn about this animal, their indifference, which is always based on ignorance, will be replaced by fascination, which is based on knowledge. I haven't the slightest doubt that their feelings about whales will change, and of course, they'll decry whaling, just as other peoples of the world have."

"The Japanese people have been good at protecting cranes, albatrosses, and other endangered animals," I mentioned.

"I have no quarrel with the Japanese people, only with their whalers—ruthless hunters who have no future," Roger said. "I had a grandfather, a lumberman, who cut nothing but walnut trees, sometimes for whole years at a time, and that excess on his part, and on the part of his contemporaries, ensured that I would never have walnut except as the most exotic of woods. He was shortsighted. Was anyone warning him? I bet there was. Going on with the destruction of a species until it's brought to the point of extinction is madness—not just a little mad or slightly mad. It's authentic madness."

In the evening I shifted my gear to the corrugated-metal hut on top of the hill behind the house, from which I'd have a panoramic view of the bay. This meant climbing a steep, skiddy winding path for three hundred feet whenever I needed something. But the hut rattled wonderfully in a dozen registers of metal and wood, and became an instrument played by the Patagonian winds. The walls gyrated like a rocket during lift-off. The wind slaloming through the dunes made a hallucination of footsteps outside. Quite often, the roof banged so hard at opposite corners that it sounded as if a hand were ripping it straight off. Inside, a narrow bed attached to one wall had a small window beside the pillow, cut there at the request of a young woman who wanted to see the moon rising as she fell asleep. On another wall, a window looked out over camp and the sea. A third wall was a bookcase with peeling shelves. The fourth had nails as clothes hooks, with a warped table beneath. The entire hut was only about six feet by eight feet, and perhaps seven feet high. A candle sat in a wobbly three-legged holder, and poured wax down its shoulders as it guttered in the draft. Although the hut got hot during the day, it was not wise to leave the door open, because sheep or guanacos or pit vipers might wander in.

At sunset, Roger and I sat on the jawbone bench on the porch of the main house and watched the horizon's simmering cauldron of red. Enthralled by Doug's account of swimming close to whales, I was puzzled by how few of the people in camp had been tempted to do the same.

"It's those last ten feet," Roger said, leaning against the wall that had grown warm from the late-afternoon sun. "That's where most people find their nerve breaks down."

"But that's what life's all about," I said. "That's where you find all the intimate details. How awful it would feel, at the end of your life, to look back and know that if you had just stayed in there a few more feet, you would have witnessed something truly astonishing."

Roger nodded. He had spent his life walking the narrow corridor between the whale's world and the human's world. "I think you can know people quite well by the distance at which they drop back. Think how many miles all the people here had to fly, how many hardships they had to endure, how many hours they had to wait, how many people they had to deal with, just to get down here. It's like that every year. Some people drop out before they ever leave the States. Some are fine doing research on the shore. Some can even tough it out in the boats, but they panic at the thought of being in the water with whales. Some can get into the water and watch at a distance—but the last ten feet horrify them. Despite all the rigors and turmoil they're gone through to get here, despite their fascination with whales, which they spend their lives studying, they just can't face those last few feet. I don't think this is limited to whales. It has to do with the way a person needs to know life."

At the south end of the bay, a whale lifted its tail into the air and held it there, drifting downwind for five minutes. Then it swam back upwind, turned around and put its tail in the air, and drifted downwind again. Roger slapped his knee in delight. The whale was "sailing," using its broad tail in place of canvas and catching a stiff breeze to blow it across the bay. Right whales sometimes practice sailing for half an hour at a time; it appears to be one of their favorite sports. You'd think many animals would sail, since it saves energy and is probably fun. But the only other animals that do it are three species of jellyfish. When you get into the upper latitudes—the roaring 40s, the frantic 50s, and the screaming 60s, as scientists refer to them—you have perfect conditions for sailing. Why waste all that time and energy wiggling your tail violently back and forth to swim if you can just put it up in the air and sail?

As evening deepened, we sat quietly, watching the upside-down whale, the wind behind its broad tail, still sailing merrily across the bay. Close in, the ocean seemed to be moving fast from right to left. But on the horizon, it didn't seem to be moving at all.

"The whole thing is a giant wheel," Roger said, holding an open hand up and tilting it slowly, "turning just as the planet is turning." Three oystercatchers flew low across the sand in front of us, scolding a petrel until it flew out of their territory.

We say dawn breaks, as if something were shattering, but what we mean is that waves of light crest over the earth. The next morning, rinsed by those light waves, I walked along the beach, beside overhanging cliffs, and realized what an ancient place the camp was based on. The cliffs were almost solid fossil—uplifted prehistoric seabeds. Fossil oysters large enough to have held more than a pound of meat jutted out from the top, and fossil sand dollars perhaps seventy million years old lay at the base. Fossil sea lions, crabs, and whales littered the beach. There was an array of dead penguins and other birds on the beach, too. In the tide wrack were feathers, flippers, mummified animals, and countless shells. Dunes of stones led down to the water. One thing the ocean does exceptionally well is sort according to size. There were fields of large stones, then ridges of medium-size ones, then areas of even smaller stones. Looking out at the water, I saw a mother and baby whale lolling in the shallows. When had they arrived? Rolling on her side, the mother whale swung her flippers up and nursed the baby. When a pack of seals appeared, and began playfully to pester them, the baby snuggled up to its mother and cupped its flipper around her. The whales appeared to have stopped in the water, but the faster I walked toward them, the more they seemed to be just another yard ahead of me. Finally, I left them and headed for breakfast at the Peludo Palace.

After coffee, cheese, and cereal-crackers, Roger, Judy Perkins—who was at the field station to collect skin samples from whales so that she could map their genealogy—and I climbed into a car with Rubén, the pilot, and set out for the airstrip half an hour away. Roger pushed the windshield-washer button, but nothing happened. "No skunks," he said in Spanish to Rubén. Patagonians call the squirting washers "skunks." As a car passed us from the opposite direction, its driver put a hand against the front window. Roger did the same. In Argentina, car windows are made to shatter utterly on impact, so that someone thrown through the window in an accident won't get slashed by glass. Unfortunately, a sharp flying stone can shatter the glass, too, so locals mistakenly think they can hold the windshield together with one hand. Whenever they pass an oncoming car, they prop a hand against the windshield.

Rubén's Cessna 182 was hangared at a nearby *estancia*, next to a long dirt airstrip. Each year Rubén flies Roger and other camp people out over the bays, to photograph whales. Because the plane's tail letters are LV-JCY, Roger's children used to call it Love Juicy. We climbed aboard and headed for the southern bay, which was said to be packed with whales. Rubén spotted whales in the water, flew straight to them, and did steep turns around them at three hundred feet, while Roger knelt and shots pictures of each animal. On an outline of the peninsula, I penciled in ♀ + ♀ + (two females, with one calf each) at our approximate position and, a little farther along, another ♀ +. As Roger finished each roll of film, I handed him a fresh one and marked the number of the roll and the date on the used one. After an hour of steep turns, we headed back to the airstrip. Rubén rolled out a yellow drum of gas and attached a green hand pump to it that looked like a coffee grinder. Judy pumped gas from it into a hose, which Rubén fed into a can topped with chamois (to filter out contaminating water), and pumped the gas from the can into the wing. It was a lengthy process. Then Rubén and Judy climbed aboard and in a moment we were airborne again, flying over the great flat deserts. Sheep trails converged and overlapped at the far-flung water tanks. In a few minutes, Rubén landed on a dirt road, paused just long enough for me to get out, turned the plane around, and took off to spend the day photographing whales. Three kilometers from camp, at the spot where the camp road meets the main one, I began walking down roads that resembled gutted riverbeds. A herd of ten guanacos took flight when they saw me. Two mares ("rabbits with white miniskirts," Roger called them) scampered away as I passed, and lizards swaggered under bushes. In an hour, I stood on the rise overlooking camp. Two boat trails leading from the boathouse to the water told me that the station's graduate students were already out at work. When I got to the house, I was struck by the stillness and silence. Everyone was gone. Climbing up to my hut, I took off my jacket and walked out to the cliff hut, a little less than a mile away. An icy morning had turned into a torrid noon, which would no doubt drop to near freezing by nightfall. From the cliff hut, I saw below in the water the same mother and baby I had seen earlier. She had a large, distinctive wound on one flank, and the callosities on her snout formed a sort of parenthesis. To some earlier observer, they resembled fangs, and thus she was named Fang. Her new calf nestled beside her. They had spent all morning close to camp. The sunlight made a glittering path over the water. Each time the whales surfaced, drops of water sparkled around them.

Fang and her calf were close below me, but the whole bay was a waltz of mother and baby whales. Right whales are pregnant for only about a year, which seems like a short time. After all, an elephant calf gestates for twenty-two months, and a whale is larger than an elephant. When an elephant calf is born it has to scramble up onto its legs, but a whale calf can go straight from the amniotic fluid of its mother's womb into the womb of the ocean. It doesn't have to support itself. Whales, being warm-blooded mammals, which breathe as we do, could, in principle, live on land, but if a whale were on land, its organs would be crushed under its own weight. It needs the water to support its massive size, which is one of the reasons stranded whales fare so poorly. Because a whale baby doesn't have to stand up, its bones are so flexible that you could take the rib bone of a baby whale and bend it back and forth as if it were made of hard rubber. Baby whales are virtually weightless. It's as though they were flying. Another lovely thing about whale mothers and babies is that a mother whale is herself 97 percent water. When she speaks, the sound she makes travels directly through the water, through her body and her womb, and her baby hears it. But because there is no air in the womb, the baby can't speak back. The baby must wait in the mother's womb for a year, listening, until it's born into a world where it can finally answer.

A newborn whale calf does not leave its mother's side but often swims along eye to eye with her. Sometimes the mother whale swims so that with every downstroke of her tail, she touches the calf. Sometimes the calf gets obstreperous and bangs into its mother, or even breaches onto its mother's back. Finally, she will lose her patience and punish it by rolling over quickly onto her back as the calf is ready to ram her for, say, the fifteenth time. Then she catches it by the small of its tail and holds it underwater so that it begins spluttering, wheezing, sneezing, coughing. In a little while she lets it go. After that, the calf resumes its eye-to-eye position and is careful not to act up again. Hungry calves will butt their mothers, climb all over them, and slide off them, trying to get their mothers to roll over and let them nurse. Occasionally, a mother will calm a hyperactive calf by sliding underneath it and turning over to pick it up out of the water and balance it on her chest, holding it between her flippers. Every now and then, with a flipper the size of a wall, a mother reaches over and pats the calf sweetly.

For hours, I sat quietly and watched the busy nursery bay. Fang rolled onto her weighty side, and her baby nursed. Then the baby got rambunctious and strayed a little too far. Mother lowed to it in a combination of foghorn and moo, calling it back within eyeshot. From time to time, Fang submerged slowly, her tail hanging limp and loose, trailing one tip of a fluke in the water. She made burpy sounds, with occasional moans, and I think she may have been napping.

When a whale sleeps, it slowly tumbles in an any-old-crazy, end-over-end, sideways fashion, and may even bonk its head on the bottom. Or it just lies quietly, looking like a corpse. When it rises again to breathe in the midst of its sleep, it comes up as slow as a dream, breaks the surface, breathes a few times, and, without even diving, falls again slowly toward the bottom. Right whales sometimes sleep in the mornings on calm days in Argentina, and some of them seem to be head-heavy, with light tails. The result is that they fall forward and their tails rise out of the water. They're so fat that they float when relaxed, and they spend a lot of time with their backs in the air. When they're asleep at the surface, their breathing rate drops tremendously, they don't close their nostrils completely between breaths, and so sometimes they snore. In fact they make marvelous, rude, after-dinner noises as they sleep. When they wake, they stretch their backs, open their mouths, and yawn. Sometimes they lift their tails up and shake them, and then they go about their business. Often, they sleep at the surface so long on calm days that their backs get sunburned; and then they peel the same way humans do, but on a big, whale-size scale. The loose skin from their backs falls into the water and becomes food for birds. When they breach, they shed a lot of loose skin as they hit the water, and seagulls, realizing this, fly out fast to a breaching whale. Not much skin sheds from the tail. The gulls know that, and when a whale is merely hitting its tail on the water, they don't bother with it.

A gull swept down, pulled a piece of skin from Fang's back, and Fang, in obvious pain, shook her head and tail simultaneously, flexed almost in half, then dove underwater. The gull flew to another pair of whales nearby, attacked them, and went off. A bizarre habit had developed among the gulls in this bay. Instead of waiting for the whales to shed skin, they landed on the backs of whales and carved the skin and blubber off. Two species of gulls—the brown-headed gulls and kelp gulls—yanked off long strips of skin and set up feeding territories on the backs of their own particular whales. When Roger first started studying right whales at Valdés Peninsula, he noticed that only brown-headed gulls were peeling the skin off the backs of sleeping, sunburned whales. Soon, however, the kelp gulls not only learned this technique but also began carving holes in backs. The result was that whales like Fang were pitted with craters made by gulls. When a gull landed on a whale's back, the whale panicked. This year there were fewer whales in the bay, and Roger thought the kelp gulls might have been chasing them away, to bays where kelp gulls don't yet know the tricks.

Juan, a graduate student, appeared at the edge of camp, on foot, apparently hiking in from a walk to a neighboring bay. By the time I got back to the main house, he was just arriving, wearing shorts, a T-shirt, and a knitted hat.

"Tired?" I asked with an inflection that said, *I really hope you aren't.* "Want to go find some whales?"

He grinned. "Just let me get a Coke, then *vamos.*"

I put on a leotard and tights and began crawling into a half-inch-thick wetsuit that included Farmer John overalls, a beaver-tail jacket, boots, gloves, and a hood. There was so much neoprene in the suit, trapping air, that I'd need to wear weights around my waist to keep from bobbing on the surface.

Sitting on the porch whale skull, John Waters watched me suit up. He looked anxious. "Be careful," he said. "This morning, I was out in a boat with Tom collecting breath samples and the calf of that mother over there"—he pointed to Fang and her baby, just around the curve of the beach—"rocked the boat with its flipper and gave us a scare."

To tell the truth, if I was going swimming I'd have felt much safer with Roger on board, but I had been waiting all week for the water to calm down and all afternoon for Roger to get back from flying. It was already past four, and I very much doubted that he intended to return before sunset. So, some of my caution evaporated, and I knew it was now or never.

Juan returned from the Peludo Palace and tugged on a thin wetsuit and boots, and we went down to the beach, where Minolo, another graduate student, joined us in the Zodiac. As we pulled out, I saw John and Tom on the porch, standing next to the sighting scopes. Heading north along the bay, we came upon two mothers and calves, but the mothers were naturally protective of their calves and hurried them away. We wanted to find a young adult. Juan had been collecting loose skin for Judy and then going into the water to photograph the heads of the whales it came from in order to identify them. I hoped to join him. We searched for an hour but found none in the mood to be approached. Finally, we headed back toward camp and, coming around a bend, discovered Fang and her calf still playing. We cut the motor about two hundred yards from the whales. Juan and I slipped over the side of the boat and began to swim toward them, approaching as quietly as possible, so that they wouldn't construe any of our movements as aggressive. In a few minutes, we were only yards from the mother's head. Looking down, I saw the three-month-old baby beside her underwater, its callosities bright in the murky green water. Slowly, Juan and I swam all the way around them, getting closer and closer. The long wound on Fang's flank looked red and angry. When her large tail lifted out of the water, its beauty stunned me for a moment, and then I yanked Juan's hand, to draw his attention, and we pulled back. At fifty feet long, weighing about fifty tons, all she would have needed to do was hit us with a flipper to crush us, or swat us with her tail to kill us instantly. But she was moving her tail gently, slowly, without malice. It would be as if a human being, walking across a meadow, had come upon a strange new animal. Our instinct wouldn't be to kill it but to get closer and have a look, perhaps touch it. Right whales are grazers, which have baleen plates, not teeth. We did not look like lunch. She swung her head around so that her mouth was within two feet of me, then turned her head on edge to reveal a large white patch and, under that, an eye shaped much like a human eye.

I looked directly into her eye, and she looked directly back at me, as we hung in the water, studying each other.

*I wish you well*, I thought, applying all the weight of my concentration, in case it was possible for her to sense my mood. I did not imagine she could decipher words, but many animals can sense fear in humans. Perhaps they can also sense other emotions.

Her dark, plumlike eye fixed me and we stared deeply at one another for some time. The curve of her mouth gave her a Mona Lisa smile, but that was just a felicity of her anatomy. The only emotion I sensed was her curiosity. That shone through her watchfulness, her repeated turning toward us, her extreme passivity, her caution with flippers and tail. Apparently, she was doing what we were—swimming close to a strange, fascinating life-form, taking care not to frighten or hurt it. Perhaps, seeing us slip over the side of the Zodiac, she thought it had given birth and we were its young. In that case, she might have been thinking how little we resembled our parent. Or perhaps she understood only too well that we were intelligent beasts who lived in the strange, dangerous world of the land, where whales can get stranded, lose their bearings and equilibrium, and die. Perhaps she knew somehow that we live in that desert beyond the waves from which whales rarely return, a kingdom we rule, where we thrive. A whale's glimpse of us is almost as rare as our glimpse of a whale. They have never seen us mating, they have rarely if at all seen us feeding, they have never seen us give birth, suckle our young, die of old age. They have never observed our society, our normal habits. They would not know how to tell our sex, since we hide our reproductive organs. Perhaps they know that human males tend to have more facial hair than females, just as we know that male right whales tend to have more callosities on their faces than females. But they would still find it hard to distinguish between a clothed, short-haired clean-shaven man and a clothed, short-haired woman.

When Fang had first seen us in the Zodiac, we were wearing large smoked plastic eyes. Now we had small eyes shaped like hers—but two on the front of the head, like a flounder or a seal, not an eye on either side, like a fish or a whale. In the water, our eyes were encased in a glass jar, our mouths stretched around a rubber tube, and our feet were flippers. Instead of diving like marine mammals, we floated on the surface. To Fang, I must have looked spastic and octopuslike, with my thin limbs dangling. Human beings possess such immense powers that few animals cause us to feel truly humble. A whale does, swimming beside you, as big as a reclining building, its eye carefully observing you. It could easily devastate you with a twitch, and yet it doesn't. Still, although it lives in a gliding, quiet, investigate-it-first realm, it is not as benign as a Zen monk. Aggression plays a big role in its life, especially during courtship. Whales have weapons that are equal in their effects to our pointing a gun at somebody, squeezing a finger, and blowing him away. When they strike each other with their flukes in battles, they hit flat, but they sometimes slash the water with the edge. That fluke edge could break a person in two instantly. But such an attack has never happened in the times people have been known to swim with whales. On rare occasions, unprovoked whales have struck boats with their flukes, perhaps by accident, on at least one occasion killing a man. And there are three reported instances of a whale breaching onto a boat, again resulting in deaths. But they don't attack swimmers. In many of our science-fiction stories, aliens appear on earth and terrible fights ensue, with everyone shooting weapons that burn, sting, or blow others up. To us, what is alien is treacherous and evil. Whales do not visualize aliens in that way. So although it was frightening to float beside an animal as immense and powerful as a whale, I knew that if I showed her where I was and what I was and that I meant no harm, she would return the courtesy.

Suddenly, Juan pulled me back a few feet and, turning, I saw the calf swimming around to our side, though staying close to its mother. Big as an elephant, it still looked like a baby. Only a few months old, it was a frisky pup and rampantly curious. It swam right up, turned one eye at us, took a good look, then wheeled its head around to look at us with the other eye. When it turned, it swung its mouth right up to my chest, and I reached out to touch it, but Juan pulled my hand back. I looked at him and nodded. A touch could have startled the baby, which might not have known its own strength yet. In a reflex, its flipper or tail could have swatted us. It might not have known that if humans are held under-water—by a playful flipper, say—they can drown. Its flippers hung in the water by its sides, and its small callosities looked like a crop of field-stones. When it rolled, it revealed a patch of white on its belly and an anal slit. Swimming forward, it fanned its tail, and the water suddenly felt chillier as it stirred up cold from the bottom. The mother was swim-ming forward to keep up with it, and we followed, hanging quietly in the water, trying to breathe slowly and kick our flippers as little as possible. Curving back around, Fang turned on her side so that she could see us, and waited as we swam up close again. Below me, her flipper hovered large as a freight elevator. Tilting it very gently in place, she appeared to be sculling; her tail, too, was barely moving. Each time she and the baby blew, a fine mist sprayed into the air, accompanied by a *whumping* sound, as of a pedal organ. Both mother and calf made no sudden moves around us, no acts of aggression.

We did not have their insulation of blubber to warm us in such frigid waters and, growing cold at last after an hour of traveling slowly along the bay with them, we began to swim back toward the beach. To save energy, we rolled onto our backs and kicked with our fins. When we were a few hundred yards away from her, Fang put her head up in a spy hop. Then she dove, rolled, lifted a flipper high into the air like a black rubber sail, and waved it back and forth. The calf did the same. Juan and I laughed. They were not waving at us, only rolling and playing now that we were out of the way. But it was so human a gesture that we automatically waved our arms overhead in reply. Then we turned back onto our faces again. Spears of sunlight cut through the thick green water and disappeared into the depths, a bottom soon revealed itself as tawny brown about thirty feet below us, and then the sand grew visible, along with occasional shells, and then the riot of shells near shore, and finally the pebbles of the shallows. Taking off our fins, we stepped from one liquid realm to another, from the whale road, as the Anglo-Saxons called the ocean, back onto the land of humans.

KENNETH BROWER

# Wake of the Whale

At quarter to six, Bill tapped on my window. The stars were still bright in the sky. I found my glasses and looked for the Southern Cross, but it had set. To the east, over the black shoulder of the volcano, was a band of pearl-gray light. I pulled on my swim trunks and walked barefoot into the kitchen. Bill poured me coffee. He cut a papaya down the middle and pushed half my way. I took a sip of the coffee and began making our peanut-butter-and-jelly sandwiches. I bagged them and laid them in the ice chest, then filled our plastic bottles—guava juice for Bill, passionfruit-orange for me—and I stuffed those in too. Finishing our papaya and coffee, we began carrying the diving gear and cameras to the car.

*Bloater*, the Zodiac, waited outside in the dark, lashed on top of the station wagon. I climbed up, connected the hose of the foot-pump to a valve in the pontoon, and stomped to restore the tautness lost in the coolness of the night. As I watched, Bill, carrying an aluminum camera case, paused by *Bloater*'s bow and bent close to examine her. He rubbed his hand over a spot where the gray neoprene had worn down to fabric. "*Bloater*'s getting old," he said. He sounded a little shocked by the realization, and sad.

KENNETH BROWER has written and traveled extensively in the South Pacific. His books include *Galápagos: The Flow of Wildness; The Starship and the Canoe; Micronesia: The Land, the People and the Sea;* and *Song for Satawal.* An earlier version of this essay appeared in *Wake of the Whale,* published by Friends of the Earth in 1979. Reprinted by permission of the author.

I drove us along the Kona shore. There were no headlights on the road but ours, no sound but the surf. The air, cool still but guaranteeing heat, was full of sea smell and the fragrance of things that bloom in the night. At Keauhou, I backed the station wagon down the ramp almost to the water, then set the handbrake. We lifted *Bloater* off the top and carried her to the water. The cement of the ramp, grooved to provide traction for tires, felt good under my bare feet. The water here in the subtropics was a shock, but a very mild one. We motored slowly until we passed the last of the moored boats, then, at the entrance to the small harbor, where we began to meet swells from the open sea, I throttled up. The ocean presented its simplest face to us in the mornings, when the swells were smooth, untextured as yet by wind. West of us the clouds were turning pink, the day's first color, and I headed there.

Steering, I sat on *Bloater's* port pontoon and watched for dolphins to starboard. Bill sat across from me, watching for dolphins to port. The morning light, as always, was hardest on our eyes. The ocean was glassy then, and the light rebounded in sheets at us. We peered into the glare, looking for fins, and saw none. It had been this way for three weeks. We had come to Hawaii to photograph spinner dolphins, *Stenella longirostris*, but the dolphins were not cooperating.

We did see whales. *Megaptera novaeangliae*, the humpback whale, breeds in Hawaiian waters, and few days passed without our seeing several. Usually it was the flukes we spotted, as the whales made their terminal dives. At a distance, the flukes all looked dark, but when the whales sounded near us, we could see their piebald markings. These white, mottled patterns, on flukes or pectoral fins, distinguish individual humpbacks as surely as fingerprints distinguish us. Sometimes the whales breached, leaping partway or entirely out of the water. We were usually an instant late in seeing the whale rise, but just in time for the splash. It was easy to miss the dark form rising. It was hard to miss the white explosion of the return, for a playful humpback hits the ocean like a locomotive going off a bridge. It raises a whole topography of foam, mountains and valleys of it.

Hours passed, sometimes days, between these snowy disappearances. A hundred or a thousand swells would roll under us, raising the Zodiac high, then dropping it in the trough, each swell washing its predecessor from our recollection. Then, out of the corner of the eye, the glassy forward slope of a swell would erupt mountainously, fixing that particular swell's shape forever in memory.

When we turned in time to see the whale itself, we could never quite believe its size. It seemed to rise in slow motion and it was forever coming out. Humpbacks usually emerge doing half-twists, their fourteen-foot pectorals flopping in great arcs, sheets of spray whipping centrifugally away.

The blows of the humpbacks were like grenades going off. One moment there was blue sky, the next moment the cloud was there, full blown. That first, faster-than-the-eye expansion of vapor and water, leaving the blowhole at four hundred miles per hour, looked like white light. It could have passed for a primary source of photons. Sometimes, when the whale blew in bright, low-angle daylight, the spout for a millisecond held a spectral scatter of color, as if the whale's lungs had been bursting with atomized rainbows. The color instantly shimmered out, the spout frayed at the edges and turned into mist. After a lag the sound arrived, like a distant gunshot.

The spout's character changed with wind conditions. On most of this leeward coast, the spout was vertical and the mist hung in the air for a long time. Above Kawaihai, though, where the trade winds veered over the island's low northern tip, the blows were bent nearly horizontal and the mist was quickly erased. On some days we saw no humpbacks but heard their voices. *Megaptera novaeangliae* of all whales is the greatest singer. Dr. Roger Payne, foremost student of this species of whale, believes that solitary males do the singing. Payne has evidence that all the humpback bulls of a given region sing variations on the same song, and that the song changes each year. Because water transmits sound so well, and because the humpback's instrument is so powerful, the songs carry tens of miles, sometimes hundreds. In the pristine ocean, before the seas were polluted by propeller sound, the singing must have carried thousands of miles.

One hot afternoon, on a day we saw not a sign of whales, we went into the water to cool off and heard them clearly. There were passages of regal trumpeting, then passages of bass groans. Occasionally the whale's voice was so loud and immediate it startled us. We jerked around, expecting to see the whale looming behind us. The whale, in fact, was ten miles or more away. We came to accept this consciously—that sound traveled differently in this medium, that the voices here were larger—but we could not recalibrate our reflexes. The next time a snatch of song came, we jerked around again.

One morning we rolled into the water a quarter mile from a solitary whale. It was singing, its voice so loud we heard it with our feet and hands. We crawled hand over hand down the anchor line, stopped eight feet under, and listened until our breath gave out. We returned for air, then crawled down to listen some more. Later, back in the Zodiac, we realized we were still hearing the song. It was so faint as to be doubtful at first, but then we were sure of it, both the high notes and the low. If ever there was a spirit voice, it was that one; inhuman, originating somewhere in the waves, borne briskly toward us on the sea wind.

And there were other sorts of whales.

One day, seven miles offshore, we saw something big and distant on the water. "That's no humpback," said Bill. I sensed, too, that this was something new. For one thing, we were farther out than humpbacks like to go, in this season. And the whale was too small. It was just lying on the surface, unhumpbacklike. It had a reddish tint that humpbacks didn't. We motored to within fifty yards, and the whale dove. It was, we agreed, about the size of a minke whale. Bill guessed it was a Cuvier's beaked whale. He pulled on his wetsuit and fins and readied his camera. We waited where the beaked whale had sounded, in the remote chance it would rise near the same spot. The sea was calm. If the whale surfaced anywhere within the radius of a mile or two, we would see or hear it. The water was clear. If the whale should rise right here, we could watch it coming from a long way down.

After half an hour, Bill looked at his watch. "He's been down thirty minutes! Can you imagine what that animal is doing down there?" We sat in the Zodiac, peering into the deep blue and trying to imagine.

For a beaked whale, diving, that blue shaded rapidly into black. The pressure grew inexorably. Lungs collapsed, heart and metabolic rates slowed, and the whale began asking the blackness its sonic question. "Are you there, squid?" it clicked, in rough translation. "Are you there, squid?" came the echo-answer.

Did the squid, a mile deep in total blackness, have any sense that the whale was coming? As the sonic probes penetrated its tissues, was there a tingling, a malaise, a brief moment of premonition? Or was the squid's first intimation of its death the shock of the whale's pressure wave, and an instant later the pain of the peglike teeth?

And the whale. How did it keep its orientation down there? How, after catching its squid in the darkness, did it know which way was up?

We could not wait any longer. We were after dolphins and we had to return to that search. We motored northward and farther out, and there, an hour later, we came upon Cuvier's beaked whale again, this time a group of four of them. They rolled slowly at the surface, hyperventilating after a deep dive. Three of the whales were a reddish gray-brown, like the earlier beaked whale, and one of those three had a creamy mottling on its head. The fourth and largest whale was an albino. It had a little pigment in its dorsal fin; otherwise it was white. We were excited. An underwater photograph of a beaked whale, and an albino at that, would have been a first. The four whales took a short, fifteen-minute dive, then resurfaced in a group several hundred yards from where they had disappeared. They spent several minutes catching their breath, with the albino slowly rolling and blowing in the midst of the others. The albino was much bigger than its fellows. We wondered whether in the society of the beaked whale, as with the other large toothed whale, the sperm, it was customary for big bulls to travel in harems of smaller females. We didn't know. The Cuvier is a rare, little-studied whale; it was possible that no one knew. Was the albino's lack of pigmentation a big disadvantage under the tropical sun? We didn't know that either. The whales dove again, and this time we lost them.

We waited for a while, then gave up. Bill ceased scanning the horizon. He had been straddling the starboard pontoon in his flippers, with one leg trailing in the water. He left the leg there; he was not ready yet to go. He seemed to be listening for something. After a moment he cupped his hands to his mouth and called, in a keening whisper.

"Have youuu seeeenn the whiiite whaaaale?"

He waited, hands cupped, as if for the ghost of some Nantucketer to answer. No answer came, but he seemed satisfied.

We gave up trying to photograph spinner dolphins inshore. We decided to go offshore instead into the country of the whales. We would try our luck with spotted dolphins, *Stenella attenuata*, the day-feeding, deep-water animal the Hawaiians call *kiko*. With that decision our fortunes changed. We hired a Hawaiian friend, Chris Newbert, and Chris's Boston Whaler. The Boston Whaler was larger and faster than *Bloater*, carried more fuel, and gave us more range. We began regularly working blue water, the mile-deep ocean far from shore. I now accompanied Bill in the water, carrying the long bangstick while he carried the short one, for the country of the whales was also the country of big pelagic sharks.

Bill told us we would find the blue water strange, and he was right. Chris and I were accustomed to diving where there was a bottom and something to see—reef, kelp forest, fish. Here there was nothing but blue. We hung from our snorkels over a blue, infinite vault. Sunlight shafted downward, illuminating nothing. There was nothing to establish scale. The bright, blurry speck of a ctenophore a foot from your face mask, in that fraction of a second it took your eye to focus, left you startled and in doubt. We loved the blue water—it was as beautiful, in its simplicity, as any earthly desert—but we felt its spookiness too. The blueness pulsed with the things that might come out of it.

The humpback whales were thinning out now, for the breeding season was ending. We still saw humpbacks occasionally, and if they were nearby we visited. One day, five miles offshore, we sighted distant spouts and headed there. It was odd to see humpbacks so far from shore, but we didn't think much about it. Drawing near, we saw the whales in profile against the background of the lava flows. It struck us that these humpbacks were spending an inordinate amount of time on the surface. "Just loafing around," Bill said. Then he shouted, "Look at that!" One of the humpbacks had raised a black bulbous rostrum above the water. "It's inflated," Bill said, puzzled. It was a peculiar thing for Bill to say. Humpback whales don't inflate their rostrums. They have no means of doing so, and no reason. The whales turned our way, and we saw the dorsal fins characteristic of humpback whales. In fact there were no dorsal fins. We manufactured them in our imaginations, as cleverly as hunters make cows into deer. We had been seeing humpbacks all spring. We expected humpbacks. We saw humpbacks. The humpback with the inflated rostrum detached itself from the others and came toward us, as if to investigate. That dark, bulbous nose cruised toward us, then, eighty yards away, it disappeared beneath the surface. We were slow getting into the water. The humpback's surface behavior was so odd, so interesting, that we didn't want to miss any of it. We sat frozen, like Greek sailors after a siren song. Suddenly the black dome resurfaced, glistening, ten feet from the boat. The whale braked easily, turning away in a gentle swirl of water.

"That's a sperm whale," said Bill. In one motion he pushed his mask into place and rolled over the side.

For an instant I believed him, but by the time I had adjusted my mask and followed him, I had changed my mind. I knew that divers can't get this close to sperm whales. Bill was kidding me now, or mistaken.

Underwater I saw an enormous whale. It was so close that Bill's torso and head fit inside the silhouette. The whale filled up half the ocean. It was a sperm whale, all right, and there were two of them, a big one near us and a smaller whale behind. They were stockier and more powerful than in any sperm-whale picture I had seen. They were beautiful. I glimpsed the white of the underslung jaw and the shallowly serrate crest running down the spine. The crest ended in a high point, and it was this that our imaginations had transformed into a dorsal fin. The two whales were moving away without real haste, but they were so fast, in their effortless way, that in five seconds they were gone.

"Say, what about these whales?" asked Chris, as we chased after them in the Boston Whaler, preparing to jump in with them again.

"That's right," I said. "These are sperm whales. That's a big toothed whale."

It was a sperm whale, after all, that had carried Ahab to his grave. It was sperm whales, jaws agape, that splintered whaleboats in those old lithographs and sent the sailors in parabolas through the air. No less an authority than Baron Cuvier himself, the great rationalist who once decried "that heated imagination which leads some enthusiasts to see nothing in nature but miracles and monsters," had written, of the sperm whale, "The terrible arms, the powerful and numerous teeth with which nature has provided the cachalot, render it a terrific adversary to all the inhabitants of the deep, even to those which are most dangerous to others; such as the phocae, the balaenopterae, the dolphin, and the shark. So terrified are all these animals at the sight of the cachalot, that they hurry to conceal themselves from him in the sands or mud, and often in the precipitancy of their flight, dash themselves against the rocks with such violence as to cause instantaneous death."

From the stomachs of sperm whales, scientists have recovered skates, snappers, sardines, seals, scorpaenids, sharks, sponges, spiny lobsters, lampreys, pike, angler fish, rock cod, ragfish, rattails, crayfish, crabs, jellyfish, tunicates, rocks, sand, glass buoys, gorgonians, coral, coconuts, wood, apples, fish line, hooks, shoes, baling wire, plastic bags. A creature that gorged on gorgonians and baling wire might just as easily gorge on Billy and Chris. An animal that could catch and swallow a ten-foot blue shark—and sperm whales have done so—would have no trouble catching and downing me. I had an intuition that I was safe with these whales, but it was a shaky intuition. We had no idea what the risks were, for as far as we knew, nobody had tried this before. None of us wanted to stop. It was, I remember thinking, like a sudden invitation to join an expedition to Mars. We had a chance to see things other men haven't. Better to slide like Jonah down the gullet than to kick yourself the rest of your life.

We followed the sperm whales all morning, but they never let us close. Again and again we cut the outboards and waited ahead of them, but they always altered course. "They know right where we are," said Bill, watching the serrate backs turn aside once more. "They have all the equipment."

There were five to ten whales, at least one calf among them. They swam in a tight group, except for the large animal that had first investigated us. The big whale, an outrider, often positioned itself between us and the others. This was, I learned later, normal behavior in bull sperm whales protecting their families.

We tried swimming far off from the Boston Whaler, in hopes that the whales, in turning to avoid the boat, would come toward us. We waited, sculling in place, trying to make no noise. The underwater blue seemed as close and featureless as that dark that comes when you shut your eyes. Everything we thought we saw there was imaginary. No shape of whale appeared.

Catching my eye, Bill cupped his hand to his ear. I listened. Out of the blue came an insistent, slow, evenly spaced *tok tok tok*. It was the sperm whale sonar. It was as riveting as any humpback's song. The signal came from one of the biggest and most penetrating of cetacean instruments. It was the ratchet noise of the kikos, but played much slower and deeper, as one would expect from a creature hundreds of times larger. It charged the blue with mystery as the blue had never been charged before. The depths under you become something else again, when it's a sperm whale that might rise out of them. We observed nothing in the blue, yet, *tok tok tok tok*, we were being observed.

The day after the sperm whales, we met another pod of unknown whales to the northwest. Drawing abreast of the school, we paced it for a while, looking down on dorsal fins unlike anything we had seen in Hawaii. They were big and rather falcate with odd, rounded tips. Some of the fins were much bigger than others. The dorsals, and the blunt head that sometimes broke the surface, made us think these were pilot whales or perhaps pygmy killer whales, a rare species that frequents Hawaiian waters. The whales did not seem bothered by us. They held to the same course, and it was easy to line up in front of them. We jumped in the water and waited, spy-hopping several times to make sure we were still on line. Onward came the big fins, so we sank underwater.

The undersea that day was the blue I liked best. Little light was penetrating the clouds, and still less penetrated the ocean's surface. The blue in those conditions was dim yet somehow vibrant. The new whales took shape in that color and came out of it toward us. Two whales passed to one side of us, and several passed below. They were built on the dolphin plan, clearly, but were blunt-nosed and much bigger than the spotted dolphin and the rough-toothed dolphin and the bottlenose dolphin and Risso's dolphin—the other species we had seen here. Had it not been for the sperm whales of yesterday, these whales would have looked gigantic. They were pilots all right, *Globicephala macrorhynchus*, the short-finned pilot whale. One whale, as it ascended to breathe, emitted a voluble, birdy snatch of song. The top of its head disappeared for a moment above the surface as the whale blew, then the great back curved down again, the blowhole trailing a line of bubbles. When they had passed, we swam to the boat and clambered in. Chris started up the outboards and spun the wheel. As we sped after the whales, we began comparing notes.

The three of us had a way of collectively filling in the details of our cetaceans. We all seemed to notice different things. Just now, Bill and Chris both had been struck by the tiny, white, sharky eye of this new whale. I hadn't noticed that, but I had seen the crescentic slit of the closed blowhole as a whale passed beneath. Next time Bill and Chris would look for that, and I would look for the sharky eye.

"Sun!" pleaded Bill, gazing skyward. For photography he needed more light underwater. There were promising rents in the clouds, but the sun was not above any of them. "Come on, sun," he prayed. "Come on, sun."

We caught up with the fins again. This time, we saw two truly enormous dorsals among the others. We rolled into the water ahead. The undersea was its dim but vibrant blue again, but then the ocean brightened suddenly, as if someone had flipped a switch. The sun, in answer to Bill's prayer, had come out in the universe above. Toward us came a mother and calf, their backs and flanks veined with sunlight. The calf rolled over and began to nurse. The mother was indifferent to us. Making a slight course correction so as not to hit Bill, she passed serenely by, her calf nursing all the way. Bill made a fluid turn and followed, kicking lazily, not wanting to frighten her, his motor-drive firing away. The calf was still nursing as the two whales disappeared, and the last thing we saw of them was the white of the calf's belly, canted up toward the surface, catching the light.

We stayed with the whales nearly five hours, jumping into the water a dozen times. With each dive we fleshed out the whales a bit more. We grew familiar with the white, impacted eye; the subtle, dark cape in the shape of an hourglass atop the head and dorsum; the shallow, craterlike depressions of healed wounds inflicted by cookie-cutter sharks; the long, white, double and triple scratch lines where the whales had relieved their itches; the insignificant beak on the underside of the blunt head; the strange, pursed smile, fixed permanently in place; the communication, which reminded Bill of a beluga's canary warbling. It was a big, blunt, powerful dolphin. The caudal peduncle, the hump directly forward of the flukes, seemed stuffed tight with muscle, like the hump of a bull.

A week later, after spending our days with spotted dolphins, we met pilot whales again. After our week with the smaller dolphins, the dimensions of the pilots were momentarily disconcerting. They came at us as big as attenuated elephants but chirping like an aviary. They dove shallowly to avoid us. Their greater size and length gave them more momentum than the spotted dolphins, and on ceasing to swim they could glide much farther. They passed under us locked in motionless formation, dark torpedoes in the blue gloaming. The adult animals, as before, did not look up. We were beneath their interest, or above it, technically. They had seen it all already; nothing in the sea surprised them anymore. Their broad backs, and the scars of old episodes, sailed under us without a movement from the flukes, as if a current were running down there. The calves and juveniles were not so jaded. They rolled sideways to look at us, showing the white of their bellies.

In our second dive, one of the whales—it was impossible to tell which—repeated a single note five or six times. It was different from the usual warbling. It sounded like a query that we were supposed to answer. Probably it was something else, a poem or a curse or a grumble—it's foolish to hope for cognates in languages that diverged sixty million years ago. One group, three mothers and three calves, passed to the side, a mobile nursery.

In our third dive, a whale passed with two remoras attached. We saw another with its dorsal fin partly bitten off—a shark? A third whale swam along with its eyes closed; the eye on our side, anyway. My own eyes, tracking that whale, came to Bill and saw that he was studying the water below me. I looked down and saw a juvenile whale the size of a Volkswagen rising belly-up toward me. At one end of the pale belly was the pursed smile, at the other end the genital slit. Captive dolphins and seals are notoriously indiscriminate in their sexual advances, and I hoped pilots weren't that way. I did not want to be violated by an animal the size of a Volkswagen. The young whale ratcheted me at point-blank range, then sank again.

In our fourth dive, I was at Bill's shoulder underwater when we saw a medium-sized pilot coming for us straighter than any pilot yet had come. All we could see was a dark sphere in the water, and the pilot's genus name, *Globicephala*, became perfectly apt. The sonar dome detected us, and the whale slowed. In an attempt to see us, or to fill us in acoustically, it slowly nodded its head, which for us meant that a mouth appeared at the lower edge of the globe, migrated toward the top, then migrated back again. The whale interrupted its normal breathing sequence. It stopped short of the surface and, instead of blowing, it sank tail first. Vertical in the water, it turned slightly to put an eye on us. It took a good look, then went up quickly for the interrupted breath. It blew, dove, and continued on its way.

The last pilots of this pass disappeared in the blue. We sculled around in slow circles, looking for a straggler. We saw nothing but the familiar three hundred and sixty degrees of blue, and a single remora moving away from us. The remora swam on its side with the odd motion of the species, its oblong sucker toward us. Perhaps it had detached from a pilot whale in hopes of settling on one of us. On coming close, it had not liked the look of us. Bill handed me his camera and sprinted after the remora. He almost overtook it, but it managed to elude his fingers. After twenty yards he gave up. We returned to the boat, and the suckerfish hurried away on the trail of its whales.

The pilots were making a beeline toward a distant cluster of skiffs. There were seven or eight boats, which meant the fishermen were working and had dropped their baits on a school of spotted dolphins. Realizing that there might be a meeting of pilots and spotted dolphins, we began to get excited. We kept pace with the pilots, waiting for one or the other of the converging cetacean schools to turn off. Neither did. The big, dark dorsals of the pilots mingled with the small gray dorsals of the spotted dolphins. We raced ahead of the confluence of schools and jumped in. The first time underwater we saw nothing but kikos—spotted dolphins. We swam to the boat, climbed in, and raced ahead again. This time, after several waves of kikos shot by us underwater, we saw, distantly, a single pilot whale with an escort of fifteen kikos. The kikos cavorted in a tight group around the pilot, like gray dogs harrying a black bear, except that everyone seemed to be having fun. I had not realized, before this direct comparison, how much smaller, paler, and more flexible the kikos were. It was a nice demonstration of the diversity within the dolphin family. The kikos circled the pilot, waving their rostrums, flexing their flukes. Those kikos in front were probably jockeying for position on the larger animal's pressure wave. If a human can read anything at all in the body language of dolphins, then the kikos were in good spirits. They were enjoying this demonstration of their greater maneuverability. The pilot's body English—its body dolphinese—was more difficult to read. I have an intuition, whatever it is worth, that the pilot was enjoying the company of its cousins and this demonstration of its greater bulk and purpose.

The two months on the water had transformed us. We were burned as brown as our respective ancestries permitted. Bill's hair and mine was bleached blond-white. Chris's lips were cracking. Bill's dark-blue T-shirt retained its original color only where the shoulder straps of his wetsuit's Farmer Johns protected it; the rest had faded nearly white. We were acclimatized. We still suffered from the conditions we called Snorkel Mouth and Wetsuit Ass, but these were in remission. Snorkel Mouth was a reaction to the plastic of the snorkel mouthpiece, compounded by the irritation of salt water, and it felt like cold sores. We winced every time we had to stretch our lips around the mouthpiece. Wetsuit Ass was a rash of bumps from the friction of our wetsuits bouncing against the boat seats. There was nothing to be done about either malady, and we had been afflicted so long we scarcely noticed, anyway.

There were rough days when the Boston Whaler, planing over the sea, slapped down hard, jarring us to the bone. It was like being punched; you saw red for an instant and looked for somebody to punch back, but there was no one aboard but friends. We were friends, mostly, though the days were hot and long and sometimes argumentative.

I remember the salt that granulated our forearms, a precipitate of the spray. The same white patterns formed every day. I remember blurry days underwater, the ocean gauzy with its gelatinous disks, spheres, and filaments, as if we had been injected somehow into a macrocosmic bloodstream full of white cells and platelets. On those days we saw all our dolphins and whales through a diatomaceous curtain. I remember other days, the water so clear, so empty of organisms, that the whales and dolphins seemed to be flying through air, except for the wave-patterned sunlight that danced along the backs of those animals closest to the surface. I remember the big cane spider that stowed away in the throttle of the Boston Whaler, accompanying us seaward for two days in a row. The spider was the same pale red as the volcanic dust that powdered the cane fields. We were sorry when, on peering into the throttle the third morning, we saw that our mascot, weary of sailing, had jumped ship in the night. I remember the squid we stole from a shearwater. The squid, a big one, had drifted up half eaten in the wake of a kiko school, and the shearwater had had the meat all to itself until we robbed it, jamming head and tentacles into the ice chest to eat later ourselves. I remember entire days in which Bill and Chris communicated only in their joke CB language, and how tired I got of that. I remember the blue shark we saw under a floating can. The can was rusted. The shark was beautiful, with the sharp nose and long pectoral fins of its species. The shark moved off reluctantly as we drew alongside the can. When we pulled away, the shark returned. The shark and the can resumed their thing together, just the two of them, alone in that blue Sahara.

I remember the questions we asked ourselves. Why did kikos have more remoras than spinners did? Why were rough-toothed dolphins so scratched up? Did pilot whales regularly circumnavigate the island of Hawaii, as they seemed to, and if so, why? What went on out here, in the depths, at night?

Of the three of us, Bill best liked the elevation of the console, our crow's nest, and he spent the most time up there. On spotting dolphins, he slapped the painter like reins on the console, urging the boat on, and he gave a cowboy whoop. He whipped off his red sun-brim and waved it wildly in the air. Sometimes there were no dolphins or whales, but Bill slapped the reins, whooped, and waved the brim anyway, as if to raise a whale by sympathetic magic.

One gray day, we saw a strange blow to the northwest. Chris spun the wheel and we headed there; he standing at the helm, I at his shoulder, Billy up on his crow's nest, where he gripped the painter, his knees bent slightly to take the shock of the waves. We gazed ahead. "It's not a dolphin," Billy said. "It's not a humpback. I wonder what the hell this is."

He held his red sun-brim in his hand, extended a bit for balance. In a moment he might wave it in the air, then give his cowboy yell and slap the reins on the deck. For now the red sun-brim remained poised. Billy's eyes were rapt on the horizon.

I realized that this, for me, was the moment. Ahead, on the dark, impenetrable surface of the sea, was some unidentified cetacean. It blew again. One day, that blow had belonged to Cuvier's beaked whale. I had not known, before meeting Cuvier's whale, that such an animal existed. Another day the spout had belonged to a sperm whale, another day to the rough-toothed dolphin *Steno bredanensis*, another to *Globicephala macrorhyncus*. Today the creature ahead of us could be anything. I realized there was no place I would rather be, that I could do this happily every day for the rest of my natural life.

We closed in on the unknown whale.

KENNETH S. NORRIS

# Beluga: White Whale of the North

Perfectly white with dark lustrous eyes, the 12-foot-long beluga whale glided up and braked to a stop on the other side of a large window at the Vancouver Aquarium in Canada. Then he did a strange thing.

From the blowhole atop his head he slowly blew a big mushroom-shaped globe of air into the water. Backing away from the rising bubble, he extended his mobile, pursed lips and sucked it into his mouth.

Next the whale puffed the air back into the water ahead of him. He eyed his creation, which expanded as it rose. Then he matter-of-factly sucked it in again.

Not finished yet, he backed away a little and blew the air out once more. This time he nodded his head sharply downward, sending an invisible boil of water against the expanding bubble. It instantly became a twisting bracelet, shining and expanding until it began to break into flattened, rising spheres.

Then he sucked up the bubbles, pumped his flukes, and was off.

I didn't know what to think. In four decades of studying porpoises, dolphins, and whales all over the world, I'd never seen anything quite

---

KENNETH S. NORRIS, a preeminent authority on cetaceans, recently retired as professor of natural history at the Long Marine Laboratory of the University of California at Santa Cruz. His books include *Whales, Dolphins, Porpoises; The Hawaiian Spinner Dolphin;* and *Dolphin Days: The Life and Times of the Spinner Dolphin.* This essay first appeared in *National Geographic* in June 1994. Reprinted by permission of the author.

like it. Many animals engage in play, but this beluga seemed to be showing an interest in something more like art.

I'd watched belugas before, not only in captivity but also in the wild, but I'd never studied them seriously. Most belugas live in the icy Arctic, where only a few cetologists work. These scientists, in cooperation with native peoples and governments, have mainly done management studies to determine whether native hunting has harmfully reduced beluga populations.

But I was more interested in the beluga's personality and way of life. It seemed to be a wholly different animal from the marine mammals I know best. For 25 years I've worked with the tropical spinner dolphin off the Hawaiian Islands. This open-sea dolphin avoids any obstacle, even a rope trailed in the water, as if its life depends upon it.

The beluga, by contrast, thrives amid the jumbled sea ice of the Arctic Ocean, dodging polar bears and killer whales. Swimming for a mile or more under the ice is nothing for a beluga, which, like Arctic seals or the giant bowhead whale, somehow manages to find or create openings through which to breathe.

These mysterious little whales intrigued me. So, with a spirit of adventure, I set out to visit my scientist friends studying the beluga.

The northern coast of Somerset Island high in the Canadian Arctic is a bleak, beautiful place of dark bluffs striped with snow. Strandlines pencil its shore like contour lines on a topographic map. The coast faces Barrow Strait, whose dark indigo waters are plated with gleaming white sea ice.

The ice up here is a part of life. The stuff seems alive, moving in the currents. One day leads, or open fissures of water, will extend for miles, and the next the ice will jam into the mouths of bays, locking them tight.

Tom Smith, a research scientist with Canada's Department of Fisheries and Oceans, invited me to visit his camp here. On a sunny day in July we looked down from a 25-foot-high observation tower to see some 1,700 white whales swimming in the shallow water of Cunningham Inlet off Barrow Strait.

"You're looking at almost 15 percent of the region's population of belugas," said Tom, who has discovered much of what we know about the whales in this part of Canada. His ginger beard and deeply lined face poked out of foul-weather gear. "If the ice is right," he said, "they come here every year about this time."

Like a halo around the top of the earth, a population of 80,000 to

100,000 belugas ranges from Alaska, Canada, and Greenland to Scandinavia and Russia. As the sea surface freezes in winter, most of the far northern belugas move with the ice fronts, staying ahead of the congealing sea in great processions into the Bering Sea in the west and halfway down the coast of Greenland in the east.

Then in spring, when the winter ice begins to break up, the belugas parade back again, clustering at the newly opened Arctic river mouths. Along the way they feed on cod, squid, herring, and halibut; they also dive to the bottom to catch flounder and various crustaceans.

The belugas below us at Cunningham Inlet were yellowish white ghosts against the jade water. They wriggled against one another like tadpoles. The herd lay in a broad swath across the mouth of the Cunningham River. Many whales pounded their tails to keep stationary in the river's strong current, sending plumes of spray into the chilly air.

I looked almost directly down upon three mother whales tending their brownish gray young. A little one found a nipple on its mother's abdomen. Beluga milk can be eight times richer than cow's milk. Capable of supporting the baby's rapid growth, it quickly provides the young one with a warm blanket of blubber.

"Why do they all come here?" I asked.

"They're molting," Tom said. "Focus your binoculars on that one with the lemon yellow cast to its skin. It hasn't finished shedding." I could see tight little wrinkles of skin along the length of the whale's back. In a few days, it would turn white and smooth from swimming in the warmer freshwater and rubbing on the bottom.

Male belugas can reach lengths of 15 feet and weigh more than 3,000 pounds. Females are slightly smaller and proportionately lighter; they typically produce a calf every three years after reaching sexual maturity at around age five. The average beluga life span is thought to be about 25 to 30 years, during which time many are so wreathed in blubber that their round heads stick out from a ruff as if from the collar of a winter coat.

Though they have no back fin, which could be a terrible impediment under the ice, the belugas do possess a long, low dorsal ridge of tough, fibrous tissue. Scientists in Russia report seeing belugas using their backs to break through more than three inches of ice to create breathing holes.

It may be hard for those of us whose feet get cold easily to understand how another mammal can live its whole life immersed in icy water. Yet the worst cold a beluga faces comes not from the water, but from the air it must breathe. During the black northern winter, the air may drop to minus 60°F, cold enough to turn a breath into a shower of ice.

John Burns, retired dean of Alaska beluga scientists, once told me of flying over the frozen Chukchi Sea and spotting a herd of white whales in an open lead. The exhaled breath of each whale had built up a little dome of ice, like a tiny igloo over its exposed head, pierced by a hole through which the animal breathed.

Belugas travel in a capsule of wild sounds, their lives spent in a symphony orchestra tuning up. As Tom and I watched, a deep tuba voice blared through the air, followed by a long, wavering tone, like a novice learning the trumpet, then a series of high trilling chirps, and the sibilant sound of exhaled air, a blat, a snore.

When I picked up a pair of earphones connected to an underwater microphone in the channel, I heard a cascade of clicks. The whales send these brief, sharp sounds out into their environment as sonar, using the echoes that return to help them navigate and locate objects. Mixed in were overlapping choruses of whistles, sounds cetologists believe are used to organize groups of whales.

Sailors in centuries past heard belugas through the wood hulls of their ships and called them sea canaries. The first scientific attempt to analyze beluga sounds came in 1962. The study's authors, marine scientists Marie Fish and William Mowbray of the University of Rhode Island, nearly ran out of words, writing of yelps, clicks, creaks, canarylike whistles, blares, rasps, squawks, warbles, and trills. Such variety hints at the complexity of the beluga's experience, of birth, of nurturing and instructing their young, and of approaching death—the commerce of a seagoing life we humans can only dimly imagine.

Belugas combine these acoustic skills with a keen ability to adapt. At the mouth of the Kvichak River in Alaska, site of the world's greatest sockeye salmon run, belugas gather every year to feed. Though the river is a murky maze of mudbanks and channels where tides reach 20 feet or more, the belugas in the early 1970s were so successful that biologists worried about the salmon's survival.

To scare the belugas away, James Fish of the Naval Undersea Research and Development Center and John Vania of the Alaska Department of Fish and Game tried playing killer whale sounds underwater—clicks and long echoing screams. At first the belugas fled from the sounds of their natural enemies, swimming down channel toward the sea. After a time they returned but moved into other channels and took refuge behind submerged mudbanks to cautiously resume feeding far away from the sounds.

Tom Smith and I climbed down from the tower where we had been watching the whales, and I dipped a rubber-booted foot into the river's edge. The nearest whales, at least 30 yards away, reacted with a start, showing a sensitivity to sound far greater than even I had imagined.

"One more step," said Tom, "and they would have been gone."

Belugas also have what may be the most highly refined navigation system of all whale species. By emitting a stream of clicks in a narrow beam through the water, belugas manage to find their way in an environment replete with complex channels under the Arctic ice. They may even be able to listen around corners by bouncing echoes off the bottoms of floes.

They focus this beam of sound, some researchers believe, by changing the shape of the melon, or fatty organ on their foreheads. One moment this melon can be rounded and of normal whalelike contour, then the next it can be elongated like Pinocchio's nose until it completely overhangs the whale's snout. The beluga may focus its sounds just as you might twist a flashlight to focus a beam of light.

One great mystery about the belugas that come to Somerset Island each summer has been where they go the rest of the year. A team Tom Smith heads with Tony Martin from the Sea Mammal Research Unit in Cambridge, England, has tried to solve the puzzle by putting satellite transmitters on whales here in Canada to track them in winter, when no biologist has been able to follow them by ship or plane.

"We suspect the belugas go east across the northern tip of Baffin Island, then continue to the west coast of Greenland where the sea doesn't freeze," Tony said. "But we don't know that yet. Large numbers migrate south along the Greenland coast each year, at about the time we would expect the belugas from Canada to arrive, and they're heavily hunted— about 700 animals are killed a year. If these really are the belugas from Canada's eastern Arctic, where native hunters kill about 100 each summer, then it could spell trouble."

Tom's camp was set up at Elwin Bay on the eastern side of Somerset Island. All around I saw a swirl of life. Magenta saxifrages, pale yellow arctic poppies, and prostrate willow trees were clustered in creases scribed across the stony land. A single sandpiper was trying to sleep near my tent in the perpetual daylight, while terns wheeled and called, and low-flying eiders strung out in flocks across the water.

We had just finished breakfast one morning when Tony came bounding down the gravel barren on a four-wheeler. "There's a whale where I think we can catch him," he said breathlessly, hopping off the vehicle to get a transmitter to attach to the animal. Tom and two other team members rushed to throw on dry suits and ran for the rubber boat, swooping up nets and tail lines as they went by. I ran across to the outer beach, arriving just as the boat did.

Tom and fellow biologist Jack Orr were both braced at the bow, one on each side, hoop nets in hand. A long white shape sliced ahead of them in the shallow water, and then the whale made an error, turning in toward the ice-edged beach. Jack leaped overboard and scooped a net over the whale's head. Tom left the boat and followed with the tail noose, which he deftly slipped in place over the flukes and cinched tight.

The two men then disappeared in a cascade of icy seawater as the whale sought to escape, beating its tail frantically. They tried to keep the hoop net in place. I raced down the berm to grab the tail rope, starting to pull the flailing beluga toward the beach.

Another team member took over from me, and soon Tony was pinning a transmitter the size of two small flashlights to the whale's dorsal ridge. The animal didn't even flinch. In about 20 minutes Tom and Jack pushed the beluga back into the channel. The next we would hear about the whale would be from Tony's lab at Cambridge, where his colleagues were tracking its radio signal.

Despite their extraordinary sensory and communication skills, belugas struck me as terribly vulnerable when in shallow water, ripe for capture by humans and other predators.

One day at Cunningham Inlet as Tom and I sat watching the whales, Russ Andrews, a graduate student, ran up with an urgent message: "Pete Jess is on the radio about a bear kill." Pete, our neighbor on northern Somerset Island, had just flown over a hungry polar bear in the act of killing at least four belugas.

We scurried for a helicopter that, by chance, was in camp unloading gear. Tossing Tom's measuring and sampling equipment aboard, along with the camp's rifle, we lifted off for Cape Anne, about 20 miles to the west.

As our helicopter touched down on the gravel strand, I could see the shadowy forms of four whales lying in a still-water embayment behind the beach. They had been trapped by the dropping tide. One flopped its tail slowly up and down, breathing its last. The others were still. The whales were streaming blood, clouding a pool the size of a tennis court with red.

"When I first saw the bear, he was standing next to a young whale that had blood flowing from the top of the head," said Art Wolfe, a nature photographer who had been one of the first to reach the scene. "The bear had blood all over his mouth. He ran east along the shore, away from our airplane. I saw several more whales near the four lying in the water."

By the time we arrived, the polar bear had eaten a prodigious meal from the smallest whale. Now the bear was nowhere to be seen. Two other whales, apparently unharmed, circled nearby, keeping a somber station. Such "standing by" with injured or sick herd members is common among whales and dolphins, even when the lives of the waiting animals are in danger. Whales have even been known to press a stricken animal to the surface for vital breaths of air.

Tom and Russ pulled the dead belugas onto the beach. With a few awesome bites, the polar bear had ripped into the skin around each whale's blowhole and then begun feeding on the incapacitated animal. The technique was surgical and practiced, and the thought of sharing the shore with so efficient a predator made me a little nervous.

The bear's capacity for killing, however, paled by comparison with the slaughter once carried out by humans for profit. On the rocky beach at Elwin Bay we camped just above whitened beluga bones spread in a half-mile-long arc. A team from Montreal's McGill University led by archaeologist James Savelle had pitched a camp here. Each day they trudged out among the bones—skulls, lines of vertebrae, and thickets of ribs—to map the remains of every animal.

"What happened here?" I asked, looking at a big skull now set in a lush flower garden of moss, saxifrages, and arctic poppies.

"Well, in the late 19th century Scottish whalers would herd belugas past the point over there at high tide, trapping them in the inner part of the bay and stripping their hides and blubber," Jim said. "In 1894 they killed 820 in one hunt."

How attitudes have changed. Back in 1894 every animal in the ocean was considered fair game. Now every whale species in the world is being watched, and in North America, at least, only subsistence hunters are allowed to kill belugas, or *qilalugaiit*, as the Inuit in eastern Canada call them.

Andrew Atagotaaluk, an Inuit hunter, was raised at Creswell Bay on southern Somerset Island. His father, Timothy Idlout, kept the family here rather than settle in one of the government villages established in the north in the 1950s and '60s. Timothy wanted to live in the traditional way, which meant hunting caribou, belugas, and narwhals and sharing the bounty with others in the camp.

"We catch narwhals just down from camp," Andrew said, pointing along the deep bay, "but the belugas are caught farther out along the north shore."

Hunters here take about ten belugas a year for their meat, blubber, and muktuk, or skin with a sliver of blubber. (They sell tusks of male narwhals, many of which are exported.) Native hunters from other villages in Canada's eastern Arctic take nearly a hundred belugas a year from the 12,000 that are thought to migrate to the area—about 15 percent of the number taken in Greenland, where hunting is only beginning to be controlled. In 1989 Canada and Greenland established a joint commission on the beluga and narwhal, which collects information on the stocks of whales that will eventually help the two countries regulate hunting.

A more insidious threat to some belugas comes from industrial pollution. Far from Arctic ice floes, a remnant population of about 500 belugas travels up and down Canada's St. Lawrence estuary, where it is the focus of an environmental battle.

"A hundred years ago, there were at least ten times as many belugas here as there are today," said Pierre Béland of the St. Lawrence National Institute of Ecotoxicology. The original decline was due to overhunting. But even when commercial hunting stopped in the 1950s, after a series of bad years, the whales failed to recover. "Now they're just hanging on," said Pierre. "We're trying to find out why."

We boarded the institute vessel *Bleuvet* at Cap-à-l'Aigle, 80 miles northeast of Quebec City, and cruised out across the St. Lawrence channel, banked by the low forested hills of Quebec's Laurentian plateau. We were joined by Robert Michaud, who keeps track of the whale population for the institute. Soon we saw the gleaming white backs of belugas against the greenish water.

"Look at that one," said Robert, pointing to an animal swimming 50 yards away. "See those dark smears on its head? It's been digging in the bottom mud. We don't know why, but they do a lot of that here."

"Do they pick up poisons from the mud?"

"It's apparently not as simple as that," Pierre replied. The food the belugas catch carries the contaminants. For example, there is a big aluminum plant near here that once dumped waste containing a powerful carcinogen, benzo(a)pyrene, directly into the Saguenay River, which feeds the St. Lawrence. When a beluga ingests the pollutant, the chemical is quickly broken down, but traces called adducts remain bonded to the DNA of the whale, possibly causing tumors.

Pierre and his colleagues have measured high levels of adducts in belugas that died here. Other researchers, such as Michael Kingsley of Canada's Department of Fisheries and Oceans, are cautious when interpreting Béland's results, noting that his institute's scientists sample diseased animals and therefore don't know the incidence of adducts in the larger beluga population.

Pierre is undeterred. "We've detected more than 25 different potentially toxic contaminants in their blubber, including PCBs and DDT," he said. "Some of these were at levels rarely reported for a seal or whale."

Recently the institute's chemical sleuthing turned up another surprise in beluga tissue—a pesticide called mirex, banned in Canada and the United States since the 1970s.

"We researched the chemical and learned that it was manufactured upstream of the St. Lawrence near Niagara Falls," Pierre explained. There are few traces of mirex in the St. Lawrence. Instead, the pesticide appears to be carried to the St. Lawrence by eels migrating from the Great Lakes, where it's still found in sediment. These eels are then eaten by the belugas.

Of the 75 tumors ever recorded among the world's porpoises, dolphins, and whales, 28 have been discovered in St. Lawrence belugas, though the direct causes are still being debated by scientists.

The first reports from Tony Martin's transmitters were disappointing. Unexpectedly, the batteries had given out early, before the half dozen whales he had tagged at Elwin Bay—including one I had splashed around with—could be expected to reach Greenland. The whales had moved around Somerset and Prince of Wales Islands, then headed east toward Greenland along Canada's Devon Island shore. But the long traverse across Baffin Bay to Greenland remained undocumented.

Tony and his team went back to the drawing board, coming up with a new circuit designed to save power. The following season, transmitters featuring the new circuit were placed on nine whales—four in Canada's western Arctic and five in the eastern. The results, Tony told me when I saw him at Creswell Bay, were surprising.

"Look at these printouts from the belugas we instrumented over at Tuktoyaktuk on the Mackenzie River Delta," Tony said of the western group. "All the belugas in that area are thought to summer near the coast, then file back west along the Alaska coast. Well, look at this. Three of the whales went north, right into the heavy pack ice."

He put his pen point on one track. "This old male went northwest to about 79°N. There's more than 95 percent ice cover up there." He pointed at another track. "After we tagged this one, it turned northeast past Prince Patrick Island and has nearly reached where we are right now. That's almost 800 miles in what is supposed to be the wrong direction." He paused. "Every time I try to fix the limits of their range," he said, "they show me how little I really know."

In late 1993, Tony finally got proof of what he and Tom Smith had suspected: One of the whales he had tagged in eastern Canada reached Greenland, indicating that the two countries share the same stock of belugas. Yet much mystery remains—not only about the movements of the white whale of the north, but also about the deeper dimensions of its life. What we have learned so far suggests a creature of subtlety and nuance. What revelations await us when we know more of what goes on in the pellucid waters under the Arctic ice, where belugas sing their wild, enigmatic songs?

DAVID RAINS WALLACE

# Whales and Limits

It is such a still summer evening on the Bay of Fundy that the sound of waves on the granite shores of Campobello Island has sunk to a murmur. Bay and sky seem empty: no planes or boats are in sight. Yet occasionally there is a sharp, explosive sound, almost like a shot, although muffled from echoing across the water. It evidently comes from some distance, and in the quiet, the explosive report seems unearthly.

The sound is not really made by extraterrestrials, but if summer vacationers knew its origin, they might be as surprised as if little green men had produced it. A baby right whale lies in the water several miles offshore, slapping its flippers and flukes against the surface, and the resultant sound waves are strong enough to echo off the shore cliffs. This may seem an excessive distance for baby sounds to reach, but sound carries far over water, and six-month-old right whales are over twenty feet long. Babies tend to make surprising amounts of noise when signaling their mothers anyway, and that may be what this baby

DAVID RAINS WALLACE is the author of numerous books of natural history and two novels. A recipient of the John Burroughs Medal for distinguished nature writing, he has just completed an ecotourism guide to Central America for the Wildlife Conservation Society's Paseo Pantera Project and is working on an evolutionary natural history of Central America as a land bridge. "Whales and Limits" first appeared in a slightly different form as a chapter in *Life in the Balance*, a companion volume to the National Audubon Society television series in 1987. Reprinted by permission of the author.

is doing, although we don't know enough about right whales to be sure.

The mother left her calf at the surface while she dove to feed on a swarm of copepods. He amused himself for a while by playing with a patch of floating kelp, but whales can stay underwater for many minutes, and perhaps he has grown impatient. Or perhaps the tail-slapping is just another form of play. In any case, his mother surfaces a few minutes later, making the right whale's characteristic J-shaped double spout that once brought excited cries from the crow's nests of whaling ships. The calf hurries over and slides on her back, and she rolls and bats him away with a flipper, perhaps playfully, perhaps in annoyance at this disturbance while she is getting her breath.

Someone who could have watched her feeding underwater, or who had watched right whales surface-feeding as they do in Cape Cod Bay in the summer, might have been a little surprised at this frisky behavior. Right whales are the slowest, stoutest whales. Compared to the other group of baleen-feeding whales, the rorquals (which includes blue, humpback, fin, sei, and minke whales), right whales are what sailing ships would be to steamships. Whereas blue whales sometimes pursue their krill prey at speeds of over ten miles an hour, engulfing entire swarms with a single gulp of their expandable gullets, right whales plod along at two to six miles an hour. They simply hold their huge underslung jaws open as they swim through copepod swarms and let the screens of baleen hanging from their upper jaws filter the small crustaceans out of the water. When enough accumulates, they scrape the baleen with their tongues and throw the food down gullets about as wide as stovepipes.

Pokey as this method of feeding may seem, it suffices to nourish right whales to an average weight of seventy tons and a length of fifty feet. It also gives them the energy for other apparently playful behavior. Like their more streamlined relatives, right whales occasionally breach, leaping out of the water, sometimes almost completely, and twisting to fall on their backs or sides with thunderous splashes. Breaching may have a practical function in that it gets rid of external parasites such as whale lice, but some right-whale behavior seems purely for fun. They like to go "sailing." A whale extends its flukes in the air and lets the wind drive it across the surface as though it were a sloop. Whales have been seen sailing a certain distance thus, then swimming back to the starting point and doing it again. Off the Argentina coast, right whale calves have been observed wrapping themselves in kelp strands, rather as human youngsters do with crepe streamers at a birthday party.

The calf quiets down after his mother's slap, perhaps feeling rebuked, perhaps simply because he is tired. They have just arrived in the bay after a very long trip for an infant, even a twenty-foot-long one. Western Atlantic right whales winter off the Georgia–Florida coast, so the calf probably was born there, then followed his mother on a six-month migration up the coast to the New Brunswick shore. Nobody can be entirely sure about this, however, because nobody really knows that much about the right whales, even though they live alongshore the most populous part of the United States. They are so rare now that they are very difficult to study. Their wintering and calving grounds off Georgia and Florida went undiscovered until 1984. (Even common whales are little-known because they spend most of their lives underwater.)

What we do know about right whales suggests that they are less specialized, perhaps less intelligent than other whale species. Their brains are not as large in proportion to their bodies as those of sperm whales or some dolphin species. They don't vocalize as much as dolphins or make the eerie, majestic "songs" of humpback whales. They don't dive deeper than three thousand feet and stay submerged for more than ninety minutes, as sperm whales do.

Because we know so little about them, of course, right whales may prove to have undreamed-of talents. Yet for the present, they seem like standard models of whaledom: basic, medium-sized (for a whale), warty, black tubs ambling through the plankton. Rights certainly have been the standard whales for whaling fleets during the roughly eight hundred years of commercial whale-catching. Their slowness made them the easiest whales to catch, and their stoutness made them float after they were killed, whereas rorquals sink. That is why they are called right whales. Before modern whaling technology became fast and efficient enough to exploit more streamlined species, they were the "right" whales to hunt. Sperm or gray whales might smash a boat, and rorquals might drag it for hours and then get away. Right whales generally were neither aggressive nor fast enough to make such difficulties.

That a fifty-foot-long, seventy-ton, oceanic descendant of smaller land mammals should be considered in any way ordinary says a great deal about the extraordinary nature of that creature's habitat. Compared to the oceans, the land and sky habitats are really rather insignificant, important as they seem to the creatures that inhabit them. Indeed, land and skies would not be inhabited if not for the oceans; the water and oxygen upon which sky and land life depend come from the oceans.

Most things in the biosphere begin, end, and begin again in the oceans. They cover seventy-one percent of the globe and contain over eighty percent of its living matter, or biomass. Most of the sedimentary and metamorphic rocks that form today's continents lay under salt water once, as the seashells Charles Darwin found high in the Andes demonstrated. Most of them will lie under salt water again, once rain, wind, and glaciers have scraped them away into river deltas and estuaries. Then those deltas and estuaries will rise to mountaintops again, scraped up by drifting continents.

Almost certainly, life itself began in the oceans. Life is still mostly water, and salt water at that: blood and other organic fluids have chemistries similar to sea water. Fossils of sea life long predate those of land and skies. The question of how life might have begun in the oceans is much less certain, of course. The general belief used to be that life began at the ocean surface, where energy from ultraviolet radiation or lightning caused formation of giant, self-replicating organic chemicals dissolved into the water from the preoxygen atmosphere. More recently, scientists have come to doubt that the early atmosphere could have contained significant amounts of such unstable compounds. They suspect life evolved in the ocean bottom, in the mud, or perhaps around volcanic vents. We know such vents to be sources of methane and other organic chemicals, and in fact primitive organisms live around such vents today, hydrogen sulfide powering their metabolisms.

There is no fossil evidence to show how life began in the oceans, but there is evidence that it has been there a very long time. Concentrated masses of thick-walled cells resembling today's bacteria have been found in South African chert (a silica-based rock similar to flint) estimated to be 3.5 billion years old. Since the planet itself is roughly five billion years old, the living ocean's antiquity is impressive. Of course, the forms that ocean life took during the first two billion years were not impressive by today's standards: they were all single-celled organisms resembling bacteria and blue-green algae. But things eventually got more complicated, although, again, we have no fossil evidence of how single-celled organisms evolved into many-celled ones.

There is ample evidence that they did evolve. Remains of creatures resembling (but only distantly related to) worms and jellyfish lie in billion-year-old rocks, and by the beginning of the Cambrian period most of the animal phyla that now exist (mollusks, arthropods, chordates, and others) had appeared. There also were some phyla that *don't* exist now, which we can determine from rare deposits like the Burgess Shale of British Columbia, formed by sudden mud avalanches that buried and preserved an unusual array of 530-million-year-old soft-bodied creatures. As many as a dozen of these creatures cannot readily be placed within any living animal group: one is so weird that scientists named it *Hallucigenia*.

Since then, the oceans have repeatedly demonstrated an ability to produce the most extraordinary creatures, from the jawless fishes, scorpionlike eurypterids, and cone-shelled nautiloids of the Paleozoic era, to the sharks and lobe-finned fishes, giant marine reptiles, and giant ammonoids of the Mesozoic, to the cod and tuna, whales, and octopi of the Cenozoic. Ocean life has nearly been wiped out a number of times, including a great extinction at the end of the Permian period when trilobites died out, and another at the end of the Cretaceous period when giant reptiles and ammonoids (shell-dwelling relatives of octopi) did. Yet evolution has refilled emptied oceans gradually with forms that exceeded extinct predecessors in biological specialization. For example, ocean-going reptiles appear never to have evolved the ability to strain plankton from the water with seive-like jaw structures such as whale baleen. The nutritional advantage that this adaptation gives whales apparently has allowed them to become the biggest animals that ever lived. (The biggest whales are the baleen-feeding rorquals, like the 100-foot blue whale, although toothed sperm whales can reach 60 feet.)

For all their novelty, the oceans retain an even more impressive environmental stability. The most ancient creatures continue to inhabit them along with the most modern because the conditions that allowed life to prosper in pre-Cambrian waters still prevail. Although rain has been washing dissolved minerals into the oceans throughout life's tenure, ocean waters remain within tolerable limits of salinity. Science probably will continue to find living examples of ocean life forms once thought extinct, like the lobe-finned coelocanth discovered in deep waters off Madagascar in the 1930s.

The oceans' combination of stability and novelty produces an abundance that seems limitless from the perspective of dry-land life. Yet ocean life is limited by the same fundamental factor as land life—the availability of food—and most ocean food comes from the same basic process—photosynthesis by green plants. Considerably more photosynthesis occurs in the oceans than on land. The one-celled algae that make up

99 percent of ocean plankton are the main source of atmospheric oxygen. It doesn't occur everywhere in the oceans with equal abundance, however. In fact, rich swarms of plankton, consisting of small crustaceans and fish as well as algae, are the exception rather than the rule, because the mineral nutrients that algae need to photosynthesize are available only in certain parts of the oceans.

The oceans are not simply global fishponds. They are as moody and changeable as the skies. Like the skies, they flow and eddy constantly across the Earth's surface, driven by solar energy. Water warmed by the equatorial sun rises and flows north and south in great currents such as the Gulf Stream of the western Atlantic. Such warm tropical waters are not rich in mineral nutrients, because they flow far above the fertile ooze of the sea floor. Underneath them, however, flow other currents of cold water moving south or north from the poles. Where these currents rise to the surface, forced upward by collision with a continent or underwater plateau such as the Grand Banks off Newfoundland, they raise huge amounts of nutrients from the ocean floor to where algae can use it (there is light enough for photosynthesis only at the upper layer). Ocean life concentrates in such places, or along continental shallows, where rivers and offshore currents sweep nutrients into the water. Of the world's fish catch, 90 percent comes from 30 percent of the oceans.

Of course, there are a great many food-rich places scattered about the oceans. Since so many are located at the edges of continents, it is easy to see how a land creature can get a deceptive impression of limitless abundance. Indeed, such a creature would have to expend quite a lot of effort to discover that the abundance does have limits. The ancestors of today's whales must have made that discovery as they gradually wandered out of the food-rich rivers and estuaries in which they originally swam and into the largely barren oceans. The earliest known fossil whales, discovered in roughly 50-million-year-old shallow sea sediments in Pakistan and India, lacked the adaptations that allow their descendants to exploit the open ocean. Evolved from primitive carnivores, the early whales had ears, legs, teeth, and other features not much different from a land mammal's, and would have been unable to dive or swim the long distances their descendants can. The adaptations which give today's whales such extraordinary powers are a response to the slow discovery of ocean limits, limits which require whales to make thousand-mile migrations between feeding and breeding grounds, or to dive miles deep to find zones of food abundance.

We don't know exactly when or why humans first ventured onto salt water, but they seem likely to have done so along the routes that whales used—rivers, estuaries, and coastlines. They are also likely to have sought the same thing whales did—food. Of course, humans had not been swimming in rivers for millions of years before they entered the seas, so they had to invent boats. Most of the known Neolithic cultures that lived near water had boats of some kind: dugouts and bark canoes in North America, balsa rafts and reed canoes in South America, outriggers in Polynesia, bamboo rafts in east Asia, papyrus boats in the Near East, skin curraghs in Europe, kayaks and umiaks in Greenland. As recent experiments by Norwegian explorer Thor Heyerdahl and others have demonstrated, some of these early boats are surprisingly seaworthy: enough to get aborigines to Australia and Polynesians to Tahiti and Hawaii.

Despite their wanderings, early humans didn't really test ocean abundance. They lived in relatively small communities and caught only enough food for their own needs. If they fished out village waters, they could always move. Larger prey such as whales were sufficiently hard to catch that they were virtually invulnerable to depletion by human hunters. Although Inuit and northwest Indian whalers were highly skilled, their expeditions had relatively low success rates. It seems proba-ble that prehistoric hunters extirpated the huge Steller's sea cow from most of North America's Pacific Coast before it was finally exterminated by the Russians in the eighteenth century. There may have been other early extinctions of sea mammals, but there's no clear evidence of them.

Only with the rise of civilization did humans discover ocean limits, and the knowledge came late, even though saltwater trade routes and fisheries quickly became indispensable to growing city-states. Sailing fleets plied the Mediterranean as early as ten thousand years ago, and dried fish was a staple food throughout Greek and Roman times. Yet classical civilization did not send its fishing fleets beyond the relatively limited areas of the Mediterranean and Black seas. Past the coastal waters of Gaul and Spain, the Atlantic remained unknown territory. Not until commerce and industry had spread throughout Europe in the late Middle Ages did demand for commercial supplies of whale and seal oil, baleen (used to make items such as brushes, springs, chair seats, and knife han-dles), salt fish, and other ocean goods expand enough to send fleets across the Atlantic.

The Portuguese fishermen and Basque whalers had already depleted the right whales and herring of the Bay of Biscay, but the herds and schools they found off the coast of Newfoundland after 1535 must have made the scarcity in the Bay of Biscay seem unimportant. Nobody knows how many right whales lived in the Atlantic at the time: probably hundreds of thousands. Other fleets quickly joined the Portuguese and Basques.

The Dutch, seeking a northern passage to the Indies, chanced upon huge herds of bowhead whales (close, polar relatives of the right whale) in the waters east of Greenland; they established a town called Smeerenberg (which translates roughly as Fat City) on the island of Spitsbergen north of Norway to process blubber and baleen. English, French, German, and Danish whalers also arrived and quickly fell into various squabbles with the Dutch and one another over the whale supply. There was big money to be made. According to estimates, every whale killed by the Dutch in that period brought in the equivalent of 33,500 dollars, and the overall income of the seventeenth-century Dutch industry more or less matched that of twentieth-century whaling in Antarctica, even though the former was carried out with sailing ships and hand-thrown harpoons, the latter with factory ships and harpoon cannons.

Yet the busy fleets discovered within decades that the new whale supply wasn't as endless as it seemed. Annual catches averaging in the thousands of whales in the seventeenth century began to drop into the hundreds in the eighteenth. Despite their initial abundance, right whales proved to have a low reproductive potential. Like females of other whale species, right and bowhead females almost always bear single young and breed only every other year or so. Young whales take many years to reach maturity. Having few natural predators, whale populations are not adapted to fast growth. Although whalers haven't hunted rights significantly in over a century, and agreements have protected them completely since 1938, right numbers have never recovered from early whaling. About three thousand survive in the southern hemisphere, where hunting began later, but only five hundred are thought to live in the North Atlantic, and fewer than 200 in the North Pacific. These populations may have become so scattered that males and females simply have difficulty finding each other.

The disappearance of right and bowhead whales discouraged Basque and Dutch whalers, but not others. New England colonists had caught small numbers of right and gray whales off their coast since the mid-seventeenth century. In the beginning of the eighteenth, they ventured farther offshore to hunt a species that had not been exploited much before, the sperm whale. Sperm whales are toothed whales (like dolphins and killer whales), rather than baleen whales. They get their food by diving deep to catch squid, a much more active prey than planktonic crustaceans. Sperm whales are sleeker, faster, and more aggressive than right whales, prompting Basque and Dutch whalers to leave them alone when rights were abundant. They also spend most of their time on the open ocean instead of coastal waters like the rights, which misled some early whalers into thinking they were rare.

On the contrary, sperm whales actually were much more abundant than rights and bowheads. They were the most numerous of the great whales, and remain so even today. Their blubber might not have been as thick as baleen whales', but it and the fatty material in sperm whales' huge, bulbous foreheads produced an oil of much higher quality than right-whale oil. Although sperm whales had no baleen, their stomachs sometimes contained ambergris, an extremely valuable substance from which one could make fixatives for perfumes and volatile essences.

New England whalers discovered all this as they extended their voyages past George's Bank to the Gulf Stream and Baffin Bay. By the Revolutionary War, they had over four hundred ships, produced hundreds of thousands of dollars worth of oil annually, and had crossed the equator to African and South American coasts and down to the Falkland Islands. In the nineteenth century, ships went on two-year, worldwide voyages, killing any and all whales they could catch, the only ones they couldn't being the fast-swimming rorquals. Whaling was the third-largest industry in Massachusetts, producing about seventy million dollars of income a year at a time when the gross national product was less than ten billion. Yankee whaling eventually killed an estimated half-million whales, enough so that traditional whaling methods became unprofitable by the end of the century. Replacement of whale oil by petroleum and of baleen by spring steel contributed to the decline, but the main cause of American whaling's demise was a scarcity of whales that could be caught with available technology.

As the American whaling business collapsed, new technologies brought a revival to the industry elsewhere. A Norwegian invented a cannon that shot a grenade-tipped harpoon into whales from the prow of a small, fast ship. With this deadly weapon, whalers could finally kill rorquals (and then keep them afloat by injecting them with compressed air). Technological innovations also extended the industrial uses of whale products: as the twentieth century dawned, whale oil became an ingredient in margarine, lipstick, and machine lubricants. Like the Americans before them, the Norwegian fleet spread throughout the world, and in the 1890s, they came upon whale populations which, again, must have made depletion elsewhere seen unimportant.

An estimated eight hundred thousand rorquals then lived in the waters of Antarctica, feeding on the vast swarms of krill that thrive during short Antarctic summers. By 1912, Norwegian and British whalers were catching over twenty thousand whales a year in southern waters, twice the annual catch of the American industry's heyday. With the introduction of the factory ship, which allowed whalers simply to haul their gigantic catch aboard and process it with the latest industrial facilities, the killing increased even more. By the 1930–1931 season, the kill had doubled to 40,201.

Rorquals don't breed any faster than other whales, so one species after another dwindled: first the relatively slow humpbacks, then the huge blues, which factory-ship whalers especially coveted because one kill produced so many tons of meat and oil. After a certain point, oil production declined even though more and more whales were being caught, because the oldest and biggest whales were gone. This size reduction was an ominous sign for whale populations, because the oldest and biggest whales were also the breeders.

Yet depletion of these last whales didn't stop whalers from trying even harder to catch them. As whaling became more technologically sophisticated, it also became more capital-intensive. Whaling countries, of which there were increasing numbers, invested too much money in their fleets to let them lie idle simply because they were threatening to exterminate the whales. They would get the best return on their investment if they killed whales as long and hard as possible, then simply junked or converted the fleets.

With only a short break during World War II, the whaling countries continued in this way. Technology improved even more after the war, and demand for animal protein and fat in war-torn countries raised the price of whale oil and meat. As kills of depleted blue whales declined from 7,781 in 1948 and 1949 to fewer than 1,500 ten years later, kills of smaller fin whales increased to 25,000. As fins declined, the even smaller sei and minke whales became the prey. Although the annual kill reached an all-time high of 66,097 in 1960, Antarctic whaling declined steadily thereafter. In 1962, a jump in the price of sperm-whale oil used in industrial lubricants sent Russian and Japanese factory ships after the Pacific sperm whales, the last population that could have been called abundant. In all, the whaling industry has killed some 2,234,000 whales in this century, and has rendered most species rare or endangered to some degree.

Given the intensity of exploitation, most whale species undoubtedly would have gone the way of the mastodon if they hadn't lived in the oceans. Certainly, conservation measures taken throughout all but the last few years of whaling history had virtually no success in stopping their decimation. Whalers do not seem to have even begun thinking about conservation until the 1920s, when the British established regulations to protect breeding whales and reduce waste at their Antarctic shore stations. Other whalers simply evaded these regulations by switching their processing to floating factories, however, and this response to regulation set the tone for the next five decades.

Various agencies, first national governments and the League of Nations, then the International Whaling Commission after its founding in 1946, would set quotas, seasons, size limits, and other regulations. Established with the express purpose of conserving whale numbers, the regulations proved ineffective for reasons that became increasingly plain over the years. The whalers themselves, or the scientists and bureaucrats whose careers they could influence, established and enforced the regulations, and they did not allow those regulations to interfere with the profitable killing of whales. Thus quotas tended to be higher than the numbers of whales actually being killed. Size limits tended to reflect the convenience of factory ships more than the needs of whale reproduction. Regulators declared whale species or whaling areas protected only after whalers had depleted them.

Conservationists and the general public did not pay much attention to Antarctic whale slaughter in its heyday. It took place far from civilization at a time when communication was much slower than it is today. Moreover, people knew much less about the whales' fascinating qualities; science had yet to discover many of them. According to popular perception, cetaceans were either rather dull, or rather dangerous creatures (except the small-toothed whales—the dolphins and porpoises).

This perception has changed radically in the past three decades, largely because knowledge has increased and communication is better. With this change, the whales' prospects have improved since the late 1960s, when continued heavy exploitation by Soviet and Japanese factory fleets raised serious doubts about the survival of several species. The improvement has not come without a struggle, however, and remaining whaling nations have continued the basic bottom-line policy of trying to take as many whales as possible for as long as possible.

As though in atonement for nineteenth-century havoc, the role of the United States in modern whale conservation has been positive. (The United States does not have a modern whaling fleet, and that has been a factor.) The International Whaling Commission originated at a conference in Washington, D.C. When the IWC's failure to conserve whales finally became evident, the United States delegation to the 1972 United Nations Conference on the Human Environment proposed a resolution calling on the IWC to pass a ten-year commercial whaling moratorium. Although the conference overwhelmingly approved the resolution, the IWC did not pass the moratorium; it did, however, begin to set more biologically sound quotas. The 1972 resolution also laid the groundwork for eventual IWC passage of a moratorium in 1982.

In 1972, the United States also passed the Marine Mammal Protection Act, which set a moratorium on the taking of marine mammals by Americans and on the importation into the United States of marine mammals or products made from them. This was the first legislation to acknowledge the aesthetic and ecological values of whales as well as the commercial ones. A year later, the Endangered Species Act gave added protection to listed whale species, which include blue, bowhead, fin, gray, humpback, right, sei, and sperm whales. As well as restricting commercial taking, the Endangered Species Act requires federal agencies to ensure that their activities don't threaten listed species, and also provides for designation and acquisition of critical habitat, which may be important to survival of coastal species such as rights and grays as offshore oil drilling increases.

In 1976, Congress passed the Fisheries Conservation Management Act, which, along with other measures to conserve saltwater fisheries, extended the United States Conservation Zone (over which it claims exclusive fishing rights) from twelve to two hundred miles into the oceans. Congress approved the measure mainly to halt depletion of offshore fisheries by foreign factory trawlers, but the law also had direct and indirect applications to whale conservation. It established instant de facto whale sanctuaries within the two-hundred-mile zone, which is the largest offshore area owned by any nation. Soviet factory ships that had been catching sperm whales in Hawaiian waters had to stop.

The Fisheries Conservation Management Act also gave the United States increased leverage over whaling nations under the Packwood-Magnuson amendments passed in 1979. These required the secretary of commerce to reduce allocations of fish made to a foreign nation using

American waters (the United States still allows foreign fleets to fish with-in the two-hundred-mile limit under a permit system) if that nation jeop-ardizes the International Whaling Commission's effectiveness. The amendments came into play when Soviet whalers exceeded their quota of Southern Hemisphere minke whales in 1985. Another legislative provi-sion, the Pelly amendment to the Fisherman's Protective Act of 1967, called for the U.S. government to prohibit importation of fish products from countries known to be violating an international fisheries conserva-tion program.

In the late 1970s, the IWC became a more effective conservation body. As well as reforming its regulatory procedures, it declared the entire Indian Ocean north of fifty-five degrees latitude a whale sanctuary and banned factory-ship whaling, except for the taking of minke whales in Antarctica. These changes weren't entirely the result of a change of heart in favor of conservation among whaling nations. More and more were dropping out of the industry as whales and profits dwindled, so die-hards like the Soviet Union and Japan increasingly were outvoted. Even the die-hards had to convert most of their fleets. When the 1982 moratorium passed, it was partly a conservation victory, partly a repetition of the historical pattern in which whales had been killed as long as it paid.

The IWC moratorium didn't stop the killing of whales entirely. The main whaling nations filed objections to it and persistently sought ways to circumvent it. At least a dozen nations killed whales in 1987, the year after the moratorium went into effect. Several nations, including Japan, the Soviet Union, Iceland, and Norway, exploited a loophole in the mora-torium treaty which allowed continued taking of whales for "research." The meat was often sold commercially. Even when these nations essen-tially idled their fleets in the late 1980s, they didn't give up. Iceland, Norway, and Japan tried to get the moratorium overturned in 1990. In 1991, Iceland appealed unsuccessfully to the IWC for permission to resume whaling. In 1992, Norway announced it would resume catching minke whales in defiance of the moratorium, asserting that the species wasn't in danger. Norwegian whalers killed 226 minke whales in 1993 and planned to kill 301 in 1994. Several nations have also continued to take thousands of small cetaceans such as dolphins; in the early 1990s, an estimated half million of these were being killed yearly, particularly by Japan, Sri Lanka, and Peru.

Whaling also continued in U.S. waters, since special provisions of the Marine Mammal Act and the Endangered Species Act permitted

Alaska natives to engage in subsistence hunting of bowhead whales. The Alaska bowhead hunt brought the U.S. government in conflict with the IWC when the commission tried to lower bowhead quotas and the United States tried to raise them. The United States tarnished its whale conservation record further when the Reagan administration failed to invoke the Pelly and Packwood-Magnuson amendments to force Japan to observe the moratorium, a failure related to balance-of-trade concerns and increasingly close ties between Japanese and American fishing companies. In June 1986, the U.S. Supreme Court upheld an American-Japanese agreement that allowed continued Japanese fishing in U.S. waters if Japan was out of whaling by 1988.

Even if the moratorium lasts, illegal whaling might continue. Pirate whalers like the *Sierra* (which was sunk in Lisbon harbor by anti-whaling activists) may kill whales much more cruelly and wastefully than legal whalers. The *Sierra* took only meat, killing forty- to fifty-ton animals for two or three tons of prime cuts, and it killed whales without explosive harpoons. This saved meat, but whales sometimes took hours to die. Since the ownership and nationality of such ships is usually obscure and complicated, enforcement of laws against them is difficult.

In May 1994, the IWC voted overwhelmingly (twenty-three nations in favor, six abstaining, Japan opposed) to establish a permanent, eleven-million-square-mile whale sanctuary in the Antarctic, including all waters south of Africa, Australia, and South America. The sanctuary provided some assurance that whale protection will continue if the whaling moratorium should end, since the area is the largest feeding ground for whales, and one of the few remaining areas where populations of minke whales are large enough to support commercial exploitation. The sanctuary didn't stop "research" whaling, however, and it didn't increase protection against illegal whaling. Measures for enforcing the sanctuary were also unclear.

Of course, whales don't define the oceans' limits. If they became extinct, the oceans would continue to function. Yet civilization also has begun to deplete organisms much more basic to ocean functions, and to its own. We can function without whales but without fish we would face real difficulties. The annual global catch of fish substantially exceeds yearly beef production and provides twenty-three percent of all animal protein consumed by humans. As world population has doubled since 1950, the annual fish catch has more than tripled. A global fish depletion would cause massive malnutrition.

Until quite recently, people did not believe ocean fish could be depleted. Before 1970, fisheries experts confidently predicted that global annual catches eventually would reach two to four hundred million tons a year, an enormous increase over the roughly twenty-five million tons caught in 1950. Many nations thus invested heavily in sophisticated fishing fleets and other ocean-taming schemes. Futurologists envisioned an age of ocean settlement, when underwater or floating cities would serve domesticated fisheries, deep-sea mining, and other industries of unprecedented bounty.

Instead, fishing nations discovered limits with surprising swiftness. The fishing industry expanded rapidly for two decades, but then growth of annual catches slowed to less than one percent after 1970. Since human population is growing much faster, this has meant a per-capita decline in availability of fish as food. Even more ominously, some local fish populations began to disappear entirely, the Peruvian anchoveta being a case in point. Its disappearance destroyed a profitable guano industry, as seabirds that had fed on the fish declined. (Guano, the nitrogen-rich droppings covering seabird colonies, makes excellent fertilizer.) By the 1980s, six Atlantic fisheries and five Pacific ones were depleted to the point of collapse, and the annual global catch had declined by about eleven million tons from its peak in the early 1970s. In the 1990s, the Newfoundland Grand Banks cod fishery collapsed, the fishery which had attracted the first Portuguese fishing boats of the late Middle Ages.

Like whales, fish declined because they were being caught faster than they could reproduce; human exploitation will have to be controlled if their populations are to be restored. The establishment by many nations of two-hundred-mile coastal zones is one step in this direction; it has led many of the factory ships that once emptied vast coastlines of fish to cease operating. Leveling off of ocean catches (at about seventy million tons a year) has also encouraged considerable growth in fish farming of freshwater species such as carp, tilapia, prawns, and catfish.

Fish farming is not necessarily a boon to wildlife, since it can pre-empt wetland, riparian, and estuarine habitat and, in the case of turtle and crocodilian farms, lead to illegal trafficking in wild animals passed off as farmed ones. Fish farming or aquaculture is a highly efficient way of producing animal protein, considerably more efficient than the growing of warm-blooded livestock. While it takes seven pounds of grain to produce a pound of beef, it takes only 1.7 pounds to produce a pound of fish. Farming now produces about a sixth of the fish and other "underwater livestock" consumed worldwide, and with a growth rate of over seven percent a year, it probably will produce much more eventually.

It is unlikely, however, that futurologists will ever realize dreams of turning the oceans into giant fish farms. It would be hard to raise their productive capacity beyond what it was in the natural state. Instead, civilization is lowering that capacity by overfishing the oceans, and, even more ominously, by polluting them. The limits of the oceans' ability to absorb sewage, toxic chemicals, radioactive wastes, and oil spills are the most crucial limits of all. If we exceed them, recovery will be much more problematic than restoration of whale or fish populations.

Like water, pollutants eventually find their way into the oceans. Unlike water, pollutants are not distributed evenly throughout the ocean basins. They accumulate near their sources, the coastlines, which are also the most important areas for ocean life. Such areas may therefore reach their pollution-absorbing capacities long before entire oceans reach their limits. For example, in New York Bight, a portion of the Atlantic off New York City, a lifeless blanket of "black mayonnaise" comprising sewage sludge and other pollutants spreads for miles out to sea, and when wind and tides are right, occasionally covers beaches. Oil spills may also blanket miles of sea floor with toxic ooze that takes years to dissipate, but at least the pollution of an individual oil spill eventually does dissipate. The pollution at the mouths of the rivers into which cities, factories, and farms dump their wastes is never-ending.

Ocean pollution is a vast, complicated problem. Yet civilization's responses to depletion of whales and fish suggest what can be done to confront this more fundamental limit of the oceans. Civilization can reform its institutions as the International Whaling Commission has been reformed. It can redistribute its investments, as international banking organizations have redistributed their loans from trawler fleets to fish farms.

# Songs
# from the
# Deep

FAITH McNULTY

# The Great Whales

My quest for a glimpse of great whales first took me to Bermuda, where Dr. Roger Payne and his wife, Katy, were recording the sounds of humpbacks from a forty-four-foot motor sailer named the *Rockfish*, which had been lent them by Dr. Henry Clay Frick, a New York surgeon, who is a grandson of the steel millionaire, is a trustee of the New York Zoological Society, and has a home in Bermuda. On a choppy, windy April day, we set off from a harbor on the east end of the island, heading down along the south shore toward Challenger Bank, where the Paynes had had good luck finding humpback whales on previous trips. On board were the captain, a ruddy-faced Bermudan named Campbell O'Connor; the Paynes; Jane Frick, Dr. Frick's daughter, who is in her twenties, likes to take underwater photographs, and hopes to get some of whales; and Oliver Brazier, a quiet Bostonian who is an expert on electronic equipment. Roger Payne is a tall, dark-eyed, boyish-looking man in his late thirties, with the ability to alternate intense seriousness with easy and graceful humor. He has passionate personal feelings about whales, and writes and talks of them with a romantic eloquence that raises the hackles of some of his fellow-biologists. Most cetologists have

FAITH McNULTY's collected essays on nature writing, many of which appeared originally in *The New Yorker*, was published in 1980. She has also published books for children, including most recently *Snake in the House*. This essay was adapted from *The Great Whales*. Copyright © 1974 by Faith McNulty. Used by permission of Doubleday, a division of Bantam Doubleday Dell Publishing Group, Inc.

started out as fishery men. Haddock and herring are not such stuff as dreams are made of, and these men have viewed whales primarily as a problem in population dynamics. They have wished to save whales only to make the maximum "use" of them. Payne, who has been crusading to save whales for the sake of whales, rather than having them used as a cheap food for mink—or even for men, since he considers it wicked to encourage the further overpopulation that menaces the globe—has a quite different point of view. His initial interest, after his graduation from Harvard, was in animal behavior, and he began by doing research on the hearing of bats, insects, and owls. He was diverted to whales by an emotional experience that occurred early in his career when he was on the staff of Tufts University. Late one sleety March night when he was working in his laboratory, he heard on the radio that a dead whale had washed ashore on Revere Beach. On an impulse, he drove out to see it. Later, he wrote about standing on the deserted beach at the water's edge, looking at the whale in the beam of a flashlight:

It was a small whale—a porpoise about eight feet long, with lovely, subtle curves glistening in the cold rain. It had been mutilated. Someone had hacked off its flukes for a souvenir and two other people had carved their initials deeply into its side. Someone else had stuck a cigar butt into its blowhole. I removed the cigar and I stood there for a long time with feelings I can't describe. Everybody has some such experience that affects him for life, probably several. That night was one of mine. At some point the flashlight went out, but as the tide came in I could periodically see the graceful outline of the whale against the white foam cast up by the waves. Although it is more typical than not of what happens to whales when they encounter man, that experience was somehow the last straw, and I decided to use the first possible opportunity to learn enough about whales so I might have some effect on their future.

When Payne found that humpback whales congregate off Bermuda in winter and early spring, he and his wife made a trip there in 1967. They met Frank Watlington, then an engineer with the Columbia University Geophysical Field Station at Bermuda. Some time before, hydrophones had been installed in the ocean offshore from Watlington's office, which is on a rocky headland, to record whatever sounds came along. He had been startled to find that these included medleys of a sort of unearthly singing, grunting, wailing, and rumbling, which he could attribute only to the humpbacks that were to be seen breaching and spouting offshore at the time the sounds were recorded.

When Roger Payne, who plays the cello and loves music, heard Watlington's recordings of whale sounds, he was deeply stirred. As he later described it: "Katy and I first heard humpback sounds over the roar of a generator and blower. Even so, what we experienced in that crowded, noisy compartment were the most fascinating and beautiful sounds of the wild world I had ever heard." Watlington gave the Paynes copies of the tapes, and back home in New York they played them over and over. What impressed and fascinated Payne particularly was the variety of the sounds. At first, they seemed to come in random sequence, but after many hearings he realized that there were definite patterns, repeated from time to time. It occurred to him that these patterns—which could be called "songs" in the same sense that the characteristic sound sequences of birds are called songs—offered a valuable tool for the study of whale behavior. The study of the humpback songs thus united Dr. Payne's two main interests: the use of sound in animal communication and the behavior of whales. He found support for these studies at the New York Zoological Society, whose officers had decided to launch a full-scale campaign to save whales in spite of what looked like hopeless odds.

The next year, the Paynes went to Bermuda again, and, hoping to get close to the whales without frightening them, Payne put out to sea in a plywood rowboat. There were humpbacks surfacing around him, but he could only get about fifty feet from them. When a pair of whales that he had been vainly chasing went down for a long dive, Payne shipped his oars and waited for them to reappear. As he sat there, he suddenly heard whale music emanating eerily from the hull of the boat. Because of the different densities of air and water, very little sound from the depths can escape into the air, but wood is of an intermediate density and can act as a transducer. (Payne points out that whaling literature includes accounts of strange ethereal music reverberating through quiet ships at night, and thinks that these accounts can be explained as whale sounds transmitted through wooden hulls.) The sounds that Payne heard in his rowboat were not only clear but startlingly similar to Watlington's tapes. "This blew my mind," Payne says. "It was confirmation that not only do individual humpbacks repeat their songs but other humpbacks may sing the same song at a different time and place." His conclusion that there are definite, recurring sequences in whale song was later confirmed by spectrographic analysis. Payne lent Watlington's tapes to Scott McVay, who was then a

Princeton University administrator and who undertook to work with him on their analysis. This involved the use of a spectrograph machine, which produces a chart that shows both frequency over a period of time and amplitude, and resembles music notation. Thus printed out, the separate whale songs are as recognizable as, say, "The Star-Spangled Banner."

Katy Payne, an attractive blue-eyed young woman, is, like her husband, an accomplished musician, and she has become deeply involved in analyzing the tapes of whale music they have collected. She has even learned to sing like a whale, imitating the sounds in a high, silvery voice, and even reproducing the rude Bronx cheers and ratchet sounds that break into the lyrical passages.

When I joined the Paynes on their Bermuda expedition, they warned me that whale-watching can be a frustrating business. Whales appear briefly and unpredictably, they said, and moments of excitement are followed by long stretches of nothing but rough water. My notes on the trip follow, beginning in the morning as the six of us, in the cockpit of the *Rockfish*, braced ourselves against the surging roll of the waves en route to the banks where the whales are most often found.

Roger explains that his immediate goal is to find out how loud the whale sounds are and how far they can carry—fundamental information that would help explain the function of the sounds. He speculates that the sounds could be a means of recognition between individuals or could proclaim territory, provide contact between migrant groups, or be involved in sex recognition and attraction. Or perhaps some components of the whale's sounds could be used in echolocation, like the sonar clicks of porpoises. Is the song the whale's altimeter, telling it where it is in relation to the surface in the course of a dive? Roger suggests still another theory: "A whale herd is like a convoy of boats and the whales can't afford to collide. Their skins are very delicate. Maneuvering such a bulk must be like trying to drive a giant trailer truck in traffic. I figure whales have to be alert and communicate rapidly and precisely."

Katy asks, "Is there a sound for left and one for right?"

Roger grins and says, "I wish I knew." He would love to know how complex the communications are, he continues. Can whales convey as much information as a honeybee, which can tell other bees precisely where to find a certain supply of food? Are different components of the whale sounds used for different purposes? Is there, perhaps, one sound for close maneuvering and another that, like bird song, simply says, "I am a healthy male and I would like to meet you"?

A little later, Roger says, "Whales have the most acoustically complex life possible—more than fish, which rely on vision." He wants to know how whales get around in a nonvisual world. The more wide-ranging and unpredictable the life of a whale is, the more need it has to communicate over long distances. The food of whales drifts randomly over featureless ocean, and in order not to compete with each other they must stay far apart while feeding. Roger theorizes that sound frees individuals from the need for close contact, so they can spread out, and make the most of the food supply. But, as nomads wandering over vast distances, unable to leave a track or a scent for others to follow, they have the problem of getting back together. "If they can shout information on where they are," Roger says, "then the whole sea becomes an enormous room."

Roger explains that there is something called "the deep sound channel"—a layer of water that confines sound so that it can carry as far as halfway around the world. The sound of a dynamite blast near Australia, for instance, was once picked up by a listening device off Bermuda several hours later. Roger speculates that whales may send their signals over hundreds of miles through the deep sound channel. He is distressed because the multitude of ships churning through the ocean nowadays—there are fourteen hundred in the North Atlantic on any given day—are polluting the seas with noise. The whir of their propellers is on the same sound wavelength as the whales' noises and may mess up whale communications.

I ask Roger what other aspects of whales' lives he wants to investigate. He says he wants to know everything—where they go, what they do at each stage of their lives, and why. "A biologist wants to become part of an animal's life. I would like to be a flea on the shoulder of a bat. That's impossible, but maybe somebody will invent a little capsule in which you could attach yourself to a whale. What I want is to be *with* whales as much as possible." He says that close observations are very difficult around Bermuda, where the water is rough and the whales are rather widely dispersed, but that he has found a place off the South American coast where southern right whales gather in calm water behind a barrier reef and can be watched at close quarters. He thinks that, with enough patience, a human being will be able to get as close to whales as George Schaller and Jane van Lawick-Goodall have got to apes. He thinks that if you hang around whales long enough the older ones will come to ignore you, and you can take advantage of the curiosity of the young. But if you chase, injure, or frighten an animal, he says, you're finished. A colleague told him that a lion that was forcibly tagged didn't forget the incident for two years. On a previous expedition, Roger attempted to plant a pinger—a device that sends out a signal—in a humpback whale so that he could follow the whale, but it used its long flippers to wipe off the device. The episode frightened the whale and disturbed Roger. He has resolved to pursue his studies by methods that don't risk hurting his subjects.

Katy says that one of her objectives in analyzing whale songs is to find out whether individuals can be recognized by their songs—or, if not individuals, then groups. If so, they could be tracked by their songs, and their travels charted. She compares whale song to bird song, pointing out that because birds are small their lives are speeded up. A bird song lasts only a few seconds—or, at most, a few minutes—and the notes are very close together. She thinks whales sing huge, slow songs appropriate to their size, and that is why each note is so distinct. It sounds to human ears like a record slowed down.

We are chugging along into rising swells, and the horizon is turbulent with whitecaps. Campbell O'Connor, our captain, says it is going to get rougher and now might be a good time to eat. Katy goes below and gets us crackers, cheese, and soup. While we eat, Roger explains how he hopes to gather information on the loudness of whale sounds. He wants to record a whale's voice on tape and then, when the whale surfaces, measure its distance from the boat. There are three things to be measured at the same time: the intensity of the sound as it reaches the hydrophones, the distance to the whale, and the temperature of the water, which influences sound conductivity. Measuring the distance to a singing whale is not easy. First, the whale must be identified as the one that is being heard through the earphones, and then its position must be fixed at a moment coinciding with a certain segment of the tape recording of its song. Roger has thought of various ways to measure the distance to the whale, but fears that some of them would frighten the whale into silence and flight. He has decided to try taking simultaneous pictures from two cameras fixed a certain distance apart, and calculating the angle between the two images. As he snaps the shutter, he will record an identifying number on the tape. The camera rig is lying on top of the deckhouse.

Katy shouts, "Whale!" Roger asks O'Connor to turn off the engine. The boat drifts and rolls in the choppy waves, which whisper and splash

against its sides. Only the jib steadies us. Off to one side, there is a round
slick, as if a ship had sunk. This is characteristic of a spot where a whale
has gone down. Oliver Brazier, the sound expert, puts the hydrophones
over the side. Roger, in bathing trunks and earphones, stands tensely in
the heaving cockpit, listening, but reports that he is hearing only strum-
ming interference.

"What direction was he going?" he asks.

"East," says O'Connor, pointing ahead. We are about two miles offshore.

Roger says, "I hear a very distant whale."

I picture a vast, green chamber beneath us, and wonder if any person
will ever be able to move in it as freely as the whales do. Roger and
Oliver are fiddling with the equipment. When they finally decide that the
machinery is working right, there is no whale.

O'Connor says, "That whale's got no time to mess with you people.
He's gone to sing to his girl friend."

We raise the mainsail and go to look for other whales. We plow
through the waves with white foam at our bow. We are all getting impatient, but see nothing except gray waves hurrying past us. Then
O'Connor says, "There's one!" and points off the port bow. A second later,
I see a whale spout. The spout is like a puff of smoke. It hangs in the air,
then disintegrates. It comes again. We lower the mainsail, and Katy
throws the hydrophones over. The whale stays under for what seems a
long time—actually, it's only a few minutes—and then suddenly rises a
stone's throw away. I see a gleaming black back and patches of brilliant
white. Then it is gone, in a surge of foam. Roger is on top of the boom
struggling with the cameras. Katy says, "I'm getting great sound, but it
can't be this whale. It's too far away." She hands me the earphones. They
are filled with sound. Mixed with the gurgle and wash of water I hear
something like a baby crying very far away. Then the cry turns into a
medley of ethereal calls such as tiny translucent fairies might make. Katy
thinks we are hearing two or three whales at once. There is an impression, impossible to confirm, of calls and answers. The whale we saw
doesn't appear again. What we are hearing *must* be far away. We settle
down to wait for another strolling singer. In spite of the jib, we roll and
slat as the gray seas come past like rolling mountains. Not far beneath us,
there are real mountains, rising from a tremendous depth. They have flattened, mesalike tops that form banks a hundred and eighty feet below
the surface. At the moment, I learn, we are over the saddle between Challenger and Plantagenet Banks. The valley floor is three or four thousand

feet below the mountaintops, and the slopes are so steep, O'Connor says, that he once dropped bow and stern anchors in this area and found his bow in a hundred and eighty feet of water and his stern in five hundred. I wonder if the whales slide down the sides of the mountains, coasting like kids on snow, and then laze along the valley floor.

I ask how close we might get to a whale. Katy says that one year three whales headed straight for the boat. She jumped in the water with a mask on and, looking down, could see their giant forms and white-banded flippers gleaming right below her. She says she felt awfully small. And once, at the South American whale grounds, she and Brazier were in a small outboard motorboat when a whale came up, raised its head out of the water to peer at them, turned tail and flurried the water in threat, then thrust its flukes under the boat, lifted it into the air, and put it down. As they hit the surface, Oliver started the motor, and they scooted away. Katy noticed that there were two mother whales with calves nearby, and wondered if the whale that threatened them was a bull protecting females. It escorted them from the area. Roger says he had a similar experience when a whale followed his skiff and nudged the stern with its head. "My first reaction was delight," he recalls, "mixed with some alarm, but I decided to hang on and see what was going to happen next. Nothing did! The whale had found out what he wanted to know about me, and, I suspect, was also hanging on to see what was going to happen next. It was a marvellous meeting."

After an hour, no whale has appeared. We pull in the hydrophones and move on. Half an hour later, we haul the mainsail down again and put the hydrophones over. Katy listens, and immediately her face brightens. She says the whale sounds are very loud. Roger begins recording. I listen for a moment. There is a sound like the hinge on a creaky iron door. Then we hear what sounds like a high-low operatic duet. Is it really a duet or one whale talking to itself? Roger would give a lot to know. All at once, O'Connor sees a whale swimming parallel to us. It is surprisingly hard to estimate the distance of a whale from a boat, but this one looks huge and seems close—perhaps less than a hundred yards away. It blows. The great, gleaming black back surges out with a swift roll. There is a glimpse of the little fin near the tail, and then the whale is gone. The few minutes the whale is visible are intensely exciting and tantalizing. To be so close to something so enormous and so transient! There is a longing to detain it, explore it, touch it, make some contact—to say or do something that the whale will respond to.

Now there are four whales off the bow, blowing as they move away from us, while closer at hand two black torpedoes cut the water in front of us. The black backs roll out and under. Then three more whales appear, even closer, and they blow twice and make a leisurely turn around our stern. They are visible for a count of twelve. I can see the small eye and the smile at the corner of the mouth. Over the white bands on the flippers the water takes on a turquoise hue, as it does over white sand in the tropics. While these three are circling us, Roger thinks, they are within a hundred feet. We are up to our ears in whales—so many that there is no way to tell which are singing. Katy reports a great medley of sounds. I listen briefly, and hear groans, bleats, moos, even motorcycles starting up and receding into the distance. Now all the whales are gone. We feel left alone, like watchers when a parade has turned the corner, but through the earphones the whales can still be heard singing in the distance.

It is afternoon now, and we have been hearing continuous song for an hour without seeing a whale. This indicates to Roger that either the sound comes from very far off or the whales are staying down a very long time. Katy lends me her earphones. I hear a slightly daft siren song. The sweetest, most poetic notes, pure and piercing, are followed by low ratchet sounds and Bronx cheers. Next, there are haunted-house sounds—Cathy calling Heathcliff. Then a switch to a rural scene—somebody blowing into a jug, beagles yipping, cattle lowing.

I contemplate the endless motion of whales. They go through the water like perpetually turning wheels, doomed never to rest or to form any attachment to a single place. They are Flying Dutchmen. I mention this to Roger. He says that at the South American site the whales loll along the shore, circling there and resting on the current. Sometimes they lie on their backs and wave their gigantic flippers. He says it is a marvellous place to observe whale behavior, because you can stand on a cliff and look right down on the whales. He often saw contact between them—heads touching, sliding over each other. In greeting each other, the whales arch their backs in a peculiar way. He saw a mating. The female, with a calf beside her, lay in the water. The male slid smoothly beneath her, turned belly up, and arched his back. It lasted only a second. There are old reports of whales' mating in a vertical position, rising out of the water belly to belly, but Roger thinks that this is unlikely.

Roger's South American whales are right whales, and at this time in their lives they are silent. Humpbacks apparently cease to sing when they move to their northern feeding grounds, where they stay from May to December; sounds have been recorded, but they have not been found to be "songs." This summer silence is puzzling Roger, but he notes that the whales are particularly scattered then, and it is harder to pick up their sounds. He wonders if perhaps they have been silenced by fear of large, noisy vessels from which recording has been attempted. He thinks it very important to approach whales in a sailboat.

Since whales have a larynx but no vocal cords, we discuss the mystery of how they make their sounds. People emit air to cause sound vibration, but there are other possible techniques—stridulation, for instance. The whale might strum a taut membrane inside itself. Roger, however, thinks it most likely that whales use air, because an air-filled cavity produces a harmonic series similar to whale sounds; namely, even multiples of the fundamental. This theory assumes that the whale transfers air inside it from one cavity to another, and implies the use of some sort of plumbing, probably in the head, for the purpose. Whales have a number of cavities associated with the larynx and the nasal passage which might serve to produce sound—and the sound need not necessarily come *out* of any particular aperture. It could simply emerge through the blubber and skin.

We've just seen a black back wheel out of the water. It is coming toward us, with a smaller one just behind—a mother and a calf. They are so close that as they submerge we again see the water turn turquoise over the gleaming white on their flippers. Their skin shines like divers' wetsuits. There is a wake of champagnelike bubbles, and smooth eddies behind it. The whales blow a deep, long, sighing exhalation, quite loud—first the mother and then the baby—and sink. They surface three more times, moving slowly away. Roger photographs them, but Katy hears nothing on the earphones.

We raise the sail and start for Challenger Bank. When we reach it, we haul down the sail and drop the hydrophones over. Bermuda is barely visible. There is a whale half a mile ahead. Katy hears a distant whale sound over the earphones. On the horizon behind us I suddenly see a cigar-shaped cylinder thrust out of the water to an incredible height, like the lift-off of a rocket. It is a whale standing on its tail. I yell, and everybody sees the giant splash as it topples and hits the water. Katy says the singing she was hearing in the earphones stopped about that time, and Roger thinks perhaps we have seen Katy's singing whale. He has a theory that whales sing when they are near the surface, rising and falling in shallow dives and not travelling fast. He thinks that they lie in the water and sing, and that the sound resembling a ratchet occurs when the whale is coming to the surface for a breath.

After a while, we start moving again. O'Connor says there are fish-pots ahead, and predicts that we'll find whales among them. He says the whales like to rub their backs on the fishpots, which sometimes damages the pots' little marker flags and angers the fishermen, who often shoot at the whales. We approach a fishpot marked by a staff flying a pennant, which seems a strange touch of civilization in this empty wilderness of water. Suddenly we are in the midst of whales. A pair, with a third whale behind them, surge alongside and blow—one, two, three great sighing, steamy sounds, like those made by a steam locomotive settling down on a siding. I see an open blowhole quivering and vibrating. It is a couple of inches across. Jane has jumped overboard in her bluejeans and is pad-dling around like a seal, upright in the choppy water, wet hair streaming over her eyes, as she tries to adjust her camera. There is excited activity on board, with Katy and Oliver working the sound equipment and Roger taking pictures. The whales surge by. They surface and sink, surface and sink, with a rhythmic, easy roll that has a wonderful grace.

These whales go by very fast. I am reminded of being at the rail of a race track when the horses come swiftly toward you. For an extraordi-nary instant, they are right beside you, so that you smell the sweat and hear the panting and the creak of leather. Then they are going away. For just such an instant, the whales surface beside the boat and they hurry on past the bow, and abruptly decide to sound. They rise, then dive steeply, seeming to stand on their heads. Their huge flukes wave above the sur-face like the wings of giant black butterflies; then they sink smoothly into the sea and are gone. The waving flukes are a sign that they are heading for the depths. Everybody seems to feel very frustrated. Jane climbs back in the boat, having failed to get a picture. The deck is a tangle of wires, but the sounds that Katy heard over the earphones were distant ones and could not have been from these whales. Roger has good pictures but no whale sounds to match them.

After a dismal, letdown hour of sloshing around, we motor to a spot near another bunch of fish traps. Roger puts on earphones. He reports that he has briefly heard a whale singing, but it has quit. "I'm afraid we shut it up with the motor," he says. After a minute, his face brightens. "Watch for a blow," he says. "There's somebody close." We watch in vain. Though the sounds are tantalizingly clear, an hour or so passes and we see nothing. Now it seems miraculous that we saw the other whales so close.

We move again, and as soon as the hydrophones are down Katy reports that she hears some beautiful grunts. She passes me the earphones, and I hear sounds exactly like water chugging out of a bottle. Then comes the siren song. Now I picture dark-green corridors lined with mirrors, and sirens in diaphanous white garments drifting through them. Jane yells "Breach!" and I turn my head in time to see a giant splash a few hundred yards astern. The whale rises again, and almost its entire body is visible. It hangs above the water for an instant and falls with a loud report, amid geysers of water. It vanishes. We wait hopefully, but it doesn't reappear. Apparently, it is also silent. The sounds on the hydrophones are coming from a distance. I hand the earphones back to Katy, who sits watching the water and listening. At intervals, she says, "It's so beautiful!"

My notes on the trip end there, but I remember, perhaps best of all, what came afterward.

For several hours, we drifted over the banks, rolling steadily but less furiously than in the early afternoon. An evening calm was settling on the water. Now and then, we saw a distant spout—nothing close. (Roger suspects that a whale can exhale invisibly underwater and then surface just long enough to take a breath without being seen.) Katy sat in the stern, resting against a pile of life jackets, listening. The sun sank, and the sky and water turned mauve and gray. O'Connor planned to let us drift through the night. He lit the running lights and went below to get some supper. Oliver and Roger went down to work with the recording equipment. They wanted to run the recorder all night.

I sat in the cockpit, watching the light soften and turn silver, watching the ceaseless movement of the water, and becoming aware that our boat was shrinking—that it had become a very small platform to rest on in this endless ocean. As I gazed at the metallic surface of the waves, it occurred to me that in the fifty million years that whales have existed the land has changed beyond recognition but the sea has remained a primeval landscape, and may have looked just like this at the beginning of creation. The sky was empty. There were no clouds to keep us company, and no birds.

Katy put down the earphones and went below. After a moment, I moved to her place and put them on. Whale songs were coming through beautifully. They were lovely and fascinating, but what struck me most of all was that they had the warmth of life. The cold, empty world of the surface dropped away as I dipped into the populated depths. Far from being empty, the great chamber below was filled with life. I relaxed as I listened to its lively hum. It was like looking through a pane of glass, watching busy activities on the other side, yet not being quite able to enter. I thought about the various speculations as to why whales make their strange sounds, and the answer suddenly seemed clear: they sing their songs so that they won't be alone.

ROGER PAYNE

# Humpbacks:
# Their Mysterious Songs

At dusk I sat in the stern sheets of our small sailboat, braced against a stanchion and using the last light of day to take a final sight on Bermuda's Gibbs Hill Lighthouse, 35 miles to the northeast.

We were too far from land to return that evening; my wife, Katy, and I would have to spend the night at sea. Bermuda's treacherous reefs are difficult enough to navigate in broad daylight. In darkness they are impossible.

As night deepened, a familiar feeling came over me, one of loneliness at sea. I felt at one with the other solitary watchers elsewhere on earth— the shepherds, sentinels, and herdsmen who huddled alone beneath these same stars, feeling the night close in around them.

To break the mood, Katy and I got down to work. We brought the boat about onto the other tack and pointed her as high into the wind as we could, so that she nodded gently with the waves. After lowering a pair of hydrophones into the sea, I switched on their amplifiers and listened in stereo through the headphones.

We were no longer alone! Instead, we were surrounded by a vast and

ROGER PAYNE is one of the world's most knowledgeable whale scientists and president of the Whale Conservation Institute in Lincoln, Massachusetts. Payne's work led to the discovery that humpback whales sing, and his many honors include a MacArthur Fellowship. He is currently researching the problem of marine pollution, one of the most pressing concerns for whale survival. "Humpbacks: Their Mysterious Songs" was first published in *National Geographic* in 1982. Reprinted by permission of the author.

joyous chorus of sounds that poured up out of the sea and overflowed its rim. The spaces and vaults of the ocean, like a festive palace hall, reverberated and thundered with the cries of whales—sounds that boomed, echoed, swelled, and vanished as they wove together like strands in some vast and tangled web of glorious sound.

I felt instantly at ease, all sense of desolation brushed aside by the sheer ebullience of it all. All that night we were borne along by those lovely, dancing, yodeling cries, sailing on a sea of unearthly music.

Often during that night off Bermuda I thought how the oceans had once heard these wild cries. How, once, the echo chamber of the sea had reverberated to the haunting "songs" of whales. Then I thought of what it is like today in many of the whales' former haunts—silent, lifeless, impressing one most with a sense of what has been lost.

Humpback whales pass Bermuda each spring on their way north from southern calving grounds near Puerto Rico. During this period the humpbacks fill the ocean with complex and beautiful sounds. Many hours of these sounds were recorded and later analyzed with the help of a friend, Scott McVay, at Princeton University. The analysis showed that humpback sounds are in fact long songs. I use the term song not in a sense of beauty, although humpback sounds are indeed beautiful. By song I mean a regular sequence of repeated sounds such as the calls made by birds, frogs, and crickets.

## HUMPBACKS CHANGE THEIR TUNE

Most birdsongs are high pitched and last only a few seconds, while humpback songs vary widely in pitch and last between six and thirty minutes. Yet if you record a whale song and then speed it up about fourteen times the normal rate, it sounds amazingly like the song of a bird.

When you go out to listen to a humpback sing, you may hear a whale soloist, or you may hear seeming duets, trios, or even choruses of dozens of interweaving voices. Each of those whales is singing the same song, yet none is actually in unison with the others—each is marching to its own drummer, so to speak.

The fact that whales in Bermuda waters are singing the same song at any given moment is not surprising when you think of how similar two robins or two cardinals sound. But if you collect humpback songs for many years and compare each yearly recording with the songs of earlier years, something astonishing comes to light that sets these whales apart from all other animals: Humpback whales are constantly changing their songs.

In other words, the whales don't just sing mechanically; rather, they compose as they go along, incorporating new elements into their old songs. We are aware of no other animal besides man in which this strange and complicated behavior occurs, and we have no idea of the reason behind it. If you listen to songs from two different years you will be astonished to hear how different they are. For example, the songs we taped in 1964 and 1969 are as different as Beethoven from the Beatles.

By combining our own tapes with those of friends like Bermudian Frank Watlington, we now have a sample spanning twenty years in Bermuda.

Katy and I have analyzed this data in detail. We find that the song has been constantly changing with time. All the whales are singing the same song one year, but the next year they will all be singing a new song. The yearly differences are not random, however. The songs of two consecutive years are more alike than two that are separated by several years. Thus, the song appears to be evolving, but regardless of how complex the changes are, each whale apparently keeps pace with the others, so that every year the new song is the only one that a listener hears.

## MUSICAL TALENT MAY BE INHERITED

We have also recorded and analyzed four years of humpback songs from Hawaii, a major wintering area for humpbacks. Although songs of the same year in Hawaii and Bermuda are different, it is intriguing that they obey the same laws of change, and have the same structure. Each song, for example, is composed of about six themes—passages with several identical or slowly changing phrases in them. Each phrase contains from two to five sounds. In any one song the theme always follow the same order, though one or more themes may be absent. The remaining ones are always given in predictable sequence.

The whale populations of Hawaii and Bermuda are almost certainly not in contact. Thus, the fact that the laws for composing the songs are the same in both places strongly suggests that the whales inherit a set of laws and then improvise within them. Whether these laws are transmitted from one generation to the next genetically or by learning remains to be seen. When Katy first discovered that the songs of humpbacks were changing from year to year, a simple explanation seemed likely: Since the whales do not sing at their summer feeding grounds and since the song is complex, perhaps the humpbacks simply forget the song between seasons and improvise a new version from whatever fragments they can recall.

To test this theory, we organized a season-long study of humpbacks off the island of Maui in Hawaii.

The study had two objectives: to record a full season of songs and to make observations of the whales' behavior.

We were joined in the study by Al Giddings and Sylvia Earle, two of the most experienced divers in the world. Al, with his unsurpassed ability as an underwater photographer, and Sylvia, with her background in both diving and science, were ideal partners, as were our two graduate students, Jim Darling and Peter Tyack.

## SONGSTERS PICK UP WHERE THEY LEFT OFF

To me, the results of the study are fascinating. Over a six-month period we obtained samples of songs, coupled with unique observations of underwater behavior. The subsequent analysis of our tapes has revealed an intriguing fact: The whales had not forgotten the previous season's song, for they were singing it when they first returned to Maui. Only as the season progressed did the changes gradually take place. Obviously, during the period between breeding seasons the song is kept in "cold storage," without change.

Another fascinating thing we discovered is that the whales always sing new phrases faster than the old ones. We discovered, too, that new phrases are sometimes created by joining the beginning and end of consecutive phrases and omitting the middle part—just as we humans shorten "do not" to "don't." In many other ways the introduction of new material and the phasing out of old are similar to evolving language in humans.

So far, the study of humpback whale songs has provided our best insight into the mental capabilities of whales. Humpbacks are clearly intelligent enough to memorize all the complicated sounds in their songs. They also memorize the order of those sounds, as well as the new modifications they hear going on around them. Moreover, they can store this information for at least six months as a basis for further improvisations. To me, this suggests an impressive mental ability and a possible route in the future to assess the intelligence of whales.

Songs are not the only vocalizations of humpbacks; we often hear grunts, roars, bellows, creaks, and whines. These sounds sometimes accompany particular types of behavior, suggesting that they may have specific social meaning.

One such association between sound and behavior has been documented by Charles Jurasz, an independent researcher in Glacier Bay,

Alaska. Chuck's twelve-year study has added significantly to our knowledge of whales. On a recent visit with Chuck I recorded the underwater sounds of a humpback in the act of "spinning its net." Such sounds consist solely of expelled air. There are no accompanying social or vocal noises, which suggests to me that bubble netting is a deliberate act—that of a whale setting a trap.

## ARE WE KILLING WHALES WITH KINDNESS?

Only a few years ago the chief threat to humpback whales was the men who hounded them dangerously close to extinction. Today international agreement forbids the killing of humpbacks, but in some areas man threatens to love them to death.

In Hawaii increasing numbers of well-meaning tourists now converge on the breeding grounds in small boats to observe and photograph the great creatures at close range. Observation can sometimes edge over into harassment, which is illegal under both the Marine Mammal Protection Act and the Endangered Species Act.

In 1976 I tackled the problem with Nixon Griffis, a longtime friend of humpbacks. Together we called on Elmer Cravalho, mayor of Maui County, who appointed Jim Luckey, manager of Maui's Lahaina Restoration Foundation, to be chairman of a citizens' committee to explore the problem. The result is an official organization to educate the public and so prevent harassment of the whales. Thus the citizens of Maui have taken a major initiative in generating local government and citizen concern for protecting a marine mammal on the endangered species list.

Plans are now under way to establish a Pacific Marine Research Center at Lahaina with support not only from Hawaiians but also from worldwide subscription.

Happily for whales, such efforts are on the increase. One recent development may have spread the songs of humpbacks not just from the oceans to the land, but throughout the galaxy. Since late summer of 1977, *Voyagers 1* and 2—spacecraft launched from Cape Canaveral, Florida, toward other worlds in our galaxy—carried aboard unique recordings that included the works of Bach, Mozart, and a rock group, as well as a section entitled "The Sounds of Earth."

In the latter section delegates from sixty member countries of the United Nations offered a greeting in fifty-five languages. The messages were followed by a somewhat longer "greeting" from a humpback whale, recorded by Katy and me off Bermuda in 1970. In some ways this constitutes a step beyond all my dreams, in seeing whales become a symbol for the hope that there is still intelligent life on earth.

The expected lifetime of the records is a billion years. Should they be encountered by some other space-faring civilization, they would bear a message that had lasted longer than perhaps any other human work.

Could it be that mankind is simply the humpbacks' guarantee that its songs will be heard throughout the galaxy?

JOHN K. B. FORD

# Family Fugues

The phone rang, rousing me from a deep sleep. As I groped for the bedside telephone, I saw that it was just past midnight. On the line was Jim Borrowman, a friend who lives in the small boardwalk village of Telegraph Cove, about 250 miles northwest of my home in Vancouver, British Columbia. "You've gotta listen to this, John . . . I don't know who it is!" Jim exclaimed. With that, he held the phone up to a speaker located in his living room but connected by a half mile of cable to a hydrophone placed on the bottom of Johnstone Strait in 200 feet of water.

Wide awake now, I listened carefully as the familiar screams and squeals of a group of killer whales echoed down the line. I immediately recognized the distinctive calls N33 and N34, which meant that the whales had to belong to either R1 or W1 pod, part of a community of sixteen pods that can be found in the area. These two groups share a repertoire of eight vocalizations that differ from those of any other pod. Next came several repetitions of call N32, subtype II, a version of a shared call that is used by only one of the two pods. "That's R1 pod, Jim!" I shouted into the phone. "They haven't been seen in the strait for over a year. It's great to have them back!"

JOHN K. B. FORD is a curator of marine mammals at the Vancouver Aquarium and an expert on orca vocalizations. He has traveled throughout the world to study killer whales, humpbacks, bowheads, and narwhals. "Family Fugues" was first published in the March 1991 issue of *Natural History*. Copyright © the American Museum of Natural History, 1991. Reprinted with permission from *Natural History*.

In 1978, a decade earlier, I had begun what was intended to be a two-year graduate study of the underwater communication of killer whales in British Columbia. Instead, this study continues as an open-ended quest to describe and understand a remarkable system of vocal traditions in this largest member of the dolphin family. Prior to my investigation, little was known about the subject. The vocalizations of the species had been taped before, but mostly in aquariums or during brief encounters with groups at sea. The inner coast of Vancouver Island had long been known to be one of the best places in the world to find "blackfish," as local fishermen call these whales. I reasoned that if I spent enough time following the pods around in a small boat, their typical behavioral and vocal patterns would be revealed to me, leading, I hoped, to greater understanding of social communication in this species.

Fortunately, studies of the killer whale population in British Columbia were well under way when I started my research. In 1972, Graeme Ellis, Ian MacAskie, and the late Michael Bigg, working out of the Pacific Biological Station in Nanaimo, British Columbia, began an intensive investigation of the numbers, distribution, and social organization of the species in local waters. Early in their study, they developed a technique for identifying individuals (based on distinctive natural markings), and after hundreds of encounters with pods, the whales' basic natural history was becoming clear.

A killer whale pod, Bigg and his colleagues found, was a group of apparently related animals that consistently stayed together. Certain pods were encountered frequently, and these they called residents. Resident pods, typically ten to twenty whales, were seen most frequently in summer and early fall when salmon, the whales' main prey, were migrating along the coast toward river mouths. Resident pods were highly social, frequently traveling and foraging with other pods in a larger resident community. Two such communities lived along the British Columbia coast. The northern community, with sixteen pods, ranged from central Vancouver Island to southeast Alaska. The southern, with three pods, moved throughout the waters off southern Vancouver Island and Puget Sound in Washington State.

Bigg and his colleagues also occasionally encountered groups of one to five killer whales they called transients. These whales behaved differently from the residents and even looked different, the tips of their dorsal fins being somewhat sharper than those of residents. Unlike the fish-eating residents, transients seemed to prefer marine mammals, mostly harbor seals, sea lions, and porpoises. Strangely, transient pods were seen to travel only with other transients, and residents only with other residents.

Working closely with Mike Bigg and Graeme Ellis, I traveled to Telegraph Cove on northeastern Vancouver Island to look for resident pods in Johnstone Strait and nearby Blackfish Sound. This is the heart of the northern community's range, where whales can reliably be found from June to September. Making my base camp on a small island, I followed the pods in a seventeen-foot runabout and collected dozens of tapes of their underwater vocal exchanges as they went about their normal, daily routines. At this stage, unfamiliar with both the whales and their vocalizations, I simply photographed as many individuals as possible, recorded as many sounds as I could, and took notes on the activities of the pods.

At the end of the summer, I moved to the waters off southern Vancouver Island, where I encountered the three southern resident pods. Upon lowering my hydrophone into the midst of these eighty whales, I was astonished at how different they sounded. Their calls had tonal qualities and pitch patterns unlike any I had heard from any northern pod. That winter, as I went over my tapes carefully by ear and with a sound-spectrum analyzer, I found differences not only between the northern and southern residents but also within each community. Certain sounds were recorded in the presence of some pods but not others.

The prospect of discovering that killer whale pods have dialects, that is, distinctive call repertoires, was exciting. Mammal vocalizations are typically consistent within a species (regional differences in isolated populations notwithstanding). Local dialects, such as those heard in bird songs, however, were rare, and variations among interacting social groups were known only in humans.

To investigate the possibility of group-specific dialects among killer whales, I first needed to record each pod separately. This task was to take me five more years, but eventually I obtained enough recordings to confirm that most resident pods in British Columbia have their own dialects. Recording the transient pods has proved more challenging, and that aspect of the research continues. Mike Bigg's study on the social organization of the resident population also continues, with invaluable contributions from researchers Ken Balcomb, David Bain, and many others. This intensive field effort has yielded much new information about the social lives of resident whales, which has thrown light on the origin and development of dialects. Likewise, studying the similarities and differences in the dialects of resident pods has provided insight into the evolution of populations.

Like all members of the dolphin family, killer whales rely heavily on underwater sound for both navigation and communication. (The whales' eyesight is good, but underwater visibility in coastal waters is usually less than 100 feet, and at night it is negligible. Underwater sound, on the other hand, travels better—faster and farther—than sound in air.) By forcing air through elaborate structures in the nasal passage beneath the blowhole, a killer whale can generate ultrasonic clicks less than a millisecond in duration, canarylike whistles more than ten seconds long, or loud, complex calls that may be heard for five miles underwater. A special body of fat within the melon, the fleshy bulge atop the animal's head, has acoustic properties that focus the higher-frequency sounds into a cone-shaped beam directed ahead of the whale. The whale's ear canal is closed; the animal receives sound mainly with its lower jaw. Sounds penetrate the thin bone of the mandible, then are conducted directly to the middle ear. With these structures, killer whales can hear with exceptional sensitivity.

From experiments in captivity, we know that the rapid series of clicks produced by killer whales and other dolphins are used for echolocation. Echoes from these clicks allow the animals to form an image of their surroundings. Resident killer whales are often heard clicking at various rates and frequencies, probably to locate prey and to find their way through the convoluted channels and passes along the coast. Whistles and calls, on the other hand, seem to be used mainly for social signaling within and between pods. Calls are more common than whistles, dominating vocal exchanges in most contexts. Typically less than two seconds long, calls are made up of bursts of pulses generated at rates of up to several thousand per second. Such pulse bursts produce high-pitched squeals and screams not unlike the sounds made by rusty hinges on a quickly closing door. By varying the timing of these bursts, the whales can generate a variety of complex signals.

After recording the whales on many occasions over several years, I learned that most resident pods repetitively emit about a dozen different types of what I term discrete calls—each distinct enough to be identified by ear. Some pods use as few as seven or as many as seventeen discrete calls. These calls seem to function as contact signals, coordinating group behavior and keeping pod members in touch when they are out of eyeshot. While searching for salmon, for example, pod members fan out, sometimes covering several square miles. When separated, they regularly exchange sounds, 90 to 95 percent of which are from their repertoire of discrete calls. Most calls contain sudden shifts or rapid sweeps in pitch, which give them distinctive qualities easily recognizable over distance and background noise. Calling rates vary according to the number of whales in the group and their location. Large pods seldom fall silent, but smaller pods may forage quietly for an hour or more between bouts of calling. When a pod nears a junction of channels, the whales usually exchange calls for several minutes before choosing a path.

My field recordings, as well as those made of captive whales taken from local pods, demonstrated that each animal emits most or all of the entire call repertoire of its group. All calls in a pod's repertoire can be heard regardless of whether the group is foraging, traveling, socializing, or rubbing on pebble beaches. (Rubbing is a popular, presumably pleasurable behavior of whales in the northern resident community.) Some calls tend to be heard more often in some situations than in others, but no call seems to be produced exclusively in any specific context. When pod members are grouped together and resting, for instance, the whales usually restrict themselves to one or two call types, but the animals also use these calls when they are fully alert and active. Nor do the calls seem to be given in any consistent sequence or syntax; rather, the whales often seem to be inspired by one another. If one emits a particular call, for example, others may respond with the same call type before moving on to another.

Whenever a pod is routinely foraging or traveling, calls tend to be stereotyped, varying only slightly in duration or pitch. Some situations create great excitement among the whales, however, such as when two pods meet after an extended period of separation. Then vocal activity is often intense, and the calls produced tend to be higher in pitch, shorter in duration, and repeated more rapidly than the same calls given by relaxed or resting whales. And when whales are interacting physically—chasing, pushing, and nipping each other—or when juveniles play together, they incorporate many aberrations into their normal calls and emit an array of squeaks, squawks, and whistles that are seldom, if ever, repeated in the same form.

The richness and variety of calls emitted by these whales appear to be a result of how dialects develop. Killer whales are part of a select group of mammals capable of learning to reproduce sounds that they hear. Such learning, once thought to be exclusive to birds and humans, is now known in a few primate species, some seals, and the dolphin family. Killer whale call repertoires are most likely learned rather than determined genetically, and as has been observed in a recent study of vocal development in a captive-born individual, young whales probably learn by mimicking their mothers. For their first year, while they are nursing, calves rarely stray far from their mothers' sides, and this period seems to be when the repertoire is acquired.

Since each pod consists of several related matrilineal groups made up of females and their offspring, maternal influence has far-reaching consequences. Females can live to seventy or eighty years of age, so pods may contain up to four generations of animals. What is especially striking about pod organization is that individuals, and thus their repertoire of calls, seem to stay in the group for their entire lives. In more than seventeen years of study, no whale has yet been seen to transfer permanently from one group to another. The pod's large bulls—once thought to be the breeding "harem masters" of the group—are simply the mature male offspring of the females in the pod. New pods seem to form gradually through the splitting of old, larger pods along matrilines, a process that we are now witnessing in the northern resident community. It may take a decade or longer before new, descendant groups spend enough time apart to be considered separate pods.

Each of the two resident communities in British Columbia contains groups of pods that have a number of calls in common. Most shared calls are not identical, however, differing in accent from pod to pod. I call these groupings of related yet distinct pods a clan because I believe they may have all descended from a common ancestral pod. On the British Columbia coast, there are four clans, three in the northern resident community and one in the southern community. Clans can be distinguished even by an untrained ear. Each has a distinct vocal tradition, branching out among the pods within the clan into a system of related dialects.

Based on our current understanding, the following hypothetical model for the evolution of dialect patterns within a clan seems reasonable. Many years ago, a pod arrived on the coast, probably from a distant location, and brought with it a unique repertoire of discrete calls. This pod became established in the area, grew slowly in size, and then began to divide. As the new pods spent more and more time apart and developed their own social identities, their repertoires of calls began gradually changing through a process of cultural drift. Such drift could result from the accumulation of imperfections in vocal copying across generations, as well as from innovation and the loss of calls in certain pods and not others. Other clans, with entirely distinct sets of calls, may be independent maternal lineages founded in this way at other times.

If the model is correct, pods in each clan with very similar dialects probably split from a common group in the recent past. Other pods, with fewer acoustic similarities, may be related through older linkages in the lineage. An accurate time scale of clan evolution cannot yet be determined, but I suspect that some relationships are ancient. Killer whales are long-lived animals, and pods grow very slowly. Females give birth for the first time at about fifteen years of age, and, for unknown reasons, less than 60 percent of calves survive their first year of life. Before ceasing reproduction at forty years, cows may produce only four or five surviving offspring. Since the overall population growth rate is less than 3 percent per year, large resident clans containing many pods may be centuries old.

Dialects, too, are slow to change. The southern community pod J1, for example, is making the same calls today as in 1958, when the Canadian navy made recordings of an unidentified killer whale group they encountered during sea trials off southern Vancouver Island. The well-known killer whale Namu, captured on the British Columbia coast in 1965 and taken to the Seattle Marine Aquarium, produced the entire call repertoire that can still be heard from his natal pod, C1, of the northern resident community.

What, if any, function is served by vocal dialects in killer whales is not certain. If calls are used to maintain contact among pod members and to coordinate their behavior, having a set of unique calls must be of some advantage to the group. Resident pods frequently travel in the company of other pods, especially during the summer, when salmon are concentrated in coastal waterways. We have occasionally observed superpods with more than 100 whales from ten or more pods mixed together. At such times, dialects may be important to help individuals differentiate the calls of their fellow pod members from those of other whales. Having a repertoire of several pod-specific calls instead of only one may improve the accuracy and reliability of this acoustic "family badge." Dialects may also play a role in breeding by enabling whales to distinguish between relatives and nonrelatives. Some have suggested that dialects in certain species of songbirds have this type of function, serving as a behavioral mechanism to avoid inbreeding. Killer whales have seldom been observed mating in the wild, but males probably breed with females outside the pod. Some pods contain no mature bulls, yet cows in these groups regularly give birth.

Because pods from different clans in the northern community frequently mix and interact, and each continues to use its own set of calls while doing so, one wonders what kind of communication takes place between these groups. I'm sure individuals are able to identify whales from other pods by their dialects, but I suspect that more information than simple pod affiliation is exchanged. As mentioned earlier, while the calls themselves are remarkably unchanging, the manner in which they are made depends on what the whales are doing: traveling, playing, or meeting up again after a separation, for example. Whales might thus be able to recognize the behavioral state of animals from other pods or clans, much the same way that we can recognize heightened emotions in foreign-language speakers without understanding the words being used. I also expect that each whale produces calls with minor but consistent structural variations that allow recognition of individual identity, as has been discovered in some primate calls.

Whatever the function of dialects may be, they have provided us with an excellent tool for revealing details about the life of killer whales. For example, we have been able to construct a "family tree," based on acoustic similarities and differences, for all resident pods in British Columbia. Pod relationships indicated by dialects are different from what would be predicted by studying association patterns of pods. Some pods seldom travel with others having a similar dialect but associate with distantly related pods in their own clan, or even with pods from different clans. Social factors, such as the number of breeding cows or mature bulls in each pod, may be more important than ancestry in determining traveling associations.

Dialects have also provided us with a way to track pod movements. Over the last five years, I have established several underwater listening stations at manned lighthouses and other strategic sites scattered along the coast, such as the system installed in Jim Borrowman's home at Telegraph Cove. Whenever whales are heard, those tending the equipment make a taped sample of the vocalizations. From the sample, I can determine which pod or set of pods was present. In time, a clearer picture of year-round pod movements in remote regions will result.

Colleagues are now studying killer whales in many parts of the world, using the same photo-identification and acoustic techniques, and early results from research in Norway, Iceland, Alaska, and the sub-Antarctic indicate that local vocal traditions with pod-specific dialects may be typical of killer whales wherever they are found. With luck and perseverance, we may eventually be able to construct a global lexicon for this most exceptional species.

LINDA S. WEILGART AND HAL WHITEHEAD

# Moby's Click

Thomas Beale, a surgeon on a nineteenth-century whaleship and generally considered the first scientific expert on the sperm whale, called this largest of the toothed whales "one of the most noiseless of marine animals." A different opinion was held by some whalers who, hearing "knocking" or "hammering" sounds through the hulls of their ships, dubbed the sperm whale the carpenter fish. Time has proved the whalers closer to the truth than the expert: sperm whales produce loud, steady clicks almost continuously while underwater. Most other toothed whales also emit clicks, among other sounds, but those of sperm whales are much louder, more continuous, and are repeated more slowly—usually one click every half second.

The huge forehead of the sperm whale is thought to hold the mystery of how the animal produces its sounds. It is almost entirely filled with a large sac of high-grade, waxy oil—the spermaceti. (Whalers mistakenly

LINDA S. WEILGART and HAL WHITEHEAD, wife and husband, are based in Nova Scotia and have studied whales in the Indian Ocean, the Caribbean, the Pacific Ocean near the Galápagos Islands and Ecuador, and in the North Atlantic. The author of *Voyage to the Whales*, Whitehead is currently researching the social organization of whales, especially sperm whales and northern bottlenose whales. Weilgart is currently working on the coda repertoires and changing dialects of sperm whales off the Galápagos Islands. "Moby's Click" was first published in the March 1991 issue of *Natural History*. Copyright © the American Museum of Natural History, 1991. Reprinted with permission from *Natural History*.

believed this to be the whale's sperm, hence the name. Spermaceti oil was much sought after for use in lamps and as an industrial lubricant.) In 1972, Kenneth Norris, of the University of California at Santa Cruz, and George Harvey, then of the Oceanic Institute, proposed that a cartilaginous clapper system (colorfully termed the monkey's muzzle by whalers) found at the front of this sac produces the click. They suggested that the click then reverberates back through the spermaceti and is reflected off an almost perfectly parabolic skull and various air sacs, located outside the sac of spermaceti, that function as sound mirrors. This highly evolved reverberation chamber, surrounded by a complicated system of nasal passages that conduct and recycle air for sound production and breathing, may explain why the sperm whale can produce its characteristically loud clicks. This is only a theory, however.

Much of the whales' clicking pertains to feeding, as the animals echolocate in search of food, usually squid. Sperm whales dive down a thousand feet or more and spread out to feed, but since their clicks travel for several miles, our underwater microphones frequently pick up the sounds of as many as fifty whales. Their nearly constant clicking sounds like the hoofbeats of galloping horses. Occasionally, a series of powerful "clangs," repeated about once every six seconds, stands out above this background patter. These dramatic slow clicks seem to be produced by the mature males, which can be three times the size of the females. The preferred catch of whaling ships in the past, big males are now rare, so the regular half-second clicks are the usual sounds we hear when near sperm whales.

After half an hour or more of hearing almost uninterrupted, evenly spaced clicks, a listener might conclude that sperm whale sounds are rather dull, a poor contrast to the variety of squeals, whistles, squawks, chirps, moans, and grunts heard from other whales and dolphins. But when not feeding, sperm whales sometimes gather at the surface to rest in large, tight aggregations. Then, intriguing new vocalizations can be heard, still clicks, but arranged in novel patterns bearing some resemblance to Morse code.

William Watkins and William Schevill, of the Woods Hole Oceanographic Institution, described these repetitive click patterns and named them codas. A coda is usually three to ten clicks and is often part of an exchange between males. One individual, for instance, may emit a coda of eight regularly spaced clicks and then pause, after which a second whale may respond with a seven-click coda. Most of the codas we recorded off the Galápagos could be categorized into twenty-three distinct types, based on the number and spacing of clicks. Certain coda types were much more likely to follow others, and the whales seemed to be responding differently to different coda types. We are far from knowing what the whales may be "saying" to one another, but these codas do seem to be a form of social communication. Many exchanges, for example, begin with a coda of five evenly spaced clicks. Perhaps this is a sperm whale equivalent of our "Hi!" or "Gimme five!"

These periodic gatherings may be a chance for group members to reaffirm social bonds or "touch base" with one another after hours of feeding separately. Female sperm whales and their offspring form stable groups, within which there seems to be cooperative care of the young. (Mature males tend to be loners.) In such a socially complex species, a fairly advanced system of communication would be expected. Other toothed whales, including most oceanic dolphin species, pilot whales, and belugas, probably also have a highly developed social system, but these species are thought to communicate mainly through whistles. Sperm whales are the striking exception—they alone seem to have adopted a form of communication based solely on clicks. While codas may not be as tuneful or pleasing to human ears as the high-spirited whistles of dolphins, these mysterious conversations, echoing over the deepest expanses of ocean, are no less fascinating.

CHRISTOPHER W. CLARK

# Moving with the Heard

Bellowing out of the black depths, as if to challenge the frozen sentinels of ice and awaken them from the numbing cold, a bowhead whale, *Balaena mysticetus*, announced its presence. This call, a deep, undulating glissando that rises to a crescendo for a second or two, reverberates off underwater caverns and propagates for tens of miles through the arctic sea.

Unseen by the searching eyes of human observers perched on an ice ridge but clearly heard over our hydrophones suspended beneath the ice, this whale had given away its location and identity. Half a minute later an answer was received from a different voice, this one more distant and farther to the north. Now we knew there were at least two whales within range of our ears, if not our eyes.

In this subtle game of hide-and-seek, we were spies, taking advantage of the bowheads' propensity to produce a rich variety of sounds. Our mission was to listen, follow, and count them during their spring migration. Bowhead whales are the most vocal of the large whales, and their repertoire is one of the most complex of any mysticete, or baleen whale. Like humpbacks, bowheads sing, often producing two different

CHRISTOPHER W. CLARK, a biomedical engineer, is director of the Bioacoustics Research Program at the Cornell Laboratory of Ornithology. His studies have included southern right whales off Argentina's Peninsula Valdés and bowhead whales in the Arctic. This essay is reprinted from the March 1991 issue of *Natural History*. Copyright © the American Museum of Natural History, 1991. Reprinted with permission from *Natural History*.

sounds simultaneously with a voice that covers a range of seven octaves. They also imitate sounds in their environment, from the whining groans of slipping ice to the shrill screams of belugas. And throughout their spring migration, they make loud, low calls.

Their annual migration brings them 1,800 miles from the Bering Sea in late winter, up along the eastern edge of the Chukchi Sea, through the mosaic of ice off Point Barrow, Alaska, and into the Beaufort Sea, where they spend the summer feeding. The ice off Point Barrow, where we pitched our census camp, is a complex amalgamation of young ice that has formed throughout the last year and old, multiyear pack ice that has built up over many seasons. Young ice first forms on the Arctic Ocean in thin sheets and then grows up to two inches per day for several months until it is about eight feet thick. These pans of young ice grind, collide, and override one another to form twenty-five- to thirty-three-foot ice ridges. The constant growth and action of the ice results in a rugged terrain of ridges, rubble, and slabs.

Visibility in these arctic waters is poor, tens of feet at most. And even if the visibility were good, there are no dependable underwater landmarks by which the whales could orient and navigate by sight. The ice is constantly changing, and for a good part of the year the sun never rises above the frozen horizon, rendering the seas essentially black.

Bowhead whales live in this world of water and ice for most of their lives. The water, at 30°F, feels cold and inhospitable to the thin-skinned human visitor, but it is actually the warmest available habitat in the Arctic. When threatened by hunters, the whales swim into and under the pack ice to escape. If caught in the vise of dynamic ice floes, they can become trapped and die there, but this happens rarely, for if necessary, the forty- to fifty-ton bowheads can push up through ice three feet thick, using the massive arch of the head or the front of the chin to bend and fracture the frozen surface of the ocean.

Most of the time, however, bowheads have no need to crash through the obstacles in their environment; their great skill lies in getting around them. As a result of differences in density, sound travels five times faster and much farther in water than in air. The sounds of many marine animals, especially the large baleen whales that produce loud, low sounds, can be detected as far away as tens and sometimes hundreds of miles. And as I was to discover, the sounds they produce are the key to the bowheads' success in the Arctic.

My first experience with bowheads was in 1979, when I was invited to join a project, under the direction of the National Marine Fisheries Service, aimed at determining the size of the bowhead population. Acoustic results from these early years demonstrated how remarkably vocal the whales were during their migration, so there was reason to hope that by listening to them we could provide visual observers with clues as to when whales were in the area, generally where they were, and possibly how many there were. A good visual count was still the only basis for deriving a population estimate.

Unfortunately, there was to be a three-year hiatus, from 1981 to 1983, in my acoustic research effort, largely due to the serious reduction of federal support for Arctic research made by the Reagan administration. I bided my time, however, and in 1984, under the direction of Thomas Albert, of the North Slope Borough's Department of Wildlife Management in Barrow, I got another chance. This time I joined with William T. Ellison and Kim Beeman to implement a "passive acoustic" technique to detect, locate, and track vocalizing whales. We set up an array of three to four hydrophones arranged in an approximate line along the shorefast edge of the ice. Shorefast ice is typically so thick that it is partly grounded on the sea bottom, making it a safe place on which to establish a base camp. An additional advantage is that whales can't swim behind us. But in 1984, as it turned out, whether whales swam behind us or not was the least of our worries.

The census effort began the second week of April, when the research team of twenty-five to thirty brave souls, led by John Craighead George and Geoff Carroll, assembled in Barrow. At this time of year it was still cold, often bitterly so at -20°F to -40°F, but we expected easterly winds to push the pack ice offshore by late April, thus creating a matrix of open-water channels, or leads. During their migration out of the northern Bering Sea, the bowheads travel up this complex system of leads along the west coast of Alaska to Barrow and into the Beaufort Sea.

But in 1984, the easterly winds never came, and the unusual, yet persistent, northwesterly winds kept the temperatures below -20°F and constantly pushed the offshore pack ice into the shorefast ice, creating massive pressure ridges and endless fields of ice rubble. There was rarely an open lead in which observers could look for whales, and only several hundred whales were seen during the entire ten-week season. We did manage, however, to install and maintain arrays of hydrophones beneath the ice and record for more than 600 hours.

Working under those conditions was difficult at best. The hydrophones had to be spaced 2,000 to 3,000 feet apart. Trails had to be cut through ridges and miles of ice rubble, an exhausting task that often took days to complete. A hole for each hydrophone had to be drilled or chopped through four- to eight-foot-thick sections of pan ice so that the instrument could be suspended twenty-five to thirty-five feet below the frozen surface. Occasionally, we were lucky and found a small polynya (the Russian word for "open water") in which to install a hydrophone. Finally, once they were in the water and connected to their individual FM radio transmitters, we had to survey the positions of the hydrophones to determine the exact geometry of the array, important for locating a whale that might be calling ten miles offshore. After all this, we could only hope that the ice wouldn't cut the cables or bury the radios or that a polar bear wouldn't meander by and destroy one of these alien electronic systems.

Despite the hardships, installing hydrophones had its own, unexpected rewards. Once, as I rappelled down to a small polynya from a fifteen-foot-high ice ridge gilded in the glory of a midnight sun, I was startled by an adult bowhead, measuring more than forty-five feet in length, as it surfaced with a thunderous exhalation just three feet below me. It was soon joined by a second bowhead and a group of four beluga whales, arctic whales with white, Pillsbury doughboy bodies and incredible voices that have earned them the common name sea canary. The precariousness of my position was forgotten as I stared down at the broad, black backs of the two bowheads. The six whales remained in the polynya to breathe for several minutes before diving beneath the ice.

During the many periods when the icescape appeared impenetrable and there seemed no place for a whale to breathe, we consistently heard the whales calling. Later analysis showed that the whales were migrating and that the majority were over the horizon from our camps and arrays of hydrophones, out of eyeshot even if there had been open water. And when, for a brief three-day period in late May 1984, the ice did break open to provide a clear lead of open water, many of the whales we heard, and knew to be close enough to be seen, were never spotted.

Counting the whales by sight was just not going to give us the whole picture. Over the years, we have had to discard the notion that the acoustic work would primarily serve to confirm what we could see. Looking and listening are complementary, simply having different fields of "view." The visual range is roughly a half circle with a radius of about two miles, while the acoustic range is a 120° truncated cone with a ten-mile radius. Given these pronounced differences, the total number of whales counted by the two methods are bound to disagree. What was surprising was that the two methods do not necessarily find the same number of whales even in the area where the fields overlap. The reason, we have learned, is that there are periods when whales are seen but never call, and other times when they call but are not seen. In general, about half of the whales within the shared field of view are both seen and heard. One result of adding acoustics to the traditional visual census has been an increase in the estimated size of the bowhead population, thought to be about 1,500 whales in 1976 but now put at 7,800.

For me, the most exciting benefit of our eavesdropping is that we are now beginning to learn about whale communication and perception. Acoustics enable us to "see" over the horizon, to perceive more the way a whale does and less like a human. And once that transition is made, our world expands by an order of magnitude. You can get some idea of this expansion if you imagine having a conversation with someone who is ten miles away, without the aid of a telephone or any other electronic device, simply talking and listening as you normally would. We all have some experience with perceiving our world out to distances of ten miles, say, from a visit on a clear day to the top of New York's World Trade Center, but we do this with our eyes, not our ears. Similarly, a human's sense of space is based on visible features. To gain some idea about a whale's sense of space and its position in it, we must understand that its spatial maps are primarily derived and memorized through sound, not sight.

But every bowhead call that we can detect and locate is more than a point on some acoustic map. Hours spent poring over the physical details of different calls, the timing between them, and the spatial distribution of the whales making them have persuaded us that bowheads call to communicate with one another and to coordinate both individual and group movements through the ice-bound Arctic. First of all, whales are polite. Rarely do two whales vocalize at the same time or interrupt each other. In 1985, for example, when more than 35,000 calls were noted during a six-week period, two calls occurred at the same time on only nineteen occasions. During the peak of the migration, when twenty to thirty whales were within range of our hydrophones, we sometimes heard more than 400 calls per hour, and none overlapped. The strong suggestion is that the whales listen carefully to one another.

Calls do, however, come close together, only seconds apart, with the same calls produced in clusters. For example, we may hear a low upsweep "whoop," followed ten seconds later by a "purr," then a "groan"—three sounds from three different whales in three different locations many miles apart. Twenty minutes later those same three sounds occur again, with the whoop, purr, and groan coming from the same general directions as they did in the first episode but shifted to the northeast in the direction of the migration. Initially, these episodes of countercalling seemed rare, but now that we are aware of them, we find that they are quite common.

The timing and composition of these countercalling episodes were intriguing. We began plotting the details and found clear cases when each of the whales involved was adopting its own distinctive call signature— one whooping, for instance, the second purring, and the third groaning. As we looked further, however, we sometimes observed that one animal in a group of countercallers would switch its call type to that of another member of the group. In the extreme case, all the callers in the group produced the same call, reminding me of the wonderfully unnerving occasions when children ape every utterance out of each other's mouths. So these calls are temporary acoustic badges, not unique signatures or voice prints. Since bowheads are both good mimics and good listeners, I assume that one bowhead can imitate any other it hears I also assume that at close range they recognize one another by the subtle characteristics of their individual voices, but work on that topic remains to be done.

At this point we do not know the age, sex, or relationship of the whales in acoustic groups. Neither do we know how stable acoustic groups are, since we can only follow them for up to five hours. But we do know that there can be at least ten to fifteen whales in a group, with individuals distributed over a four- to eight-square-mile area and with very few of the whales within sight of one another. We do not know what rules, if any, determine which call to adopt, when to switch, and whom to imitate, but we are certain that all the vocal banter we hear over the hydrophones is not just idle chatter. It is an open roll call whereby members of the herd remain in contact. Like migrating Canada geese honking on their way south in the fall or wild steers moaning as they move over the prairie, the bowheads call to maintain cohesion in the widely dispersed herd.

I believe, however, there is more to it than that, and the "more" is directly related to the acoustic environment of the Arctic. Over an expanse of 100 square miles, the herd must find its way in ice conditions that are often life threatening. Fortunately for the whales, simply by listening to the ice, or to how ambient noise varies subtly from one type of ice environment to another, they can learn to discriminate between grounded ice, moving ice, flat ice, or deep, heavily keeled ice. A wall of grounded ice, for example, imparts a rich reverberation to all sounds, giving a human listener the impression of standing in the nave of a cathedral. Pan ice cloaks the ocean like a quilt, dampening background noise and thus enabling other sounds to stand out clearly, crisply. When a pan collides with another pan or a ridge of grounded ice, the result is a rhythmic series of groans, squeals, and screams that can resemble a cat fight, a steam-driven engine, a lone wolf howl, or the thunderous roar of an avalanche.

Since we cannot manipulate their environment, we have no easy way of proving that whales use these acoustic clues, but I do know that I and others who have spent many years listening under the ice have learned to associate certain ice noises with particular ice conditions. Whales should be able to do the same. Furthermore, a whale can listen to echoes of its own calls, and the calls of other whales, bouncing off the ice. They can then translate any degradation or distortion of those sounds into meaningful images of the underwater environment. Bill Ellison used a computer model to test this concept. He first projected a typical bowhead call through conditions characteristic of young pan ice and then of thick (ten to twenty-five feet) multiyear ice. The results were dramatically different. Thin ice appears acoustically similar to open water: when a bowhead makes a call in young ice, there is essentially no echo reflecting back to the caller from the underwater surfaces of the ice. Any whale listening to the call would hear a relatively undistorted version. In contrast, when a bowhead makes a call in multiyear ice, a complex of echoes reflects off vertical underwater ice keels. The differences between sound reflections in these different ice conditions is similar to what you would hear if someone called you, first, across an open field and then, through a forest.

In 1985, we observed a group of 100 to 120 whales detouring around a large, four-square-mile multiyear ice floe. The whales were distributed over a six-by-fifteen-mile area with individuals at least 600 feet apart. As the first whales in the herd approached to within a half mile of the floe, they called more and more frequently, much as echolocating bats and dolphins click faster as they approach a target. Between 600 and 1,500 feet from the edge of the floe, when still too far away to see it, they changed direction to avoid the ice. The whales behind these leaders began their detour when they were even farther away—up to 5,000 feet from the floe—and did so without stepping up their own calling. The followers must have been listening, either to the changing location of the leaders' voices or to the echoes of the leaders' calls off the ice, and altered their own course accordingly.

Bowheads are not the only large baleen whales to use sound for communication and navigation, but living in the ice-cluttered world of the Arctic has honed their skills beyond those of whales in the world's more open, temperate oceans. Toothed cetaceans are in a similar situation. Belugas, which, like bowheads, are found primarily in arctic waters, have the most extensive, richest acoustic repertoire of any toothed whale and are much better than bottle-nosed dolphins of temperate climates at detecting objects in their environment.

But wherever they are—in cold polar waters or equable tropical seas—whales depend on sound. For humans, the importance of recognizing this dependence is not restricted to basic biological research. Whether exploring oceans for fossil fuels or dabbling in them for sport, we must all be aware of and make serious efforts to reduce the noises from all our activities—seismic exploration, drilling operations, dredges, helicopters, cruise ships, motorboats, and jet skis—noises that are degrading the whales' world. For the whales, a clean ocean is one free of the noise debris of human activities, a kind of pollution we can't see but the whales can't escape.

KATHERINE B. PAYNE

# A Change of Tune

Humpback whales are only distantly related to bow-heads, but these two species of baleen whales are the only ones that sing complex songs. Because humpback males sing primarily on their breeding grounds, songs may function in competition between males. We assume that the songs also play a role in courtship; humpbacks, however, have never been observed mating.

There is at least one population of humpback whales in each of the world's major oceans. Within each population, all humpbacks share the same song, a long sequence of varied sounds organized in patterns that, by analogy with human music, can be described as having phrases (groups of notes that are roughly the same each time they are repeated) and themes (groups of similar phrases). Since a single song lasts ten to thirty minutes, performing it is a feat of memory particularly remarkable because each population's song is constantly evolving. A detailed analysis of songs from two populations (one that breeds near Hawaii; the other near Bermuda) has documented the changes that have taken place in

KATHERINE B. PAYNE has studied whales in the waters near Bermuda, the Hawaiian Islands, Argentina, and elsewhere. She has been a research associate at Cornell University's Bioacoustics Research Program and a conservation fellow with the New York Zoological Society. She is currently studying acoustic communication and behavioral ecology in elephants as well as whales. "A Change of Tune" was first published in the March 1991 issue of *Natural History*. Copyright © the American Museum of Natural History, 1991. Reprinted with permission from *Natural History*.

each population's song over the course of five and nineteen years, respectively, and has shown that individual whales always keep up with the current version of their population's song.

Since whales are relatively silent during the six months of each year when they are on their feeding grounds in colder waters (the Hawaiian humpbacks go to waters off Alaska; Bermuda whales head for Newfoundland), one might imagine that the reason songs change is that whales forget how the last year's song went. But not so. When humpbacks return to their breeding grounds, the song they sing is little changed from that of six months earlier. Singing, not silence, is what brings on change, and the song changes most and fastest when the most whales are singing.

After five or ten years the material in any humpback population's song, and even some of the ways in which the material is organized, are radically altered. The process is not unlike linguistic drift in human speech, but the pace is so rapid that songs recorded ten years apart in one population are as different from one another as from the song of a different population. Every theme changes—in pitch, rhythm, or numbers or durations of notes—or drops out or is replaced.

How do humpback whales remember the changes in their songs? One possibility is that whales, like human bards, sometimes use rhymes to help recall their lines in a long oral performance. Analysis of the songs shows that when they contain many themes, they also include rhymelike material, phrases with similar-sounding endings that link dissimilar but adjacent themes. When songs contain few themes and are presumably not so hard to remember, we do not hear this sort of material.

What do the song changes, and the preference for novelty that they seem to reflect, mean in the life of humpback whales? What drives tomorrow's song to be just a little different from yesterday's, and all singers to keep up with the latest version? Can we speculate about this, and about whales' use of rhymes, without thinking of human beings and wondering about the ancient roots in nature of even our aesthetic behavior?

# Sightings
# of the
# Leviathan

CHARLES BERGMAN

# So Ignoble a Leviathan

I

For all its infinite reach and scope, you don't really see the ocean from the bow of a small boat. You *feel* it. The wilderness offshore tosses itself into your face with the spume of a sickening beauty.

I sat spraddle-legged on the bow of the 29-foot *Harry Lee II*, named for Robert E. Lee's father, as we chugged out of the mouth of the St. Mary's River dividing Florida from Georgia. Squalls from a threatening storm whipped the ocean surface into whitecaps. Low clouds smothered the sea in a sepia wash, with lurid greens mixed in, and waves beat the hull in 5-foot breakers. One of the volunteers puked aft over the railing. My face dripping with salt spray, I rode the boat as if it were a rodeo bull as it crashed through the breaking waves, making our way a few miles offshore. At the shock of each wave, I held on tight and felt the boat shiver through my thighs. The sea as an assault to our senses: I kept thinking of James Joyce's description of the ocean in *Ulysses*: "the snot-green sea, the scrotum-tightening sea."

The solidity of our bodies is an illusion: The body is its own ocean. Though I live with the firmness of my flesh every day, my body is a *mare incognita* to me. Our skin and bones and muscles are liquid—waters of

CHARLES BERGMAN is chair of the English department at Pacific Lutheran University in Tacoma, Washington. *Wild Echoes: Encounters with the Most Endangered Animals in North America*, from which "So Ignoble a Leviathan" was adapted, was published in 1990 by McGraw-Hill, Inc. Reprinted with permission of the publisher.

the body held in fragile membranes—made up of some 65 percent water. And the seas are only apparently water: They are heavy, firm, tangible in their substance when they pound into us, hit us in the face. It must be that this is why I love to live by the sea, why I keep making trips out onto the sea, why I have taken so many chances to go offshore looking in the fecund barrenness of the surface of the sea for albatrosses and petrels, turtles and whales. Some physical pull, some response in the body, exerts its sway over me, and I keep going back, as if the sea is a moon to my tides.

Rocking over the breakers in the *Harry Lee II*, my head and shoulders swung in wild circles while my stomach swam in my guts, and I realized I was answering the sea with my body.

We were looking for whales in the Atlantic Ocean, just off the coast of Amelia Island, at the extreme northeastern corner of Florida. In their size, whales are prodigious creatures, living hyperboles. They answer some need I have to be reduced, to be humbled, to be reminded of how little I am, like Job struck dumb before the invocation of the monster of creation, Leviathan: "Shall not *one* be cast down even at the sight of him?"

Each of the great whales has come to embody a particular meaning for us in the ecological renaissance they helped create. The humpback whales: the most popular of all, probably the current ideal—a "gentle giant." Their eerie and reverberating songs, first recorded in the late 1960s, evoke the lyricism of the sea. And they are one of the most playful of the whales, white flanks shining as they breach. The bowhead whales: associated with Eskimo subsistence hunting and the unending allure for Americans of Arctic hardships. The gray whales: famous for their resort to calving grounds in the tropical waters of Baja California and for their long annual migrations up and down the west coast. The orca, or killer, whales: known for their bold black and white markings, their predatory habit of eating salmon, and their place on the totem poles of the coastal Indians of the Pacific Northwest. The fin and sei whales: both rorquals and less well known, but sleek creatures of speed. The narwhals: renowned for their strange and enigmatic tusks, reminiscent of the magic ascribed to the unicorn. The blue whales: over 100 feet long and 160 tons in weight, the biggest creatures ever to have lived on the earth.

And sperm whales: perhaps the most important animals in the American experience. Through Herman Melville's imaginative vision, sperm whales helped create the American identity. They have huge, blunt foreheads and toothed jaws. They prefer the deep seas all around the world. And they have a propensity to ram big whaling ships in anger and to stove smaller whaleboats in a rage of self-defense. Altogether, sperm whales have offered Americans dramatic narratives and noble opponents. They were transformed in whalers' stories into the symbol of our epic aspirations, of our defiance of the "demoniac indifference" of the universe, of our will to conquer the world. They have summarized our vision of the heroic and the tragic in our battles with nature.

But another species of whale has been overlooked, neglected, even spurned: the North Atlantic right whale. Its Latin name is *Eubalaena glacialis*. Its common name indicates its former importance to whalers, who considered it the "right whale" to hunt. Yet its significance—biological, historical, and psychological—has been largely forgotten, even though it was the most important whale in American culture until Melville popularized the sperm whale.

Even if the right whale has been silent to us for over a century, even if we have not heard much about it since Melville's epic, there is something important in this blankness. It was my experience with the right whale off the coast of Florida that first made the significance of its silence come alive for me.

Shrimpers had reported right whales off the coast of Amelia Island that morning, at the mouth of the St. Mary's River, and I was looking for them with biologists and volunteers. Though they were not easy to pick out against the textured but featureless face of the sea, we didn't have to go far to find the two right whales. During a lull in the gathering storm, the seas settled into a wind-fretted chop, and we found the whales cruising along the surface about 5 miles offshore. They plugged slowly into the waves, doing no more than 3 or 4 knots. If we ran the boat at anything above a "fast idle," we punched right past them. In their dark profile, their heads rested partly exposed above the water in an outline like a huge 747 airliner—the same high and rounded shape of the cockpit, sloping up to the blowholes and tapering off to a broad back.

After a couple of hours of gathering data on the whales' breathing patterns—part of a study these researchers were conducting for the New England Aquarium in Boston—we edged in closer, and the whales began to take on dimension and substance. The mother was unwary; as we approached, it became easy to see why, for early natural historians like the Elizabethan Bartholomew, the whale "for greatness of body . . . seemeth an island."

Though not the biggest of the whales, this right-whale mother logged in the water with a staggering bulk, waves washing over her back as if she were shoals. She was about 45 feet long, her back perhaps 12 feet across and very flat. Though her head was long and narrow, she swelled into a monstrous girth just behind her curling mouth. Right whales are the fattest of the whales, with their girth just before their flippers totaling more than half their body length. Their weight in tons is equal to about three times their body length in meters: 15 meters in length, 45 tons in weight. The males have a 12-foot-long penis, and each testis weighs a ton. The right whales also have the smallest brain in proportion to body size of all the whales. The big female near us probably weighed about 45 tons. As we idled up next to her, she seemed massively indifferent to us, her black bulk inert and sulking in the white froth of waves on her flanks. She dwarfed the boat that we were on, and she dwarfed all of us on board, too, as we scurried around to get nearer to her.

It was impossible not to be overwhelmed by her sheer size, by her physical presence. For Western sensibilities, animal life has always been associated with the physical body, and our own bodies are the signs of our animality. But in her the idea of a body had been taken to outrageous and almost transcendent proportions. I stared at her slate-gray flesh and saw some fundamental ground of existence, the space in which life is contained and must live out its time: a living body.

As if her size were not enough of a challenge to comprehension, her face was its own affront. Above a jutting lower jaw, her face was pinched by thick lips that bowed up and inward. On her narrow rostrum (the top of a whale's head from the blowholes to the tip of its snout), she wore crusty, jagged growths of black skin, called callosities, that look vaguely like uncut fingernails curling upward in bizarre shapes. Colonies of "whale lice" clung to these callosities and clustered on her lips, making up patches of white and orange and pink. The lice are little crustaceans called cyamids.

This combination of the fat and the ugly in the right whale has left the American imagination uninspired. Herman Melville, in *Moby Dick*, granted his tribute to the right whale, but it was a grudging tribute, a kind of dismissal or displacement in favor of the nobler sperm whale. Writing of the right whale, Melville invites the reader to "fix your eye upon this strange, crested, comb-like incrustation on the top of the mass—this green, barnacled thing . . . you would take the head for the trunk of some huge oak, with a bird's nest in its crotch." He goes on: "This mighty monster is actually a diademed king of the sea, whose green crown has been put together for him in this marvellous manner. But if this whale be a king, he is a very sulky looking fellow to grace a diadem. Look at that hanging lower lip! what a huge sulk and pout is there! . . . a sulk and a pout that will yield you some 500 gallons of oil and more."

The right whale was slow, found near shore, and buoyant with all its blubber, so it was easy to catch and process. But these same qualities, plus its ugliness, led nineteenth-century whalers to view it with disgust. As the crew of the *Pequod* prepares to lower for a right whale, Melville writes: "All hands commonly disdained the capture of those inferior creatures." And after the crew kills the whale, Melville reports the headsman's attitude: " 'I wonder what the old man [Ahab] wants with this lump of foul lard,' said Stubb, not without some disgust at the thought of having to do with so ignoble a leviathan."

So ignoble a leviathan: given a kind of practical tribute only as the source of immense yields of oil and baleen.

It is not the right whale itself being loathed by the *Pequod*'s crew. It is the right whale as body, with its weird incrustations and its larded bowels, that made our Puritan forefathers, turned Yankee whalers, condemn the right whale even as they killed it. All this immodest bulk and all these strange imperfections of appearance—they are too much of the body. The New England clergyman Cotton Mather has a diary entry from 1700 in which he makes very clear his anxiety over the way his bodily functions connect him too intimately with the beasts:

> I was once emptying the cistern of nature, and making water at the wall. At the same time, there came a dog, who did so too, before me. Thought I; 'What mean and vile things are the children of men . . . How much do our natural necessities abase us, and place us . . . on the same level with the very dogs!'
>
> My thought proceeded. 'Yet I will be a more noble creature; and at the very time when my natural necessities debase me into the condition of the beast, my spirit shall (I say *at the very time!*) rise and soar.'

So the redoubtable divine resolved in the future to make peeing "an opportunity of shaping in my mind some holy, noble, divine thought."

Captain Ahab transmutes the attempt to deny nature as expressed in the body, transforming a Puritan anxiety into a heroic monomania. His is one side of the essentially modern quest—to travel beyond life, to define the self by throwing it outward through the universe, to tear through the limits of the body and the masks of life. For Ahab, the sperm whale is the embodiment, the great theme and metaphor, of the quest for the self accomplished through metaphysical heroics, of breaking through the walls of the physical to the ultimate and the transcendental, of writing the self through action upon the face of the unknowable. As Ahab says, "All visible objects, man, are but as pasteboard masks. But in each event—in the living act, the undoubted deed—there, some unknown but still reasoning thing puts forth the mouldings of its features from behind the unreasoning mask. If man will strike, strike through the mask! How can a prisoner reach outside except by thrusting through the wall? To me, the white whale is that wall, shoved near to me. Sometimes I think there's nought beyond . . . That inscrutable thing is chiefly what I hate."

It was under this metaphysic of the sperm whale that the right whale was lost.

The right whale announces a different side, a different aspect of the modern quest. The sperm whale has a huge square head, inspiring thoughts of the mind-in-nature, but the right whale gives the figure of the massive body. Unlike Moby Dick, the right whale is found not in the "midmost ocean of the world" but closer to home; it is a creature not of far seas but of shorelines.

The white sperm whale Moby Dick, which Ahab chased around the world, implies boundlessness; the right whale suggests the quest for historical roots. It is the story of origins: of the origins of Western whaling by the Basques in the Bay of Biscay and of the origins of American whaling along the shores of New England.

In the silence of the right whale, there is a quieter story, a more humble story, less pretentious but closer to home, anchored to where we actually live. Through Moby Dick, the sperm whale locates us in the grand struggle, in the quest for the future, in the impulse to overcome nature—which is so central to the American experience of its own identity. It is as if we are in nature but somehow always moving through nature. But the right whale recalls us backward, into our own history; it locates us not outside of time but in the forgotten past.

There is as well a psychological correlative to this cultural theme. The right whale suggests not just the shorelines of the American continent but the shoreline of the body, which is the ground and background of our lives in nature. It is through the experience of my body that I have my own place in time. It inserts me into the chronology of things. It gives me the space I occupy in the world. And if I am able to discover myself through animals, this is probably their most basic revelation: They summon me to a simple contact with a being which just is—this stupid body, this animal life, which is the basis of desire.

We stayed with the two right whales for the whole afternoon. The captain killed the engine and we drifted with them, chatting among ourselves, taking notes on their behavior, rocking with the swells, enjoying being near the whales. The flat outline of Cumberland Island, off the coast of Georgia, hovered in the distance, through a foggy mist. Gannets flew past us in the poor light, their wings thin and pointed, their beaks thick and heavy, giving their darkened shapes a look reminiscent of ancient pterodactyls. The mother whale loomed beside us, passive for the most part, resting.

Her baby, however, was coltish and frisky, playing around its mother with a surprising, winsome grace. It rested its head across its mother's snout and then slid slowly backward into the water, bubbles gurgling up around it as it vanished. It reemerged in a headstand, tail first. Its broad, flat flukes, outlined in elegantly bold curving lines, unfurled before us like a flag. Slipping once again out of sight, the calf reappeared by its mother's tail, nuzzling and pushing, perhaps nursing.

Several times, the baby whale swam up to our boat, curious as right whale babies are. Only about 2 weeks old, it was already about 16 feet long, over half the size of our boat. On the port side, I leaned down and watched the calf nudge the bow with its head, which was still smooth and did not yet have clusters of whale lice. Its sides bulged in sleek curves and young dark flesh. It dove under the boat and resurfaced on the starboard. I scrambled across the deck to stare at it again, from barely 2 feet away. I could have reached out and touched it; I was so excited I could have jumped in with it. But I didn't want to touch it. I didn't want to break the magic of the moment. I wanted just to be close to it, feeling it define my space by the immediacy of its presence.

## II

The current fashion is to consider the North Atlantic right whale and the South Atlantic right whale as two separate and distinct species, since neither population crosses the equator. If so, the North Atlantic right whale may be the rarest and most endangered whale in the world.

Such a claim is difficult to make. The North Pacific right whale is also extremely rare—for decades, only a handful of sightings of this whale have been recorded along the coasts of Washington, Oregon, and

California. Not only is the current estimate of 200 to 250 animals alarmingly low, but it is also a shot in the dark.

The bowhead whale was circumpolar, and it is now given five separate stocks. One of these stocks, the bowheads of the once heavily hunted Greenland and Barents seas, is very near extinction. Two of the other stocks have only about 100 whales left, and another has just a few hundred. The only strong population left, ironically, is the one that received so much media attention because of Eskimo subsistence hunting: the bowheads of the Chukchi and Bering seas. They number between 1000 and 3000. (Before whaling, however, this stock may have contained 18,000 to 36,000 whales.)

According to Randall Reeves, who works at the Arctic Biological Station at Ste-Anne-de-Bellevue, Quebec, and is the coauthor of *The Sierra Club Handbook of Whales and Dolphins*, we don't know just how close to extinction the right whale came. For over a decade, Reeves has studied the hunting records and sightings of the species, and he speculates that the low point came early in the twentieth century with only "a few dozen individuals."

Protected by international agreement since 1937, the right whale in the North Atlantic was known from only a handful of sightings through the 1950s and 1960s, many of those coming from the waters around Cape Cod and Florida. But the reports were so scarce that they seemed to represent the trailing wake of a species headed almost certainly toward extinction.

No whale has gone extinct in modern times. Although many species of whales are cosmopolitan—widely distributed in the world's seas—they form isolated, separate stocks, which are the equivalent of races or nations among humans. One stock—the gray whale of the North Atlantic—has gone extinct, entirely exterminated by whaling. The North Pacific stock of the gray whale, considered extinct on two separate occasions, was compared to the North Atlantic right whale in its precarious status. The protection it received in 1937 was seen as a gesture flung into the teeth of inevitable extinction. Nevertheless, the gray whale along the Pacific coast has recovered: Its current numbers are perhaps 15,000, rivaling the stock's original population.

But if the gray whale on the Pacific coast has recovered so well, why hasn't the North Atlantic right whale? Several recent discoveries of sizable groups of right whales along the Atlantic coast have lead to a virtual reinvention of the species. As the enthusiasm grew with increasing knowledge over the last decade, research efforts intensified and led to a slowly evolving picture of the right whale's current status. It is a species we are learning to see and appreciate anew.

On the basis of a catalog of thousands of photographs, Scott Kraus of the New England Aquarium in Boston has identified 230 individual right whales. He estimates there might be anywhere from 300 to 600 in the North Atlantic. Kraus's research is primarily devoted to gathering empirical information on the most crucial, most basic biological questions about an endangered species: How many are there, and where are they?

Underlying the numbers is the simplest, most basic question of all. It is a question not of data, of hard facts gleaned from the field, but of interpretation: Is the North Atlantic right whale making a comeback, or is it still heading toward extinction?

The major breakthrough in studying the right whale, the discoveries that led to the new efforts to understand the species, came in the lower Bay of Fundy. For cetologists, as for the whalers before them, the Bay of Fundy was largely uncharted and unknown, a broad watery wedge separating Maine from Nova Scotia in its lower reaches. A few whalers ventured into the bay, but the historical records show only a scant, casual use of these waters. Mostly, whalers bypassed the bay on their outward-bound journeys, heading for pelagic whale grounds in the Arctic.

Over the last half century, the right whale has been sighted along the Atlantic coast, most notably in Cape Cod Bay. By 1979, right whales were known to be in the Bay of Fundy, with reports coming in from ferry crews and fishermen. On July 10, 1980, flying over the Bay of Fundy while conducting a systematic inventory of cetaceans (whales, dolphins, and porpoises), Scott Kraus and Randall Reeves found a large number of right whales, their "only real surprise." In that field season, which lasted until October 30, they sighted twenty-six right whales in the area of The Wolves and Grand Manan, including four different cow-calf pairs. The numbers were modest, but for an endangered and unstudied animal, they represented a large concentration and major discovery.

Realizing that the right whales in the Bay of Fundy were significant, Kraus began a major research effort to learn as much as possible about the species. He and a crew of biologists and volunteers have returned to the Bay of Fundy every summer since 1980.

The second major discovery of right whales in the North Atlantic came from Browns Bank, about 35 miles south of the tip of Nova Scotia. It repeated the pattern of the discovery of the whales in the Bay of Fundy: scant and sketchy historical data preceding a stunning confirmation of large groups of whales from aerial surveys. Flying for the University of Rhode Island and the Cetacean and Turtle Assessment Program (CeTAP), which covered the entire coast in aerial surveys from North Carolina to Nova Scotia, Greg Stone surveyed the area of Browns Bank in 1981. On August 27, he saw forty-six right whales, the largest right-whale sighting in the North Atlantic.

Another important location for right whales was discovered off the southeast coast. In winter, small numbers of right whales—between six and ten pairs of mothers and calves—occur off the coasts of Florida and Georgia.

Scott Kraus has organized research in all three areas on an annual basis—Bay of Fundy, Browns Bank, and the Florida coast. A man with sharp, heronlike features, he told me: "In right whales, nobody knows about them, so we're on the front edge. Not many places you can still do that kind of work. We're still working on the basic questions."

The answers to those questions come from observation in the field and from studying over 16,000 photographs. The study of cetaceans depends upon the identification of individual animals—that is how population size, distribution patterns, and reproductive trends can be determined. Each right whale has a distinctive and unique pattern to the callosities that form on its bonnet and lips. Growing in islands and peninsulas that stay constant for each whale, the callosity pattern is a "fingerprint." Photographs of these callosity patterns are the coin of the realm in right-whale studies: Spending long, dull hours sorting through the photographs, researchers have compiled a catalog of 230 individual right whales.

Using this catalog, Kraus has documented migrations between all three of the major locations so far discovered, and he believes these whales constitute one large population of right whales, not separate groups. Browns Bank seems to be a place for sexually active whales: The whales are active in courtship groups, and Kraus has seen one whale insert his penis into a female, though he carefully points out that this does not confirm that conception took place. In the Bay of Fundy, about half of the sixty or so whales that gather in late summer and fall are cows with 1- and 2-year-old calves. The rest are a miscellany of males and nonreproductive females. These Bay of Fundy whales tend to stay closer to shore. Florida is the only known calving ground for the species, with about ten pairs of mothers and calves seen there in the winter.

A great deal about the species remains unknown. For example, if Florida is the only known wintering ground, with twenty whales, where

do the other 200 or more right whales spend the winter? From old whaling records, some cetologists suspect the whales go farther out to sea.
Also, females devote tremendous amounts of energy to raising their
calves—the right-whale calf may be the fastest-growing mammalian infant
in terms of adding body weight. So, after raising their babies, the mothers
appear to take a year off, during which they fatten and recoup their
strength. Where do the females spend their off year? Finally, Browns Bank
is the place for courtship, and if right whales are like other large whales,
the gestation period is twelve months—though this is *not* documented for
right whales. But if so, why do the right whales give birth off Florida in
January? Is the gestation period longer than thought? Or do the whales
actually mate in some as yet unknown place in January?

Why haven't right whales returned as forcefully, as prolifically, as gray
whales? No one knows for sure yet, but the question is being researched.
One fear is that at least part of the reason may be the pollution of the seas.
This is the biggest problem now facing marine mammals, and it drives
cetologists nearly to despair. The right whale, for example, is living along
the near-shore waters of the Atlantic coast in a degraded and assaulted
environment. In the Gulf of Maine, where right whales are found, harbor
seals have the highest levels of pesticides in their systems of any U.S.
mammal. Between 1987 and 1988, 750 dolphins died mysteriously along
the Atlantic coast, their snouts and flippers pocked with blisters.

As one marine biologist I spoke with said, pollution has displaced
whaling as the largest threat to cetaceans. We don't know exactly what
the effects of pesticides and PCBs and heavy-metal contaminants are on
right whales. They may suffer from malnutrition or be impaired in their
reproductive abilities. But one thing is clear: The pollution cannot be
good for them.

III

I have stood on the shores of Cape Cod, watching the sun's thin light fall
upon bleached sands and low dunes, looking out on the glaring blueness
of the sea, and I have tried to imagine what the early New England settlers saw in these waters. The sunlight doubles back from the sand, glints
off the waters, and fills the air with an intense veil of light that is
blinding. Though imposing, the dunes and sea are unlike forests and
mountains. They are stark and lonely, appealing less to the senses than to
the imagination. But it takes a prodigious act of imagination to picture
the sea as alive with whales as it once was. The early settlers' journals and

reports offer a staggering introduction to a foreign world. The seas are not dead now, but they are less alive than when the first colonists discovered them. When I try to look beyond the light and imagine the lost abundance, I can't do it. I faint under the attempt.

Though researchers are working to determine the size of the right whale's former abundance, numbers only give a plodding and prosaic way to comprehend what must have been some of the richest waters in the world for whales when the colonists arrived on the Atlantic coast. One of the pilgrims on the *Mayflower* described the scene in vivid terms as the ship lay at anchor in Cape Cod Bay, off Provincetown, in November 1620. In a document now called Mourt's *Relation*, the diarist writes of an enormous and unfrightened concentration of what must be right whales: "Great whales of the best kind for oil and bone come close aboard our ship, and in fair weather swim and play about us." He goes on:

> And every day we saw whales playing hard by us; of which in that place, if we had instruments and means to take them, we might have made a very rich return, which to our great grief we wanted. Our master and his mate, and others, experienced in fishing, professed we might have made three or four thousand pound worth of oil. They preferred it before Greenland whale-fishing, and purpose the next winter to fish for whale here.

This pilgrim betrays an ominous exuberance in his description, as if in the moment of discovery the future was defined. If their Calvinism left little room for enjoying the abundance of God's creation, the austere pilgrims were nevertheless eager to exploit what they found. With pious eyes fixed on God's face, they were from their first moments in the New World scheming to pick His bulging back pocket.

When Richard Mather arrived in Massachusetts in 1635, he wrote of "multitudes of great whales . . . spewing up water in the air like the smoke of chimneys and making the sea about them white and hoary." Yet he became so inured to their abundance that he betrayed a trace of boredom: The whales had "grown ordinary and usual to behold." And a memorandum in the British secretary of state's papers for 1667 reported, "The sea was rich in whales near Delaware Bay, but . . . they were to be found in greater numbers about the end of Long Island."

A number of researchers have recently pioneered a renewed interest in the historical significance of the right whale in North America: Randall

Reeves, on whale records in logs and newspapers; Selma Barkham, on the Basques in Newfoundland; and Elizabeth Little, on the relations between Indians and the early Yankee whalers. Elizabeth Little works with the Nantucket Historical Association. She divides New England whaling into three categories: drift whaling, along-shore whaling, and pelagic whaling. The typical account of the history of whaling in America moves quickly through the early periods to "the Golden Age of American whaling" in the pelagic period. Little's work is especially important for demonstrating the importance of the right whale in the first two stages of the whale fishery (they were virtually synonymous with the right whale), for demonstrating the rapid depletion of the right whale off the coast of New England, and for untangling the role the Indians played in teaching the early colonists to whale.

If the history of the right whale is largely an indictment of our own depleted inheritance, it is also an act of remembering the past, the prelude to our own remembering of the future.

Most modern histories are inconclusive on the contributions of Indians to the beginnings of American whaling. One tradition has it that the Indians taught the early English colonists how to whale. According to Little, this tradition is a nineteenth-century invention, when writers like Herman Melville displaced the legendary skill of the Indian whalemen backward in time. Though the Indians were famous for their seamanship (Crévecoeur described them as "fond of the sea and expert mariners"), Little says, "In spite of the tradition, I can find no evidence that Indians of New England routinely killed whales at sea." The only account of Indian whaling during the "Contact Period," when Europeans were exploring the waters and coast of North America, comes from James Rosier, who accompanied George Waymouth in 1605. In cryptic syntax, he describes their custom:

> One especial thing is their manner of killing the whale, which they call powdawe; and will describe his form; how he bloweth up the water; and that he is twelve fathoms long; and that they go in company of their kind with a multitude of their boats, and strike him with a bone made in fashion of a harping iron, fastened to a rope, which they make great and strong of the bark of trees, which they veer out after him: then all their boats come about him, and as he riseth above water, with their arrows they shoot him to death: when they have killed him and dragged him

to shore, they call all their chief lords together, and sing a song
of joy: and those chief lords, whom they call sagamores, divide
the spoil, and give to every man a share, which pieces so distributed, they hand up about their houses for provision: and when
they boil them, they blow off the fat, and put their pease, maize,
and other pulse, which they eat.

For a number of reasons—location, mention of maize, the unique
account of killing by arrows—Little considers this well-known account a
muddled, second-hand report.

As Little says, "We have no evidence that Indians harpooned whales
at sea off the east coast of colonial America after 1605, until they became
involved with English along-shore whaling." She demonstrates that the
Indians from Long Island to Nantucket taught the colonists not how to
go to sea but how to harvest the whales tossed onto the beaches. The
original colonists, after all, were not sailors. The Puritans came expecting
to farm and raise sheep. The drift whales became a kind of seashore
farming and were harvested more than hunted. To this day, southern
New England is the spot in the country with the most strandings of
whales. In 1986, one right whale, two humpback whales, about eighty
pilot whales, and innumerable dolphins and porpoises inexplicably
stranded themselves on the beaches of Cape Cod.

Strandings must have been an even more fertile source of whales in
colonial and precolonial times, and Little thinks that drift whales were so
numerous that the Indians felt no need to go to sea to kill them. The
cetaceans do not drift ashore or strand themselves entirely haphazardly.
They are more likely to come ashore at certain beaches than others, and
the Indian names of places betray a faint glimmer of the former importance of beached whales in their geography: If the translation is accurate,
Siasconset on Nantucket, for example, means "great bones place."

We are likely to feel pathos over the inexplicable strandings of
whales and dolphins. We still cannot explain them. These strandings
must have appeared in a much different light to the Indians: less a tragedy than a blessing. So significant were these drift whales that they were
metamorphosed by the Indians into their mythology. The Algonquin
tribes of Long Island, Martha's Vineyard, and Nantucket shared a set of
stories about a fabulous culture hero variously called Moshup, Manshop,
Moishup, or Maushop.

Moshup was said to have created Nantucket when he knocked the poke from his pipe into the sea. The fog that hangs over the sea south of Cape Cod, obscuring Nantucket, is the smoke rising from his pipe. One of the richest of the Moshup legends portrays him as the Indians' mythic whaleman. The story is quoted from historical sources by William S. Simmons in *The Spirit of New England Tribes*:

> The first Indian who came to the Vineyard, was brought thither with his dog on a cake of ice. When he came to Gay Head, he found a very large man, whose name was Moshup. He had a wife and five children, four sons and one daughter; and lived in the Den. He used to catch whales, and then pluck up trees, and make a fire, and roast them. The coals of the trees, and the bones of the whales, are now to be seen. . . . Moshup went away nobody knows whither. He had no conversation with the Indians, but was kind to them, by sending whales, etc. ashore to them to eat.

It requires a shift in our relationship with nature to understand this story. Since I pay for my groceries, I have the crazy delusion that I have actually earned my salad greens and nacho chips—an attitude inherited from the Puritan work ethic. For the coastal Indians, however, whales were not something they chased, caught, and therefore achieved. Whales were a gift from a vanished hero, a father figure. Drift whales represented the kindness of Moshup, a blessing from their hero, a symbol of their connection with both animal and place. Finding a whale on the beach must have made the world seem like a place of happy chances, and they were the lucky winners.

For the whites, drift whales quickly grew in economic significance. By 1644, within four years of settling in Southampton, townspeople had set forth rules for sharing "such whales as were by hard luck and the kindness of Providence cast up." Deeds on Long Island to important beach areas and the rights to carcasses were always carefully spelled out. The whales, in fact, contributed to a major political controversy between the colonies and England, over a century before Bostonians were protesting the tea tax. When the Dutch handed New Netherland over to the English, Long Island became the special dominion of the Duke of York. Under the "Duke's Laws," whales were declared a "Royal Fish," and a fifteenth of a gallon of oil "shall be received for whales . . . cast upon the Shoare of any Precinct." By 1660, the whales had already become a prime source of wealth, and the fiercely independent islanders resisted this taxation by the Duke's "robber governors." Ignoring the "Perills" from the law, the whalemen contrived to report no whales to their rulers, and thus resisted the taxation.

Because it was more abundant then, and because it frequented the shores so closely, the right whale probably contributed a large percentage of the drift whales on the prime beaches in southern New England. The right whale soon drew the colonists off the shore and into boats. The beaches where the whales had been cast up soon became the places where the along-shore whalers built their lookout masts and launched their boats. Over the next century, the places in New England that had been the best for drift whales became the centers of the great pelagic whaling enterprises. The leading whale ports of the nineteenth century were not the large mercantile or fishing ports of Philadelphia, New York, Boston, or Salem. Rather, they were the ports near the recorded sites of Indian drift whaling, like Nantucket, New Bedford, Sag Harbor, and Southampton. As Elizabeth Little writes, the basis for "the distribution of all three whaling activities [drift, along-shore, and pelagic] was the distribution of right whales near the east coast in colonial times."

The human geography of the eastern coast is also a map of the value of the right whale, demonstrating the significance of the forgotten whale in American history. In a metaphorical as well as an economic way, we built our cities and homes on the back of the right whale.

## IV

The move into the sea in pursuit of right whales marked the invention of a distinctly American form of whaling. Following sporadic attempts with little success, the sons and grandsons of the English settlers learned to push through the surf, dare the worst of the winter weather, and challenge a 50-ton leviathan in small boats on rough seas. Goethe writes that the days of becoming are the most invigorating and that the full realization of being always comes with a tinge of sadness for the times of struggle gone by. It must have been an exhilarating time for these early whalers, since they were in the process of inventing a way of life and of learning what they could do.

Part of what makes the enterprise so distinctly American is the relationship between the Indians and the Yankees. Documents now suggest that the English settlers provided the new enterprise of along-shore whaling with the technology and the vision, while the Indians supplied the seamanship, the talent, and the courage. It proved to be a combination that would eventually carry Ahab and Queequeq around the world.

Along-shore whaling was right whaling. As Obed Macy wrote in his 1835 *History of Nantucket*, "The whales hitherto caught near the shores were of the Right Species." He goes on to offer a picturesque story on the origins of along-shore whaling in Nantucket. He wrote, "Some persons were on a high hill . . . observing the whales spouting and sporting with each other, when one observed, 'there,' pointing to the sea, 'is a green pasture where our children's grandchildren will go for bread.'"

Along-shore whaling was also winter whaling, December to March. Macy described the conditions under which the whalers went to sea: "They sometimes, in pleasant days, during the winter season, ventured off in their boats nearly out of sight of land. It has often been remarked by the aged, that the winters were not so windy and boisterous at that time as at present, though quite as cold; and that it would sometimes continue calm a week or even a fortnight."

By separating figures for along-shore whaling from the composite accounts of early historians, Little concludes that it began in Delaware as early as 1632 and that the industry worked its way up the coast. Charted on a graph over time, the harvests of the various locations are like successive parabolas of plenty and loss. On Long Island, the along-shore whaling began officially in 1650, when John Ogden was granted the first whaling license on record for "free liberty without interruption from the inhabitants of Southampton to kill whales on the south sea." But the colonial whaling industry did not get well under way under way until 1667, when James Loper, a Dutchman, organized the Indians on the eastern end of Long Island into along-shore whaling companies. The right whales off Long Island were largely exhausted by 1718. In a peak year, eighty whales were killed. On Cape Cod, the boom began after 1680, and it crashed by 1725.

According to Zaccheus Macy, writing in 1792, Nantucket started late: "The whale fishery began at Nantucket in the year 1690. One Ichabod Paddock came from Cape Cod to instruct the people to whale in boats from the shore, and the business lasted pretty good until about 1760, and then the whales gon and prety much don." The peak year was probably 1726, when eighty-six right whales were taken.

We can get an idea of the kind of riches to be made, and the extent of the destruction of right whales, from some remarkable research on the whaling industry of the Basques on the coast of Labrador. We know the right whale was hunted by the Basques in the Bay of Biscay at least as early as the eleventh century, making the right whale the first whale to be hunted for commercial purposes.

A hardy and mysterious people, the Basques keep popping up unexpectedly in remote corners of the world. In the last decade, Canadian researchers led by Selma Barkham discovered the presence of the Basques in Red Bay, Labrador. In 1977, archaeologists entered the town to find unmistakable evidence of Basque history: in the town's gardens and on the beaches, Spanish red tiles; with just a little digging, flensing knives and cooper's tools; and under water, the biggest prize, a sunken galleon, named the *San Juan*, with 55,000 gallons of right-whale oil in its hold.

The huge yields of oil and baleen from right whales rivaled the more glittering treasures sailing back to Spain in the galleons from the Caribbean. (Environment Canada researchers estimate the hold of the *San Juan* contained about $6 million worth of right-whale oil.) Oil from these whales lit lamps throughout Europe, became tallow in candles, and was an ingredient in products like soap. Plus, the huge plates of baleen in the right whale's capacious mouth ("whale-bone," which could reach nearly 9 feet in length), stiffened fashionable women's corsets and put the elasticity into whips.

The Basques had followed the right whale around the Atlantic, whaling from shore in Newfoundland in 1530 and reaching the peak of their success in the 1560s and 1570s. The whole business for the Basques in Newfoundland was probably finished by 1620. There is some debate over how much of the catch was made up of right whales and how much was made up of bowhead whales, a near relative. But with an average catch per boat per year of about twelve whales, one estimate puts the average annual catch at about 300 to 500 whales. The total harvest between 1530 and 1610 is estimated to have been between 25,000 and 40,000 whales.

These seas must have been teeming with whales.

The drogue, or drag or drug, has played a controversial part in the research into early American whaling. Its origins usually attributed to Indians, Elizabeth Little has found its source in the Basques. Before Yankee whalers learned to fasten their boat to the whale with harpoon and line, they used a thick board about 14 inches square to keep the line afloat and tire the whale. According to Little, there is "unequivocal evidence" that the drogue originated with the Basques. In the seal of the city of Fuentearrabia, dating from perhaps 1335, Little has found a square shape attached to a whaling harpoon line flung at a whale.

The question is, how did the Yankees in New England learn to use this drogue? As mentioned, Ichabod Paddock, otherwise unknown, came from Cape Cod to teach the people on Nantucket to whale from shore. James Loper, the innovator in whaling techniques on Long Island, was also asked by entrepreneurs on Nantucket to aid them in establishing whaling companies. Little says that if we wish to speculate, perhaps Ichabod Paddock or James Loper introduced an ancient Basque technique to the Indian and Yankee whale crews. It was both intelligent and successful. As she writes, "Successful colonial American whaling appears to have begun only after the American Indians learned an archaic European method of catching whales."

If Indians did not supply the equipment for "fixeing out whaling," they indisputably taught seamanship to the New Englanders. In energetic prose, William Wood of Salem conveyed his astonishment at the skill of the Indians at sea in 1635, calling the Indians' canoes "these cockling fly-boats, wherein an Englishman can scarce sit without a fearfull tottering." According to Crévecoeur, the Indians of Nantucket dominated colonial American whaling. In a whaling boat of six men, five would be Indians and one would be white, and the white one would be the leader.

On the traditional drift-whale beaches, the whalers erected a mast or lookout, from which they watched for the spouts of whales. Huts or whale houses crouched on the shore around the mast—thatched wigwams on Long Island; small, single-story, boarded houses on Nantucket. At the sight of a whale, the lookout cried, "Awaite Pawana, here is a whale."

With what Crévecoeur calls "astonishing velocity," the men tried to pull within 15 feet of the whale—close enough for the poised harpooner to try for the thrust of death. With one leg braced in a notch in the bow, he aimed for the prime spot just behind the whale's head. In pitching seas, often in miserable winter weather, in a 20-foot boat beside a 50-foot whale, these men faced terrifying dangers. The small boat gave the men the advantage of mobility; nevertheless, to quote Crévecoeur, "Sometimes in the immediate impulse of rage, she will attack the boat and demolish it with one stroke of her tail. In an instant the frail vehicle disappears and the assailants are immersed in the dreadful element." A man who fell overboard in the winter seas stood little chance of survival if he was not immediately hauled from the waters.

The final struggle could last for hours as the whale fled or fought for life, slowly wearying from the assault. The boats closed in as the whale, pulling the drogue, tired. The men used sharp lances for the death stabs, until, in the last paroxysm, the whale spouted a crimson blow, her breath thick with blood—the sure sign of death.

Sometime before 1782, New England whalers learned to fasten the harpoon line to the boat. This technique had also been developed by the Basques, and it was used by English and Dutch whalers near Greenland. Thus began the "Nantucket sleigh ride": A captain had grown tired of losing harpooned whales and tried to convince his men to use a method, just told to them, "by boat and the line." According to Thomas Beale, who in 1839 published *The Natural History of the Sperm Whale,* the idea "seemed monstrous; the mere thought of having the boat they were in attached to an infuriated leviathan by a strong rope struck terror among the whole crew. . . . Others more daring undertook the trial soon afterward, in which they frequently came off victorious, so that the new method was established among them, and has since been much improved."

The along-shore whalers were too successful. Early in the 1700s, complaints began to surface that the whales were no longer in their usual haunts. But emboldened by their success with right whales, and hearing that the sperm whale, once thought rare, was abundant far offshore, the men on Nantucket began by 1718 to go after it. The sperm whale soon displaced the right whale as the preferred creature of the hunt.

Right whales continued to be hunted from the shore through the nineteenth century: About ninety were taken from Long Island in the last half of the century. The last one was killed off Long Island in 1918. But for the most part, whalers had turned their attention to other species and other seas. With an awful inevitability, one species after another fell under the onslaught, and even in the mid-1800s Herman Melville wondered whether "Leviathan can long endure so wide a chase, and so remorseless a havoc; whether he must not at last be exterminated from the waters."

As the waters around the world were depleted, and as the preferred species went into their predicted declines, whalers turned to new hunting grounds and new species. Advances in technology (the heavy cannon harpoon gun, faster ships, and floating factories) made it both efficient and profitable to take species that had formerly been too small or too elusive to be considered worth the pursuit. This particularly meant hunting rorquals—blue, humpback, minke, fin, and sei whales. They were the untapped reserve of the "wrong" baleen whales of earlier times.

Protection for the whales came late, and it is a sad case of trying to close the barn door after the horse has bolted. The International Whaling Commission (IWC), founded in 1946, has been plagued by controversy and ineffectualness, but it has gradually extended its protection over the large rorquals, right whale, gray whale, bowhead whale, and sperm whale. In 1983, the IWC made the historic decision to impose an indefinite moratorium on all whaling. Sadly, whaling has probably been discontinued not out of concern for the whales but because the enterprise has lost its profitability. There are still indigenous subsistence whale hunts—notably by Inuits for bowhead and Faroe Islanders for pilot whales—though this pressure on the populations is not now a major concern for most environmentalists. Only one member country of the IWC now refuses to honor the moratorium—Japan.

Though protection has helped the whales, most species are appallingly low fractions of what they once were. Even if no species has gone extinct, several of the stocks or regional populations have vanished or are in imminent danger of doing so:

*Right whales:* Precarious throughout their range, and on the verge of extinction in the North Pacific and North Atlantic.

*Blue whales:* A few hundred in the North Atlantic; of the 5000 once in the North Pacific, perhaps 1500 survive; of the 200,000 in the southern hemisphere in the nineteenth century, a recent scientific census saw only 453 animals, and estimates only 1200 to 1500 blues remain.

*Humpback whales:* Of 15,000 in the North Pacific before the onset of mechanized whaling, less than 1000 survive; the western North Atlantic has about 2000, though the eastern North Atlantic is in poor shape; in the southern hemisphere, of the 100,000 humpbacks in the nineteenth century, about 2500 are all that remain.

*Fin whales:* Severely reduced throughout the seas, perhaps by one-half to two-thirds.

*Sei whales:* Heavily exploited, suffering major declines in all areas.

*Minke whales:* Heavily exploited, largely for their meat, though they were once considered too small for whalers to waste time and effort on.

We have inherited, and created, impoverished seas. The spouting is more sporadic, gone totally from some areas of the oceans, and the whales that remain are mere relics of the swarms our ancestors wrote of with such awe. Whaling, now a small industry in terms of former glories and actual contributions to national economies, is conducted only in defiance of world opinion. Still, one nation refuses to abandon a business that has become an ethical and economic anachronism—the sad devastation for dollars that began with the right whale.

V

On the southern tip of Nova Scotia, I joined Scott Kraus and his crew of biologists and volunteers in their late-summer, early-fall research on the right whales in the Bay of Fundy and on Browns Bank, 35 miles into the Atlantic Ocean. From July to October, he bases his fieldwork out of Lubec, Maine, the northeastern-most city in the United States. The crew is made up largely of volunteers, seminomadic people really, working for nearly nothing just to live near the whales. Some were just out of college, looking for something to do that mattered to them, that was more than making money. Others worked flexible jobs so that they could follow the whales up and down the coast during the year—winter in Florida, summer in Maine.

One man, named Brian Hoover, was planning to go to graduate school soon as a student of marine biology, and he had plans to look for the probably extinct monk seal in the Caribbean. The next year, his sense of adventure led him to climb Mt. McKinley in Alaska, where he was killed; his body was never recovered.

Lubec is a small fishing town past its prime, its modest houses sprawled over a small hill above Passamaquoddy Bay. Some of the volunteers lived on the second floor of the brick-red cannery by the water. Others of us lived in one of the grand old houses higher on the hill, dilapidated and dirty, plaster falling at night from the ceilings while we slept. Though it was rundown, it gave us magnificent views of the harbor.

From Lubec, seven of us formed a research team on a rented yacht with (of all things) teak paneling and a tape deck. We dared a wild passage on heavy seas across the Bay of Fundy, then skirted the inner coast of Nova Scotia from Briar Island to Cape Sable Island, where we made port in tiny Donald Head. Just a fishing village, it had a new harbor crowded with beautiful, broad-beamed, and distinctive fishing boats—Cape Sable Islanders, painted in vivid pastels of blue and red and yellow, all of them using as well their characteristic shade of chlorine green.

Bad weather, combined with a plague of boat problems, kept us in port for a whole week; our silly yacht, rich in comparison to the Islanders and always broken down, was stupidly conspicuous. We drew two visits from customs officials, who were convinced we were drug runners.

One afternoon we forced ourselves out to sea under iffy circumstances: The sky was low, and the fog had not fully dissipated. But we wanted to get out among the whales. About 35 miles south of Cape Sable Island, between Browns and Baccaro banks, we ran into a group of at least eighteen right whales—it was hard to be sure of numbers, because the whales came at us so fast from every direction, surfacing and diving. Browns Banks is a courtship area for summer right whales, and they were active and busy.

I scooted down onto the foredeck, clinging to railings, and braced myself on the bowsprit. Always, it's a dislocating experience for me to get right down close to the ocean's surface, to feel small above the hundreds of feet of ocean below me, with nothing but miles of empty, steely ocean visible in all directions. Yawing and pitching with the swells, I dipped with the bowsprit to within inches of the sea.

At that instant, barely 10 feet from me, two huge whales broke the surface with an explosive whoosh, their characteristic V-shaped blows rising like the steam from vents on city streets, their backs flat and black as asphalt sidewalks. Fat-cheeked under the inward curves of their scalloped lips, they had mouths and snouts of startling size, maybe 15 feet long. We were so close, and the moment was so suddenly intimate, that I could hear the water dripping from their jutting lower jaws as it splashed into the vastness of the sea.

It was a jarring contrast: two massive and moving bodies, right there before me, suddenly defining the depth of field for all the empty wilderness of water around us.

They wallowed on the surface. One of the whales lifted a flipper, flat and splayed, and flailed it against the waves, and I could hear it slapping. Dropping out of sight, the whale rolled onto its back, the underside of its belly bursting out of the water, flippers at angles to each side throwing white spray. Unlike the rest of its black body, the belly was a blaze of white, as if it had been splashed with paint. Even in this dark sea, the water washed off the white blaze in ice-blue streams, clear and bright cascades.

The second whale submerged and then rose under the first. They turned belly to belly. Slow but forceful, their big bodies banged indolently, and a white froth stirred the waters around them.

Then one of them swam right up to me in an enchanted moment in the midst of the sea, intensely private and peaceful. It lifted its chin out of the water, and on the underside of its cyamid-covered head, a white blaze lit its chin. It hung there, poised, for a moment. Then it slipped backward into the water and expelled a blow. The vapor of its breath trailed just over the gray waters and drifted into my face and onto my lips.

I licked my lips and tasted the salt. The whales submerged and swam off. In the calm of that encounter, the simple peace in the midst of such huge stretches and such awful deeps of sea, there was truth for me. In fragile moments in the midst of the void, in the fleeting encounters with another living being, in the delicate feel of the breath of another on my face, I can feel my heart open up and the earth become less desolate.

I shuffled my way to the bridge, where the view of the whales was strikingly different. From the bridge, intimacy gave way to energy and power, whales visible in nearly every direction. Flukes wavered above the swells, peaks slipping beneath the peaked waves. Whales rolled over each other, more whales swam into view, whales bellied up to the surface, whales lay motionless in the lapping swells, and whales thrashed a frothing sea. Twisting, touching, stroking with flippers—the scene was too dynamic and active to comprehend fully in any one look.

Even out on Browns Bank, well into the sea, these huge whales seemed fragile and in jeopardy. These courtship grounds are right next to major shipping lanes in the Atlantic. Barely recovered from near extinction, many of the whales were banged and brutalized. We could identify many of them by scars from their collisions with boats. One of them, which the biologists had appropriately named Creases, had a gash of white scar tissue down its back; more than a meter long, the cut had probably been caused by a propeller. In recent years, three whales known to researchers had been found dead from collisions with ships.

As we were photographing and recording, the latent power of the whales broke into a thrust of pure energy. About 3 miles off starboard, through the gray sea-air, a right whale rammed up out of the sea, breaching in an extravagant release of a body out of water, physical life bursting from the elements that had contained it. Though, swimming in the water, the right whale is sluggish and slow, in the instant of the breach this creature seemed transformed by its own explosion of energy. Straining into the jump, its massive body was bent and unavoidably phallic, and water fell from its sides like clouds.

We headed straight for that whale, forgetting data, forgetting all the whales closer by.

Defying water and air and probability, the whale—all 45 tons of it— breached several times. It launched almost completely out of the water, twisting in muscled torsion, quivering on the axis of its tail, and then crashed back to the sea on its side, white sheets of water avalanching before it like snow off a mountain.

The breaches were like a storm breaking open and disturbing the surface of life, like the primitive force that every now and then, for all of us, heaves up out of its confines, insists on its own expression, and then falls back into itself. They were like life itself, flashing for one shining instant above the gulf in a superb display of will and strength.

By the time we got there, the whale had quit breaching. All its flinging into the air, all the energy of its body expressed in those fleeting and precarious moments above the yawning sea—they were gone, leaving only a vibration in the air.

The breath on my lips. The breach from the sea. I need the friction of these opposites. They give me energy, light me up. Moments of stillness and communion, acts of passion and flurry: breaking in and breaking out. I keep veering between the passion and the peace, the future very much in doubt, and I don't understand.

BARRY LOPEZ

# Lancaster Sound:
## *Monodon monoceros*

The first day I saw narwhals I knew that no element of the earth's natural history had ever before brought me so far, so suddenly. It was as though something from a bestiary had taken shape, a creature strange as a giraffe. It was as if the testimony of someone I had no reason to doubt, yet could not quite believe, a story too farfetched, had been verified at a glance.

I was with a bowhead whale biologist named Don Ljungblad, flying search transects over Bering Sea. It was May, and the first bowheads of spring were slowly working their way north through Bering Strait toward their summer feeding grounds in the Chukchi and Beaufort seas. Each day as we flew these transects we would pass over belukha whale and walrus, ringed, spotted, and ribbon seals, bearded seals, and flocks of bird migrating to Siberia. I know of no other region in North America where animals can be met with in such numbers. Bering Sea itself is probably the richest of all the northern seas, as rich as Chesapeake Bay or the Grand Banks at the time of their discovery. Its bounty of crabs, pollock, cod, sole, herring, clams, and salmon is set down in wild

BARRY LOPEZ is one of America's most eminent nature writers. For his book *Of Wolves and Men* he received the John Burroughs Medal for distinguished nature writing. His other books include *Fieldnotes; Crow and Weasel; Desert Notes; River Notes;* and *Winter Count.* In 1986 he received the American Book Award for *Arctic Dreams,* from which "Lancaster Sound: *Monodon monoceros*" was adapted. Copyright © 1986. Reprinted by permission of Sterling Lord Literistic.

numbers, the rambling digits of guesswork. The numbers of birds and marine mammals feeding here, to a person familiar with anything but the Serengeti or life at the Antarctic convergence, are magical. At the height of migration in the spring, the testament of life in Bering Sea is absolutely stilling in its dimensions.

The two weeks I spent flying with Ljungblad, with so many thousands of creatures moving through the water and the air, were a heady experience. Herds of belukha whale glided in silent shoals beneath transparent sheets of young ice. Squadrons of fast-flying sea ducks flashed beneath us as they banked away. We passed ice floes stained red in a hundred places with the afterbirths of walrus. Staring all day into the bright light reflected from the ice and water, however, and the compression in time of these extraordinary events, left me dazed some evenings.

Aspects of the Arctic landscape that had become salient for me—its real and temporal borders; a rare, rich oasis of life surrounded by vast stretches of deserted land; the upending of conventional kinds of time; biological vulnerability made poignant by the forgiving light of summer—all of this was evoked over Bering Sea.

The day we saw the narwhals we were flying south, low over Bering Strait. The ice in Chukchi Sea behind us was so close it did not seem possible that bowheads could have penetrated this far; but it is good to check, because they can make headway in ice as heavy as this and they are able to come a long way north undetected in lighter ice on the Russian side. I was daydreaming about two bowheads we had seen that morning. They had been floating side by side in a broad lane of unusually clear water between a shelf of shorefast ice and the pack ice—the flaw lead. As we passed over, they made a single movement together, a slow, rolling turn and graceful glide, like figure skaters pushing off, these fifty-ton leviathans. Ljungblad shouted in my earphones: "Waiting." They were waiting for the ice in the strait to open up. Ljungblad saw nearly 300 bowheads waiting calmly like this one year, some on their backs, some with their chins resting on the ice.

The narwhals appeared in the middle of this reverie. Two males, with ivory tusks spiraling out of their foreheads, the image of the unicorn with which history has confused them. They were close to the same size and light-colored, and were lying parallel and motionless in a long, straight lead in the ice. My eye was drawn to them before my conscious mind, let alone my voice, could catch up. I stared dumbfounded while someone else shouted. Not just to see the narwhals, but *here*, a few miles northwest of King Island in Bering Sea. In all the years scientists have kept records for these waters, no one had ever seen a narwhal alive in Bering Sea. Judging from the heaviness of the ice around them, they must have spent the winter here.* They were either residents, a wondrous thought, or they had come from the nearest population centers the previous fall, from waters north of Siberia or from northeastern Canada.

The appearance of these animals was highly provocative. We made circle after circle above them, until they swam away under the ice and were gone. Then we looked at each other. Who could say what this was, really?

Because you have seen something doesn't mean you can explain it. Differing interpretations will always abound, even when good minds come to bear. The kernel of indisputable information is a dot in space; interpretations grow out of the desire to make this point a line, to give it a direction. The directions in which it can be sent, the uses to which it can be put by a culturally, professionally, and geographically diverse society, are almost without limit. The possibilities make good scientists chary. In a region like the Arctic, tense with a hunger for wealth, with fears of plunder, interpretation can quickly get beyond a scientist's control. When asked to assess the meaning of a biological event—What were those animals doing out there? Where do they belong?—they hedge. They are sometimes reluctant to elaborate on what they saw, because they cannot say what it means, and they are suspicious of those who say they know. Some even distrust the motives behind the questions.

I think along these lines in this instance because of the animal. No large mammal in the Northern Hemisphere comes as close as the narwhal to having its very existence doubted. For some, the possibility that this creature might actually live in the threatened waters of Bering Sea is portentous, a significant apparition on the eve of an era of disruptive oil exploration there. For others, those with the leases to search for oil and gas in Navarin and Norton basins, the possibility that narwhals may live there is a complicating environmental nuisance. Hardly anyone marvels solely at the fact that on the afternoon of April 16, 1982, five people saw two narwhals in a place so unexpected that they were flabbergasted.

---

* The narwhal is not nearly as forceful in the ice as the bowhead. It can break through only about six inches of ice with its head. A bowhead, using its brow or on occasion its more formidable chin, can break through as much as eighteen inches of sea ice.

They remained speechless, circling over the animals in a state of wonder. In those moments the animals did not have to mean anything at all.

We know more about the rings of Saturn than we know about the narwhal. Where do they go and what do they eat in the winter, when it is too dark and cold for us to find them? The Chilean poet and essayist Pablo Neruda wonders in his memoirs how an animal this large can have remained so obscure and uncelebrated. Its name, he thought, was "the most beautiful of undersea names, the name of a sea chalice that sings, the name of a crystal spur." Why, he wondered, had no one taken Narwhal for a last name, or built "a beautiful Narwhal Building?"

Part of the answer lies with a regrettable connotation of death in the animal's name. The pallid color of the narwhal's skin has been likened to that of a drowned human corpse, and it is widely thought that its name came from the Old Norse for "corpse" and "whale," *nár* + *hvalr*. A medieval belief that the narwhal's flesh was poisonous has been offered in support of this interpretation, as well as the belief that its "horn" was proof at that time against being poisoned. The eighteenth-century naturalist Buffon characterized the animal for all the generations that would read him as one that "revels in carnage, attacks without provocation, and kills without need." Among its associations with human enterprise in the inhospitable north is the following grim incident. In 1126, Arnhald, first bishop of Iceland, was shipwrecked off the Icelandic coast. Drowned men and part of the contents of the ship's hold washed up in a marsh, a place afterward called the Pool of Corpses. Conspicuous among the items of salvage were a number of narwhal tusks, "with runic letters upon them in an indelible red gum so that each sailor might know his own at the end of the voyage."

W. P. Lehmann, a professor of Germanic languages, believes the association with death is a linguistic accident. The Old Norse *nárhvalr* (whence the English *narwhal*, the French *narval*, the German *Narwal*, etc.), he says, was a vernacular play on the word *nahvalr*—the way *highbred corn* is used in place of *hybrid corn*, or *sparrowgrass* is used for *asparagus*. According to Lehmann, *nahvalr* is an earlier, West Norse term meaning a "whale distinguished by a long, narrow projection" (the tusk).

Some, nevertheless, still call the narwhal "the corpse whale," and the unfounded belief that it is a cause of human death, or an omen or symbol to be associated with human death, remains intact to this day in some quarters. Animals are often fixed like this in history, bearing an unwarranted association derived from notions or surmise having no connection at all with their real life. The fuller explanations of modern field biology are an antidote, in part, to this tendency to name an animal carelessly. But it is also, as Neruda suggests, a task of literature to take animals regularly from the shelves where we have stored them, like charms or the most intricate of watches, and to bring them to life.

The obscurity of narwhals is not easily breached by science. To begin with, they live underwater. And they live year-round in the polar ice, where the logistics and expense involved in approaching them are formidable barriers to field research, even in summer. Scientists have largely been limited to watching what takes place at the surface of the water in the open sea adjacent to observation points high on coastal bluffs. And to putting hydrophones in the water with them, and to making comparisons with the belukha whale, a close and better-known relative. About the regular periodic events of their lives, such as migration, breeding, and calving, in relation to climatic changes and fluctuations in the size of the population, we know next to nothing.*

Scientists can speak with precision only about the physical animal, not the ecology or behavior of this social and gregarious small whale. (It is the latter, not the former, unfortunately, that is most crucial to an understanding of how industrial development might affect narwhals.) Adult males, sixteen feet long and weighing upwards of 3300 pounds, are about a quarter again as large as adult females. Males are also distinguished by an ivory tusk that pierces the upper lip on the left side and extends forward as much as ten feet. Rarely, a female is found with a tusk, and, more rarely still, males and females with tusks on both sides of the upper jaw.

From the side, compared with the rest of its body, the narwhal's head seems small and blunt. It is dominated by a high, rounded forehead filled with bioacoustical lipids—special fats that allow the narwhal to use sound waves to communicate with other whales and to locate itself and other objects in its three-dimensional world. Its short front flippers function as little more than diving planes. The cone-shaped body tapers from

---

* The knowledge and insight of Eskimos on these points, unfortunately, are of little help. Of all the areas of natural history in which they show expertise, native hunters are weakest in their understanding of the population dynamics of migratory animals. The reason is straightforward. Too much of the animal's life is lived "outside the community," beyond the geographic and phenomenological landscape the Eskimos share with them.

just behind these flippers—where its girth is greatest, as much as eight feet—to a vertical ellipse at the tail. In place of a dorsal fin, a low dorsal ridge about five feet long extends in an irregular crenulation down the back. The tail flukes are unique. Seen from above, they appear heart-shaped, like a ginkgo leaf, with a deep-notched center and trailing edges that curve far forward.

Viewed from the front, the head seems somewhat squarish and asymmetrical, and oddly small against the deep chest. The mouth, too, seems small for such a large animal, with the upper lip just covering the edge of a short, wedge-shaped jaw. The eyes are located just above and behind the upturned corners of the mouth, which give the animal a bemused expression. (The evolutionary loss of facial muscles, naturalist Peter Warshall has noted, means no quizzical wrinkling of the forehead, no raised eyebrow of disbelief, no pursed lip of determination). A single, crescent-shaped blowhole on top of the head is in a transverse line with the eyes.

Narwhal calves are almost uniformly gray. Young adults show spreading patches and streaks of white on the belly and marbling on the flanks. Adults are dark gray across the top of the head and down the back. Lighter grays predominate on top of the flippers and flukes, whites and light yellow-whites underneath. The back and flanks are marbled with blackish grays. Older animals, especially males, may be almost entirely white. Females, say some, are always lighter-colored on their flanks.

The marbled quality of the skin, which feels like smooth, oiled stone, is mesmerizing. On the flukes especially, where curvilinear streaks of dark gray overlap whitish-gray tones, the effect could not be more painterly. Elsewhere on the body, spots dominate. "These spots," writes William Scoresby, "are of a roundish or oblong form: on the back, where they seldom exceed two inches in diameter, they are the darkest and most crowded together, yet with intervals of pure white among them. On the side the spots are fainter, smaller, and more open. On the belly, they become extremely faint and few, and in considerable surfaces are not to be seen." These patterns completely penetrate the skin, which is a half-inch thick.

In the water, depending on sunlight and the color of the water itself, narwhals, according to British whaling historian Basil Lubbock, take on "many hues, from deep sea green to even an intense lake [blue] colour."

Narwhals are strong swimmers, with the ability to alter the contours of their body very slightly to reduce turbulence. Their speed and maneuverability are sufficient to hunt down swift prey—Arctic cod, Greenland halibut, redfish—and to avoid their enemies, the orca and the Greenland shark.

Narwhals live in close association with ice margins and are sometimes found far inside heavy pack ice, miles from open water. (How they determine whether the lead systems they follow into the ice will stay open behind them, ensuring their safe return, is not known.) They manage to survive in areas of strong currents and wind where the movement of ice on the surface is violent and where leads open and close, or freeze over, very quickly. (Like seabirds, they seem to have an uncanny sense of when a particular lead is going to close in on them, and they leave.) That they are not infallible in anticipating the movement and formation of ice, which seals them off from the open air and oxygen, is attested to by a relatively unusual and often fatal event called a savssat.

Savssats are most commonly observed on the west coast of Greenland. Late in the fall, while narwhals are still feeding deep in a coastal fiord, a band of ice may form in calm water across the fiord's mouth. The ice sheet may then expand toward the head of the fiord. At some point the distance from its landward to its seaward edge exceeds the distance a narwhal can travel on a single breath. By this time, too, shorefast ice may have formed at the head of the fiord, and it may grow out to meet the sea ice. The narwhals are thus crowded into a smaller and smaller patch of open water. Their bellowing and gurgling, their bovinelike moans and the plosive screech of their breathing, can sometimes be heard at a great distance.

The Danish scientist Christian Vibe visited a savssat on March 16, 1943, on the west coast of central Greenland. Hundreds of narwhals and belukhas were trapped in an opening less than 20 feet square. The black surface of the water was utterly "calm and still," writes Vibe. "Then the smooth surface was suddenly broken by black shadows and white animals which in elegant curves came up and disappeared—narwhals and white whales by the score. Side by side they emerged so close to each other that some of them would be lifted on the backs of the others and turn a somersault with the handsome tail waving in the air. First rows of narwhal, then white whales and then again narwhals—each species separately. It seethed, bobbed, and splashed in the opening. With a hollow, whistling sound they inhaled the air as if sucking it in through long iron tubes. The water was greatly disturbed . . . and the waves washed far in over the ice." The splashed water froze to the rim of the breathing hole, as did the moisture from their exhalations, further reducing the size of the savssat. In spite of the frenzy, not a single animal that Vibe saw was wounded by the huge tusks of the narwhal.*

The narwhal is classed in the suborder Odontoceti, with toothed whales such as the sperm whale, in the superfamily Delphinoidea, along with porpoises and dolphins, and in the family Monodontidae with a single companion, the belukha. In contrast to the apparently coastally adapted belukha, biologists believe the narwhal is a pelagic or open-ocean species, that it is more ice-adapted, and that it winters farther to the north. Extrapolating on the basis of what is known of the belukha, it is thought that narwhals breed in April and give birth to a single, five-foot, 170-pound calf about fourteen months later, in June or July. Calves carry an inch-thick layer of blubber at birth to protect them against the cold water. They appear to nurse for about two years and may stay with their mothers for three years, or more. Extrapolating once again from the belukha, it is thought that females reach sexual maturity between four and seven years of age, males between eight and nine years.

Narwhals are usually seen in small groups of two to eight animals, frequently of the same sex and age. In the summer, female groups, which include calves, are sometimes smaller or more loosely knit than male groups. During spring migration, herds may consist of 300 or more animals.

Narwhals feed largely on Arctic and polar cod, Greenland halibut, redfish, sculpins, and other fish, on squid and to some extent on shrimps of several kinds, and on octopus and crustaceans. They have a complex, five-chambered stomach that processes food quickly, leaving undigested the chitonous beaks of squid and octopus, the carapaces of crustaceans, and the ear bones and eye lenses of fish, from which biologists can piece together knowledge of their diets.

Two types of "whale lice" (actually minute crustaceans) cling to their skin, in the cavity where the tusk passes through the lip, in the tail notch in the flukes, and in wounds (all places where they are least likely to be swept off by the flow of water past the narwhal's body). The tracks of the sharp, hooked legs of these tiny creatures are sometimes very clear on a

---

* Eskimo hunters killed 340 narwhals and belukhas at this savssat in a week, before the ice fractured and the rest escaped. In the spring of 1915, Eskimos at Disko Bay took more than a thousand narwhals and belukhas at two savssats over a period of several months. Inattentive birds, especially thick-billed murres and dovekies which require a lot of open water to take off, may also suddenly find themselves with insufficient room and may be trapped.

narwhal's skin. Older animals may carry such infestation of these parasites as to cause an observer to wince.

If you were to stand at the edge of a sea cliff on the north coast of
Borden Peninsula, Baffin Island, you could watch narwhals migrating
past more or less continuously for several weeks in the twenty-four-hour
light of June. You would be struck by their agility and swiftness, by the
synchronicity of their movements as they swam and dived in unison, and
by a quality of alert composure in them, of capability in the face of whatever might happen. Their attractiveness lies partly with their strong,
graceful movements in three dimensions, like gliding birds on an airless
day. An impressive form of their synchronous behavior is their ability to
deep-dive in groups. They disappear as a single diminishing shape, gray
fading to darkness. They reach depths of 1000 feet or more, and their
intent, often, is then to drive schools of polar cod toward the surface at
such a rate that the fish lose consciousness from the too-rapid expansion
of their swim bladders. At the surface, thousands of these stunned
fish feed narwhals and harp seals, and rafts of excited northern fulmars
and kittiwakes.

Watching from high above, one is also struck by the social interactions of narwhals, which are extensive and appear to be well organized
according to hierarchies of age and sex. The socializing of males frequently involves the use of their tusks. They cross them like swords
above the water, or one forces another down by pressing his tusk across
the other's back, or they face each other head-on, their tusks side by side.

Helen Silverman, whose graduate work included a study of the social
organization and behavior of narwhals, describes as typical the following
scene, from her observations in Lancaster Sound. "On one occasion a
group of five narwhals consisting of two adult males, one adult female,
one [calf] and one juvenile were moving west with the males in the lead.
The group stopped and remained on the surface for about 30 [seconds].
One male turned, moved under the [calf], and lifted it out of the water
twice. There was no apparent reaction from the mother. The male then
touched the side of the female with the tip of its tusk and the group continued westward."

Sitting high on a sea cliff in sunny, blustery weather in late June—the
familiar sense of expansiveness, of deep exhilaration such weather brings
over one, combined with the opportunity to watch animals, is summed
up in a single Eskimo word: *quviannikumut*, "to feel deeply happy"—

sitting here like this, it is easy to fall into speculation about the obscure narwhal. From the time I first looked into a narwhal's mouth, past the accordian pleats of its tongue, at the soft white interior splashed with Tyrian purple, I have thought of their affinity with sperm whales, whose mouths are similarly colored. Like the sperm whale, the narwhal is a deep diver. No other whales but the narwhal and the sperm whale are known to sleep on the surface for hours at a time. And when the narwhal lies at the surface, it lies like a sperm whale, with the section of its back from blowhole to dorsal ridge exposed, and the rest of its back and tail hanging down in the water. Like the sperm whale, it is renowned for its teeth; and it has been pursued, though briefly, for the fine oils in its forehead.

Like all whales, the narwhal's evolutionary roots are in the Cretaceous, with insect-eating carnivores that we, too, are descended from. Its line of development through the Cretaceous and into the Paleocene follows that of artiodactyls like the hippopotamus and the antelope—and then it takes a radical turn. After some 330 million years on dry land, since it emerged from the sea during the Devonian period 380 million years ago, the line of genetic development that will produce whales returns to the world's oceans. The first proto-whales turn up in the Eocene, 45 million years ago, the first toothed whales 18 million years later, in the Oligocene. By then, the extraordinary adjustments that had to take place to permit air-breathing mammals to live in the sea were largely complete.

Looking down from the sea cliffs at a lone whale floating peacefully in the blue-green water, it is possible to meditate on these evolutionary changes in the mammalian line, to imagine this creature brought forward in time to this moment. What were once its rear legs have disappeared, though the skeleton still shows the trace of a pelvis. Sea water gave it such buoyancy that it required little in the way of a skeletal structure; it therefore has achieved a large size without loss of agility. It left behind it a world of oscillating temperatures (temperatures on the Arctic headland from which I gaze may span a range of 120°F over twelve months) for a world where the temperature barely fluctuates. It did not relinquish its warm-blooded way of life, however; it is insulated against the cold with a layer of blubber two to four inches thick.

The two greatest changes in its body have been in the way it now stores and uses oxygen, and in a rearrangement of its senses to suit a world that is largely acoustical, not visual or olfactory, in its stimulations.

When I breathe this Arctic air, 34 percent of the oxygen is briefly stored in my lungs, 41 percent in my blood, 13 percent in my muscles, and 12 percent in the tissues of other of my organs. I take a deep breath only when I am winded or in a state of emotion; the narwhal always takes a deep breath—its draft of this same air fills its small lungs completely. And it stores the oxygen differently, so it can draw on it steadily during a fifteen-minute dive. Only about 9 percent stays in its lungs, while 41 percent goes into the blood, another 41 percent into the muscles, and about 9 percent into other tissues. The oxygen is bound to hemoglobin molecules in its blood (no different from my own), and to myoglobin molecules in its muscles. (The high proportion of myoglobin in its muscles makes the narwhal's muscle meat dark maroon, like the flesh of all marine mammals.)

Changes in the narwhal's circulatory system—the evolution of *rete mirabile*, "wonder nets" of blood vessels; an enlargement of its hepatic veins; a reversible flow of blood at certain places—have allowed it to adapt comfortably to the great pressures it experiences during deep dives. There is too little nitrogen in its blood for "the bends" to occur when it surfaces. Carbon dioxide, the by-product of respiration, is effectively stored until it can be explosively expelled with a rapid flushing of the lungs.

It is only with an elaborate apparatus of scuba gear, decompression tanks, wet suits, weight belts, and swim fins that we can explore these changes. Even then it is hard to appreciate the radical alteration of mammalian development that the narwhal represents. First, ours is largely a two-dimensional world. We are not creatures who look up often. We are used to exploring "the length and breadth" of issues, not their "height." For the narwhal there are very few two-dimensional experiences—the sense of the water it feels at the surface of its skin, and that plane it must break in order to breathe.

The second constraint on our appreciation of the narwhal's world is that it "knows" according to a different hierarchy of senses than the one we are accustomed to. Its chemical senses of taste and smell are all but gone, as far as we know, though narwhals probably retain an ability to determine salinity. Its tactile sense remains acute. Its sensitivity to pressure is elevated—it has a highly discriminating feeling for depth and a hunter's sensitivity to the slight turbulence created by a school of cod cruising ahead of it in its dimly lit world. The sense of sight is atrophied, because of a lack of light. The eye, in fact, has changed in order to accommodate itself to high pressures, the chemical irritation of salt, a constant rush of water past it, and the different angle of refraction of light underwater. (The narwhal sees the world above water with an eye that does not move in its socket, with astigmatic vision and a limited ability to change the distance at which it can focus.)

How different must be "the world" for such a creature, for whom sight is but a peripheral sense, who occupies, instead, a three-dimensional acoustical space. Perhaps only musicians have some inkling of the formal shape of emotions and motivation that might define such a sensibility.

The Arctic Ocean can seem utterly silent on a summer day to an observer standing far above. If you lowered a hydrophone, however, you would discover a sphere of "noise" that only spectrum analyzers and tape recorders could unravel. The tremolo moans of bearded seals. The electric crackling of shrimp. The baritone boom of walrus. The high-pitched bark and yelp of ringed seals. The clicks, pure tones, birdlike trills, and harmonics of belukhas and narwhals. The elephantine trumpeting of bowhead whales. Added to these animal noises would be the sounds of shifting sediments on the sea floor, the whine and fracture of sea ice, and the sound of deep-keeled ice grounding shallow water.

The narwhal is not only at home in this "cacophony," as possessed of the sense of a neighborhood as we might conceivably be on an evening stroll, but it manages to appear "asleep," oblivious at the surface of the water on a summer day in Lancaster Sound.

The single most important change that took place in the whale's acoustical system to permit it to live in this world was the isolation of its auditory canals from each other. It could then receive waterborne sound independently on each side of its head and so determine the direction from which a sound was coming. (We can do this only in the open air; underwater, sound vibrates evenly through the bones of our head.) The narwhal, of course, receives many sounds; we can only speculate about what it pays attention to, or what information it may obtain from all that it hears. Conversely, narwhals also emit many sounds important, presumably, to narwhals and to other animals too.

Acoustical scientists divide narwhal sound into two categories. Respiratory sounds are audible to us as wheezes, moans, whistles, and gurgles of various sorts. The second group of sounds, those associated

with, presumably, echolocation and communication, scientists divide
into three categories: clicking, generated at rates as high as 500 clicks per
second; pulsed tones; and pure tones. (Certain of these sounds are audible to someone in a boat in the open air, like an effervescence rising from
the surface of the water.)

Narwhals, it is believed, use clicking sounds to locate themselves,
their companions, their prey, and such things as floe edges and the trend
of leads. Pulsed tones are thought to be social in nature and susceptible
to individual modification, so each narwhal has a "signature" tone or call
of its own. Pure-tone signals, too, are thought to be social or commu-
nicative in function. According to several scientists writing in the *Journal
of the Acoustical Society of America*, the narwhal "seems much less noisy
[than the belukha], appears to have a smaller variety of sounds, and produces many that are outside the limits of human hearing." A later study,
however, found narwhals "extremely loquacious underwater," and noted
that tape recordings were "almost saturated with acoustic signals of highly variable duration and frequency composition." The same study
concluded, too, that much of the narwhal's acoustically related behavior
"remains a matter of conjecture."

I dwell on all this because of a routine presumption—that the
whale's ability to receive and generate sound indicates it is an "intelligent"
creature—and an opposite presumption, evident in a Canadian government report, that the continuous racket of a subsea drilling operation,
with the attendant din of ship and air traffic operations, "would not be
expected to be a hazard [to narwhals] because of . . . the assumed high
levels of ambient underwater noise in Lancaster Sound."

It is hard to believe in an imagination so narrow in its scope, so cal-
loused toward life, that it could write these last words. Cetaceans may
well be less "intelligent," less defined by will, imagination, and forms of
logic, than we are. But the idea that they are intelligent, and that they
would be affected by such man-made noise, is not so much presumption
as an expression of a possibility, the taking of a respectful attitude toward
a mystery we can do no better than name "narwhal." Standing at the
edge of a cliff, studying the sea-washed back of such a creature far below,
as still as a cenobite in prayer, the urge to communicate, the upwelling
desire, is momentarily sublime.

I stare out into Lancaster Sound. Four or five narwhals sleep on the
flat calm sea, as faint on the surface as the first stars emerging in an
evening sky. Birds in the middle and far distance slide through the air,

bits of life that dwindle and vanish. Below, underneath the sleeping narwhal, fish surge and glide in the currents, and the light dwindles and is quenched.

The first description of a unicorn, according to British scholar Odell Shepard, appears in the writings of Ctesias, a Greek physician living in Persia in the fifth century B.C., who had heard reports of its existence from India. The existence of such an animal, a fierce, horselike creature of courageous temperament, with a single horn on its forehead, gained credibility later through the writings of Aristotle and Pliny and, later still, in the work of Isidore of Seville, an encyclopedist. The Bible became an unwitting and ironic authority for the unicorn's existence when Greek translators of the Septuagint rendered the Hebraic term *re'em* (meaning, probably, the now extinct aurochs, *Bos primigenius*) as "the unicorn."

The legend of the unicorn, and the subsequent involvement of the narwhal, is a story intriguing at many levels. Until well into the Middle Ages the legend passed only from one book to another, from one learned individual to another; it was not a part of the folk culture of Europe. During the Renaissance, scientists, scholars, and theologians put forth various learned "explanations" for the unicorn's existence. However far-fetched these explanations might have seemed to skeptics, the concrete evidence of a narwhal's tusk to hand seemed irrefutable. Furthermore, no Christian could deny the unicorn's existence without contradicting the Bible.

Scholars argue that the animal in Ctesias' original report from Persia represents the transposed idea of an oryx or a rhinoceros. It went unquestioned, they speculate, because Greeks such as Ctesias took "the grotesque monstrosities of Indian religious art" rendered in the Persian tapestries they saw for real animals. In medieval Europe, trade in rare narwhal and walrus tusks, confusion with the mythical animals of Zoroastrian as well as Christian tradition, and the bucolic practice of making bizarre alterations in the horns of domestic animals, all lent credence to the legend. The interest of the wealthy and learned in this regal animal, moreover, went beyond mere fascination; it was also practical. European royalty was besieged with politically motivated poisonings in the fourteenth and fifteenth centuries, and the unicorn's horn was reputedly the greatest proof against them.

In *The Lore of the Unicorn*, Odell Shepard writes of the great range of appreciation of Renaissance people for the unicorn's horn; it was "their companion on dark nights and in perilous places, and they held it near their hearts, handling it tenderly, as they would a treasure. For indeed it was exactly that. It preserved a man from the arrow that flieth by day and the pestilence that walketh in darkness, from the craft of the poisoner, from epilepsy, and from several less dignified ills of the flesh not to be named in so distinguished a connection. In short it was an amulet, a talisman, a weapon, and a medicine chest all in one."

The narwhal's tusk, traded in bits and pieces as the unicorn's horn, sold for a fortune in the Middle Ages, for twenty times its weight in gold. Shepard estimates that in mid-sixteenth-century Europe there were no more than fifty whole tusks to be seen, each with a detailed provenance. They were gifted upon royalty and the church and sought as booty by expeditionary forces who knew of their existence. Two tusks stolen from Constantinople in 1204 were delivered by Crusaders to the Cathedral of Saint Mark in Venice, where they may be seen to this day.

The presence of these tusks in Europe depended upon Greenlandic and Icelandic trade. The oddity was that they were delivered to Europe by men like those who drowned with the Bishop of Iceland, sailors with no notion of unicorns and no knowledge of the value of the tusk to those who did know. On the other hand, the tusk was frequently bought by people who had not the remotest notion of the existence of such an animal as the narwhal.

The first European to bring these disparate perceptions together, it seems, was the cartographer Gerhard Mercator, who clearly identified the narwhal as the source of the unicorn's horn in 1621. In 1638, Ole Wurm, a Danish professor and a "zoologist and antiquarian of high attainment," delivered a speech in Copenhagen in which he made the same connection. But by then the story of the unicorn was simply too firmly entrenched at too many levels of European society to be easily dispelled, and the horn itself was too dear an item of commerce to be declared suddenly worthless. Besides, it was argued, was not the tusk simply the horn of the unicorn of the sea? Why shouldn't it have the same power as the horn of the land unicorn?

Over time the narwhal's tusk lost its influence in medical circles, trade dwindled, and the legend itself passed out of the hands of ecclesiastics and scholars to the general populace, where it became dear to the hearts of romantics, artists, and poets. It was passed on, however, in a form quite different from the secular tradition in Ctesias. In its secular rendering the unicorn was a creature of nobility and awesome though benign power. It was a creature of compassion, though solitary, and indomitably fierce. It became, as such, the heraldic symbol of knights errant and of kings. It was incorporated into the British coat of arms by James I in 1424, and in 1671 Christian V became the first Danish king to be crowned in a coronation chair made entirely of narwhal tusks.

Under Christian influence, the story of the unicorn became the story of a captured and tamed beast. The animal lost its robust, independent qualities, that aloofness of the wild horse, and was presented as a small, goatlike animal subdued by a maiden in a pastoral garden. The central episode of its fabulous life, its power to turn a poisonous river into pure water so that other creatures might drink, as Moses had done with his staff at the waters of Marah, passed into oblivion. The creature of whom it was once written in Solinus' *Polyhistoria*, "It is an animal never to be taken alive—killed possibly, but not captured," became a symbol of domestic virginity and obeisance.

One winter afternoon in Vancouver, British Columbia, I spoke with the only person ever to have succeeded in putting an adult narwhal, briefly, on display. (The six animals, brought back from northern Canada in 1970, all died of pneumonia within a few months.) Murray Newman, director of the British Columbia Aquarium, explained the great difficulties inherent in capturing such animals and later of maintaining them in captivity, especially the male, with its huge tusk. He doubted any aquarium would ever manage it successfully. The description from Solinus' *Polyhistoria* seemed at that moment, as we gazed across the aquarium's trimmed lawns toward Vancouver's harbor, oddly apt and prophetic.

A narwhal's tusk, hefted in the hands, feels stout but resilient. It is a round, evenly tapered shaft of ivory, hollow for most of its length. (The cavity is filled with dental pulp in the living animal.) A large tusk might weigh twenty pounds, be eight or nine feet long and taper from a diameter of four inches at the socket down to a half-inch at the tip. The smooth, polished tip, two to three inches long, is roundly blunt or sometimes wedge-shaped. The rest of the tusk is striated in a regular pattern that spirals from right to left and may make five or six turns around the shaft before fading out. Often a single groove parallel to the spiraling striations is apparent. The tusk also shows a slight, very shallow ripple from end to end in many specimens.

The striated portion is rough to the touch, and its shallow grooves are frequently encrusted with algae. These microorganisms give the tusk a brindled greenish or maroon cast, contrasting with the white tip and with the ten to twelve inches of yellower ivory normally embedded in the upper left side of the animal's skull.

Well into the nineteenth century there was a question about which of the sexes carried the tusk (or whether it might be both). Although many thought it was only the males, a clear understanding was confounded by authenticated reports of females with tusks (a female skull with two large tusks, in fact, was given to a Hamburg museum in 1684 by a German sea captain), and an announcement in 1700 by a German scientist, Solomon Reisel, that some narwhals carried "milk tusks." It did not help matters, either, that there was much conjecture but no agreement on the function of the tusk. (A more prosaic error further confused things—printers sometimes inadvertently reversed drawings, making it seem that the tusk came out of the right side of the head instead of the left, and that it spiraled from left to right.)

Several certainties eventually emerged. The tusk spirals from right to left. In normal development, two incipient tusks form as "teeth" in the upper jaw of both sexes, one on each side. In the female, both teeth usually harden into solid ivory rods with a protuberance at one end, like a meerschaum pipe (these were Reisel's "milk tusks"). In males, the tusk on the right remains undeveloped, "a miniature piece of pig iron," while the one on the left almost always develops into a living organ, a continually growing, fully vascularized tooth. On very rare occasions, both tusks develop like this, in both sexes. And both tusks spiral from right to left (i.e., they are not symmetrical like the tusks of an elephant or a walrus). Viewed from above, twin tusks diverge slightly from each other. In some males the left tusk never develops (nor does the right in these instances). In perhaps 3 percent of females a single tusk develops on the left.

Solving this problem in sexual systematics and physiology proved simpler than determining the tusk's purpose. It was proposed as a rake, to stir up fish on the seabed floor; as a spear to impale prey; and as a defensive weapon. All three speculations ignored the needs of narwhals without tusks. In addition, Robin Best, a Canadian biologist with a long-standing interest in the question, has argued that the tusk is too brittle to stand repeated use as a rake or probe; that attacking the sorts of fish narwhals habitually eat with the tusk would be difficult and unnecessary and getting large fish off the tusk problematic; and that there are no records of narwhals attacking other animals or defending themselves with their tusks.

The fact that narwhals frequently cross their tusks out of water and that the base of the tusk is located in the sound-producing region of the narwhal's skull led to speculation that it might serve some role in sound reception or propagation (again ignoring the female component of the population). Oral surgeons determined that the tooth's pulp does not contain the bioacoustical lipids necessary for echolocation, but this does not mean that the narwhal can't in some way direct sound with it and, as some have suggested, "sound-joust" with other males. (On their own, the oral surgeons speculated that because the tooth was so highly vascularized, the narwhal could get rid of a significant amount of body heat this way, which would presumably allow males to hunt more energetically. The biologists said no.)

William Scoresby, as bright and keen-eyed an observer as ever went to sea, speculated in 1820 that the tusk was only a secondary sexual characteristic, like a beard in humans, and was perhaps used to fracture light ice when narwhals of both sexes needed to breathe. Scientists say narwhals are too careful with their tusks to subject them to such impact, but on the first point Scoresby was correct.

Male narwhals engage in comparative displays of their tusks, like the males of other species, but they also appear to make some kind of violent physical contact with each other occasionally. The heads of many sexually mature males are variously scarred, and scientists have even found the broken tips of tusks in wounded narwhals. (A scientist who made a detailed examination of the narwhal's musculature said the muscles are not there in the neck to allow the animals to parry and thrust with rapierlike movements. Indeed, males appear always to move their tusks with deliberation, and dexterously, as at savssats.) The circumstances under which head scarring might occur—the establishment and continual testing of a male social hierarchy, especially during the breeding season—are known; but how these wounds are suffered or how frequently they are inflicted is still widely debated. One plausible thought is that males align their tusks head-on and that the animal with the shorter tusk is grazed or sometimes severely poked in the process.

A significant number of narwhals, 20 to 30 percent, have broken tusks. Some broken tusks have a curious filling that effectively seals off the exposed pulp cavity. Oral surgeons say this rod-shaped plug is simply a normal deposition of "reparative dentine," but others have long insisted it is actually the tip of another narwhal's tusk, to which it bears an undeniable resemblance. (The broken tips of other narwhals' tusks are filled with stones and sediment.)

Exposed tooth pulp creates a site for infection, not to mention pain. That animals would try to fill the cavity (if "reparative dentine" didn't) makes sense. That one narwhal entices another into this ministration is as intriguing a notion as the thought that males put the tips of their tusks on the opposite male's sound-sensitive melon and generate a "message" in sound-jousting. It would be rash to insist categorically that narwhals don't do *something* odd with the tusk on occasion, like prodding a flatfish off the sea bottom. (Herman Melville drolly suggested they used it as a letter opener.) But it seems clear that its principal, and perhaps only, use is social. Robin Best argues, further, that because of its brittleness, its length, and the high proportion of broken tusks, the organ may have reached an evolutionary end point.

A remaining question is, Why is the tusk twisted? D'Arcy Wentworth Thompson, a renowned English biologist who died in 1948, offered a brilliant and cogent answer. He argued that the thrust of a narwhal's tail applied a very slight torque to its body. The tusk, suspended tightly but not rigidly in its socket in the upper jaw, resisted this force with a very slight degree of success. In effect, throughout its life, the narwhal revolved slowly around its own tusk, and over the years irregularities of the socket gouged the characteristic striations in the surface of the tooth.

Thompson pointed out that the tooth itself is not twisted—it is straight-grained ivory, engraved with a series of low-pitched threads. No one has disproved, proved, or improved upon Thompson's argument since he set it forth in 1942.

Because the ivory itself dried out and became brittle and hard to work, the greatest virtue of a narwhal tusk to the Eskimos who traditionally hunted the animal was its likeness to a wood timber. Some of the regions where narwhals were most intensively hunted were without either trees or supplies of driftwood. The tusk served in those places as a spear shaft, a tent pole, a sledge thwart, a cross brace—wherever something straight and long was required.

Narwhals were most often hunted by Eskimos during their near-shore migration in spring, and in bays and fiords during the summer. To my knowledge, Eskimos attach no great spiritual importance to the narwhal. Like the caribou, it is a migratory food animal whose spirit (*kirnniq*) is easily propitiated. The narwhal does not have the intercessionary powers or innate authority of the polar bear, the wolf, the walrus, or the raven.

Beyond its tusk, Greenlanders valued the narwhal's skin above all other leathers for dog harnesses, because it remained supple in very cold weather and did not stretch when it became wet. The sinews of the back were prized as thread not only for their durability but also for their great length. The outside layer of the skin was an important source of vitamin C, as rich in this essential vitamin as raw seal liver. The blubber, which burned with a bright, clean yellow flame, gave light and warmth that were utilized to carve a fishhook or sew a mitten inside the iglu in winter. A single narwhal, too, might feed a dog team for a month.

It is different now. The hunter's utilitarian appreciation of this animal is an attitude some now find offensive; and his considerable skills, based on an accurate and detailed understanding of the animal and its environment, no longer arouse the sympathetic admiration of very many people.

In the time I spent watching narwhals along the floe edge at Lancaster Sound in 1982 no whale was butchered for dog food. The dogs have been replaced by snow machines. No sinews were removed for sewing. Only the tusk was taken, to be traded in the village for cash. And muktuk, the skin with a thin layer of blubber attached, which was brought back to the hunting camp at Nuvua. (This delicacy is keenly anticipated each spring and eaten with pleasure. It tastes like hazelnuts.)

The narwhal's fate in Lancaster Sound is clearly linked with plans to develop oil and gas wells there, but current hunting pressure against them is proving to be as important a factor. In recent years Eskimo hunters on northern Baffin Island have exhibited some lack of discipline during the spring narwhal hunt. They have made hasty, long-range, or otherwise poorly considered shots and used calibers of gun and types of bullets that were inadequate to kill, all of which left animals wounded. And they have sometimes exceeded the quotas set by Department of Fisheries and Oceans Canada and monitored by the International Whaling Commission.* On the other side, Eskimos have routinely been excluded from the upper levels of decision-making by the Canadian government in these matters and have been offered no help in devising a kind of hunting behavior more consistent with the power and reach of

---

* These charges are detailed in K. J. Finley, R. A. Davis, and H. B. Silverman, "Aspects of the Narwhal Hunt in the Eastern Canadian Arctic," *Report of the International Whaling Commission* 30 (1980): 459–464; and K. J. Finley and G. W. Miller, "The 1979 Hunt for Narwhals (*Monodon monoceros*) and an Examination of Harpoon Gun Technology Near Pond Inlet, Northern Baffin Island," *Report of the International Whaling Commission* 32 (1982): 449–460.

modern weapons. For the Eskimos, there is a relentless, sometimes condescending scrutiny of every attempt they make to adjust their culture, to "catch up" with the other culture brought up from the south. It is easy to understand why the men sometimes lose their accustomed composure.

In the view of Kerry Finley, a marine mammal biologist closely associated with the Baffin Island narwhal hunts, "It is critical [to the survival of narwhals] that Inuit become involved in meaningful positions in the management of marine resources." The other problems, he believes, cannot be solved until this obligation is met.

I would walk along the floe edge, then, in those days, hoping to hear narwhals, for the wonder of their company; and hoping, too, that they would not come. The narwhal is a great fighter for its life, and it is painful to watch its struggle. When they were killed, I ate their flesh as a guest of the people I was among, out of respect for distant ancestors, and something older than myself.

I watched closely the ivory gull, a small bird with a high, whistly voice. It has a remarkable ability to appear suddenly in the landscape, seemingly from nowhere. I have scanned tens of square miles of open blue sky, determined it was empty of birds, and then thrown a scrap of seal meat into a lead, where it would float. In a few minutes an ivory gull would be overhead. It is hard to say even from what direction it has come. It is just suddenly there.

So I would watch them in ones and twos. Like any animal seen undisturbed in its own environment, the ivory gull seems wondrously adapted. To conserve heat, its black legs are shorter in proportion to its body than the legs of other gulls, its feet less webbed. Its claws are longer and sharper, to give it a better grip of frozen carrion and on the ice. It uses seaweed in its nest to trap the sun's energy, to help with the incubation of its eggs. To avoid water in winter, which might freeze to its legs, it has become deft at picking things up without landing. In winter it follows the polar bear. When no carrion turns up in the polar bear's wake, it eats the polar bear's droppings. It winters on the pack ice. Of the genus *Pagophila*. Ice lover.

And I would think as I walked of what I had read of a creature of legend in China, an animal similar in its habits to the unicorn but abstemious, like the ivory gull. It is called the *ki-lin*. The *ki-lin* has the compassion of the unicorn but also the air of a spiritual warrior, or monk. Odell Shepard has written that "[u]nlike the western unicorn, the *ki-lin* has never had commercial value; no drug is made of any part of his body; he exists for his own sake and not for the medication, enrichment, entertainment, or even edification of mankind." He embodied all that was admirable and ideal.

With our own Aristotelian and Cartesian sense of animals as objects, our religious sense of them as mere receptacles for human symbology, our single-mindedness in unraveling their workings, we are not the kind of culture to take the *ki-lin* very seriously. We are another culture, and these other times. The *ki-lin*, too, is no longer as highly regarded among modern Chinese as it was in the days of the Sung dynasty. But the idea of the *ki-lin*, the mere fact of its having taken shape, is, well, gratifying. It appeared after men had triumphed over both their fear and distrust of nature and their desire to control it completely for their own ends.

The history of the intermingling of human cultures is a history of trade—in objects like the narwhal's tusk, in ideas, and in great narratives. We appropriate when possible the best we can find in all of this. The *ki-lin*, I think, embodies a fine and pertinent idea—an unpossessible being who serves humans when they have need of its wisdom, a creature who abets dignity and respect in human dealings, who underlines the fundamental mystery with which all life meets analysis.

I do not mean to suggest that the narwhal should be made into some sort of symbolic *ki-lin*. Or that buried in the more primitive appreciation of life that some Eskimos retain is an "answer" to our endless misgivings about the propriety of our invasions of landscapes where we have no history, of our impositions on other cultures. But that in the simple appreciation of a world not our own to define, that poised Arctic landscape, we might find some solace by discovering the *ki-lin* hidden within ourselves, like a shaft of light.

JOEL W. ROGERS

# Orca: Johnstone Strait to Blackfish Sound

They come out of the North Pacific depths in a coordinated attack. Orcas, the killer whales, quietly encircle the sockeye returning to the rivers of British Columbia. The salmon mill in confusion as the orcas, one by one, charge the center of the school. Those salmon prudent enough to flee discover the ring of orcas, like a net holding them in, each predator patiently awaiting its turn to feed.

It is early summer off the northwestern tip of Vancouver Island. The scent of the Fraser, western Canada's largest river, draws the salmon on as they follow their spawning urge, seeking their ancestral stream. They gather and turn south into the increasingly confining waters of Queen Charlotte Strait. The orcas follow, feeding at will.

By June, families, or pods, of orcas begin arriving at their summer "village." This gathering site is at the western entrance to a great passage of saltwater that continually floods and ebbs between the massive northern flank of Vancouver Island and the myriad islets and inlets that buffer the mainland of British Columbia. Known as Johnstone Strait, this entrance is one to three miles wide, forty-seven miles long, and over 1,000 feet deep. It is a natural gauntlet the salmon must run to find their spawning grounds. During the five months the salmon pass this way, up

JOEL W. ROGERS, an outdoor photographer and writer, has published widely in such places as *Audubon*, *Outside*, and *Sierra*. *The Hidden Coast*, from which this essay is taken, won several awards, including the Washington State Governor's Writers' Award, when it was published in 1991. Reprinted with permission from Alaska Northwest Books™.

to 170 blackfish, as orcas are also known, will congregate in these waters, herding salmon, teaching their children, families reuniting with families.

So too in June the humans come, heading north from the universities and research centers, passing through Seattle and Vancouver up the fabled Inside Passage to Johnstone. They bring with them underwater microphones, cameras, and computers. They bring, as well, a curious reverence for the orca that separates them from their brethren. For they have a common conviction that the orcas are something greater than one more precious organism swimming in the sea. They study the behavior of a marine mammal that rules the world's oceans and has captured the hearts of all who study it. Paul Spong, who initially approached studying the orcas as you would a laboratory rat, described in 1974 after six years of research a far different understanding:

> [The orca is] an incredibly powerful and capable creature, exquis-
> itely self-controlled and aware of the world around it, a being
> possessed of a zest for life and a healthy sense of humor, and
> moreover, a remarkable fondness for and an interest in humans.

This viewpoint was not easily accepted. The orcas had long been named killer whales—toothed whales that have no enemies and, in Dr. Spong's estimation, no fear. They have been witnessed by seafarers to be swift and effective hunters of all major fish and mammal stocks. The orcas themselves were hunted sporadically by the Japanese and the Norwegians, and shot at by every self-righteous fisherman out for the same catch. They were assumed to be ruthless, voracious killers. The assumption was wrong.

Into the 1970s, in both Canada and the United States, researchers' fascination with orcas and other whales resulted in a groping realization of these marine mammals' remarkable abilities. The first studies were of captive dolphins, porpoises, and, beginning in 1969, orcas, often in the circus atmosphere of the new marinelands. The first tests were simple nose-the-proper-button-and-receive-half-a-herring physiological studies. But in Paul Spong's visual acuity research, something went marvelously wrong: after 2,400 half-herrings and a 90 percent success rate, Skana, the first captive orca to be studied, began giving the incorrect answer time after time—her only way to tell the researcher, "I want a new game."

Skana continued the education of Paul Spong, at one time seeming to correct him for leaving off a pectoral fin on her portrait by pointedly wheeling about her pool, the omitted fin splashing the artist. On another,

Skana slashed her teeth across Paul's bare feet, only touching and causing no pain. He recoiled in instinctive fright but returned his foot to the original position. Skana repeated the movement, her head rising out of the quiet pool, her teeth sweeping over his extended toes. Again Paul flinched, but being a dedicated experimental psychologist, he repeatedly dangled his foot. Each time, Skana would lunge until he controlled his involuntary reaction. Skana then stopped and vocalized, staring back at Paul from the middle of the pool. He then realized that she was intentionally deconditioning his fear of her, establishing a bond of trust.

Through the 1970s, the studies of orcas evolved. No one doubted the whales' intelligence; their gentleness and family loyalty turned public opinion into a love affair, yet no one really knew the orca. Dr. Spong began studying free as opposed to captive orcas in 1974, by establishing a research station on uninhabited Hanson Island at the northern entrance to Johnstone Strait. Taping their voices and monitoring their daily patterns in the tidal wilderness, Paul's research turned personal and public. Together with a growing family of researchers, film teams, writers, and musicians, the clinician became an advocate and a voice for the orca, and Johnstone Strait rippled to the wakes of kayakers, researchers, and orcas interacting in open curiosity.

In 1981, David Arcese had caught wind of Dr. Spong's studies and asked me to join him on a kayak trip to Johnstone Strait. Quiet, soft-spoken, fascinated by whales, David's curiosity about orcas must have rivaled Spong's. We were well into September, late for seeing orcas, but going anyway, as we car-topped our kayaks along Highway One north through the clearcuts and gentle peaks of interior Vancouver Island.

Our put-in was Telegraph Cove, a tiny, protected bay rimmed by second-growth evergreens. Along the back bayshore lay an exhausted timber mill whose saws had been stilled for a decade, a general store and a boat launch for the new economy of sport fishing, and a boardwalk connecting an unplanned string of sturdy fir-framed houses. With one green exception, these houses were painted white, roofed with corrugated tin, and each was well kept and lived in. They were sited along the tideline wedged between outcrops of granite and the stumps of long-gone old growth. Spartan, clean, dotted with the passing of ravens, Telegraph Cove was as it once was, hedged in by the landform, overlooked, blessed to grow no bigger.

We paid the store owner a small sum for launching privileges, and paddled out into Johnstone and a rising southeasterly. Hoping to be with orcas and intent on making Robson Bight, eleven miles distant, we headed east hugging the Vancouver Island shore, our paddles feathered to knife the wind.

This first paddle to Robson would be a stormy one. Much of our time was spent grounded beneath a rain tarp, as a strong southeasterly tore up the strait. We saw only two orcas pass on our third day. The following morning, wet and cold, we packed and paddled back to Telegraph Cove, promising to return.

Robson Bight is not quite a bay—it is a bend in the shoreline, an indentation deep enough to warrant a name but too exposed to give a vessel safe anchorage. In the years following our paddle to Robson, the bight would gain the attention of the world for its unique orca visitations. It would also narrowly miss becoming a timber booming yard, where the great log rafts would be created and towed to market. And its uplands, the climax forests of the Tsitika River valley—the last virgin watershed on the 285-mile-long island—would be slated for clearcutting. The government of British Columbia would designate the bight a marine ecological preserve in 1982, but in the end the timber industries have been allowed to cut the valley and only a 200-foot coastal buffer has been saved.

There were other changes: new paths and new attitudes were bringing new people to the water's edge. Each year another massive ocean liner joined the popular cruise ships sailing the Inside Passage. Two or three ships a day passed the bight, immersing thousands of tourists into the magic of the forested islands, the eagles overhead, and, if they were lucky, the orcas. Telegraph Cove's old tug *Gikumi* had been converted to an orca-watching vessel, breathing new life into the Telegraph Cove economy. But one phenomenon stands out in the decade of growing interest over the orcas of Johnstone Strait: sea kayakers. These were newcomers with a relatively gentle impact, silently tracking to Robson Bight.

On a Sunday in July 1989, I returned to Johnstone Strait to meet up with David, who had founded Northern Lights Expeditions and was beginning his seventh season guiding sea kayakers into the strait. Amidst the salmon fishermen and whale watchers, we load and launch our group of twelve new kayakers into the little-changed harbor of Telegraph Cove. The weather is overcast and dry as we paddle out through the port entrance, the new seafarers bumping gunwales, hurtling this way and that as they learn to steer the fast, stable double kayaks. David and his assistant guide, Steffie Ackroyd, are moving like sheepdogs through the little flock, instructing and reassuring the neophyte kayakers, as we enter the open waters of Johnstone Strait.

As each pair of paddlers gets a rhythm going, we begin to speed up, relax, and take in our surroundings. Behind us hills of conifers rise up into the low clouds hiding the steep 3,000-foot almost-mountains that crowd the northern shore of Vancouver. Before us, two miles of open water sweep away to the east and west to form the strait. Beyond the crossing lies Paul Spong's Hanson Island, one of a hundred low-lying islands to explore.

With the chart and a firsthand look at this landscape, I can realize, almost see, the forces that have shaped the scene before us. Off our bows, miles inland, the islands turn to mainland and rise to mountains, like a mirror image of Vancouver Island. Between these two natural barriers a millennium of glaciers has come and gone, rounding the islands' edges, mining channels as deep as 1,500 feet along the strait.

As we approach Hanson Island, David steers us toward Weynton Passage and the entrance to Blackfish Sound. We cheat as only a kayaker can, and paddle behind the tiny islets that rim the west end of the island, avoiding the main channel and the beginning of the opposing flood tide surging in from the Pacific.

Once through the pass, we stretch out into the open waters of Blackfish Sound, moving at a beginner's pace. This is a casual exploration; all of us are watching for orcas, some more impatient than others. David is in no hurry. After all his summers running trips along the strait, he knows the people in his charge will settle into enjoying all there is to see and do here—and see orcas.

David is good at this business, in part because he respects the spirit of the land as well as the orcas. He knows the locals and works with the Kwakiutl people of the region to protect their heritage sites. He is respected by the long-term researchers who help him set self-imposed guidelines on kayaking in the presence of whales. And he knows the orcas from his reading, attending conferences, and simply being here in contact.

In a few days, we'll move back across Johnstone to the camps north of Robson Bight where whale sightings are routine. For now, we get to know our kayaks and our partners as we paddle our way to camp.

We beach on a small pocket bay that faces south and set to unloading the boats and putting up tents. I wander through the kitchen and discover it is possible to snitch a fresh piece of cornbread. As our dinner of fresh salad and grilled cod, salmon, and crab disappears, we idly watch the evening go by. On the far side of our vista, the last of the salmon fishermen power back to Telegraph, the whine of their outboards fading toward the setting sun. A bald eagle soars off to the left, over a perfect little island. For many of the people on this expedition, this is their first day in company with eagles. Conversation stills as we watch the great scavenger wheel away.

One of our group asks David about the small minke whale we'd seen earlier in the afternoon, when suddenly the ground begins to vibrate, strongly enough to stop the conversation. An ocean liner, massive and at speed, enters Blackney Pass southbound, passing our camp about a half-mile out. The light shines from the ship's cabins with the color of a campfire. I can almost imagine the disco music over the sound of the engines. Although we're close enough to see people, the decks are empty. The ship swings to ride the centerline of the 1,000-yard channel, comes around to port, steadies up on a course down Johnstone, and is gone. We stay quiet for a bit, to ruminate over this remarkable visitor. Elegant to some, an extravagance to others? No one says. We are undeniably on a different cruise.

The following days we explore Blackfish Sound, trailed by shy yet curious seals. Our real intent shows in our scanning of the way ahead for telltale dorsal fins, our ears tuned to the distant "whoosh" of orca breath. On the morning of our fourth day, we move our camp five and a half miles to the Vancouver Island side of Johnstone Strait for some serious orca watching. No sooner have we established camp than David spots a pod well out in the channel. We assist each other with our boats, and one by one we paddle from shore to intercept.

Whale watching is not unlike the behavior of a professional sports photographer on the sidelines of a football game. With every play, he moves farther down-field in an attempt to predict the advance of the team. The key to this analogy is that he cannot enter the field. Neither can we. Placing boats across the oncoming path of an orca pod might disrupt their activity—feeding, sleeping, playing—causing an unknown amount of stress to an already too popular mammal.

We paddle fast and hard, angling to approach the whales' course well ahead of them. David calls a halt and we gather into a group, staying still and hoping for the best. We wait. David had said that orcas have a distinctive cruising pattern of deep diving for three or four minutes at a time, then a series of shallow dives of ten to fifteen seconds duration. If we're in the right place, the pod should begin a shallow diving sequence about 200 yards off our bows. We wait and watch, necks swiveling left-right-left, fingers focusing lenses from thirty feet to infinity and back.

"They're behind us!" someone shouts, as the sudden sound of exhaling air reaches us across the water. We turn to face the pod. The whales surface again, and we do a sort of sotto-voce mutual squeal because they have turned, coming straight at us. At 100 yards, the orcas dive again and we go quiet, darting glances at each other. David says, "Just stay put."

One by one, their dorsal fins rise into the air right in front of us—so close it looks like a sure collision. At less than thirty feet, the largest bull aims right for me. I know from my reading and David's assurances that orcas do not intentionally attack or even bump kayakers in such a non-threatening situation. I'm just trying to focus my camera. They dive, the male's six-foot dorsal fin sinking with a subtle side-to-side movement, and I realize it's flexible, not knifelike, not a weapon. I look into the depths of mid-channel for the passing of the twenty-five-foot-long submarine shape, its dorsal fin faint in the watery darkness—five tons of *Orcinus orca* beneath my fifty-five-pound kayak.

We watch transfixed as the pod swims beneath us, their white-to-grey "saddles" across their backs marking their progress. The orcas make one final surface, each exhaling followed by a sharp intake of air, and they deep dive, tails rising from the water with an unhurried, fluid motion.

The water surrounding our kayaks ripples from sudden displacement. No one lifts a paddle. David suggests a course we can follow and we begin to move north toward Weynton Passage, keeping to the right of the pod's probable path.

In David's opinion, this pod is asleep. "Orcas sleep on the move, the adults taking turns on watch. See how they all breathe in unison." The pod surfaces well to our right, in easy rhythm, exhaling in the same uncanny synchronism; their high, jet-black dorsal fins rise and fall, parting the clear, jade-green water in mid-nap.

We learn that these four whales are called the C-5 subpod, a part of C pod, one of the larger resident families that summer in Johnstone Strait. The leader is C-5, the matriarch, the fifty-eight-year-old mother of C-2, a big dorsal-finned thirty-two-year-old male; C-10, an eighteen-year-old female; and C-13, a five-year-old toddler with the characteristic hook-shaped baby fin. These whales will stay together for life, a life that nearly matches ours in longevity.

Their colorless titles are disturbing—we would name them differently. David tells us that the numeric designations are a necessity for scientists.

Whales in early studies were identified by more distinctive monikers—Wavy, Saddle, Nicola—with each name identifying a particular physical feature of the individual whale. But that became unworkable with the discovery of so many more whales at Johnstone.

Our own "pod" of fourteen kayakers looks pretty professional, paddling easily. Mirrored in the reflective greens and greys of the strait, our paddles rise and fall in unison, bow and stern sailors intent on the whales. Though David rarely shows it, he is pleased with the trip. We have achieved the skills to safely travel these waters, the people have warmed to the land's character, we all have been doing our dishes, and now we are in the company of orcas.

Suddenly the orcas' cruising pattern changes. They have doubled their speed, coming farther out of the water, awake and excited. The orcas have picked up echolocations from H pod, infrequent visitors to this area, moving through Weynton Passage and headed our way.

We paddle hard to keep up, but fall far behind as the giant mammals surge up the strait to greet their friends. The first orca breaches, his full body leaving the water, a 10,000-pound silhouette on the horizon, then a mammoth splash. Other orcas are "spyhopping" or swimming in place, propelling their upper torso clear of the water to see around them. Still others below are most likely curling around neighbors in physical touch. The sounds they are no doubt making underwater—clicks, whistles, and screeches—are identifications and greetings. Another whale breaches, this time close enough for us to see the distinctive markings of the whale's white and black stomach.

David brings us to a halt well short of the melee, at a 200-yard distance, grouped, watching. Gradually the hubbub dies, and we lower our cameras. The pods deep dive, showing their tail flukes, and minutes later they surface separated. The H pod continues with the tide along the east side of the strait, and C-5 subpod crosses back toward our camp.

We have had our close encounter. In the gathering dusk, C-5 and her family swim away, and we slow to a stop to watch them go. Clustered together, our paddles resting across our neighbors' boats, we try to verbalize the sensation of paddling with orcas, David every bit as animated as the rest. But words are insufficient. One by one, our paddles bite the still waters of Johnstone Strait for the Vancouver shore.

K. C. BALCOMB III

# Kith and Kin
# of the Killer Whale

As we motored slowly out of Admiralty Inlet and headed across the Strait of Juan de Fuca, we headed into a thick blanket of fog which reduced visibility to about 50 feet. For two days we had been following reports of killer whales in Puget Sound. Three pods, J, K, and L, had come into the area to feed upon the salmon migrating toward the rivers which drain into the Sound, and we had been dispatched to find them and photo-identify each individual. On this particular morning, the whales had gathered near Possession Point, and now they were heading back out of the Sound, probably bound for Haro Strait in their endless search for food.

I checked the chart and plotted a course which would take us through the fog around Smith Island to the west side of San Juan Island, where I expected the whales to arrive in about five hours. We stopped to clean and pack our camera gear and then accelerated the Boston Whaler for the trip across the strait on compass bearings. We were maneuverable enough to avoid any other boats or ships we might encounter, and we needed some speed to avoid getting "set" by the currents. I didn't relish this crossing in the blind, but home was on the other side.

K. C. BALCOMB III is director of the Center for Whale Research in Friday Harbor, Washington. He has participated in humpback whale surveys in the eastern Pacific and in killer whale studies since 1976, when he carried out the first American field study of killer whales in Washington State. "Kith and Kin of the Killer Whale" was published in *Pacific Discovery* in spring 1991. Reprinted by permission of the author.

Ten minutes later, a group of killer whales converged rapidly upon us in the fog and crowded right around the boat, causing me to slow to idle speed. It was J, K, and L again, numbering more than 80 whales in all. Without radar, there was no way we could have found them in the fog, but they had no problem finding us. They gathered more and more tightly around us until the closest were only inches away from the hull on either side and in front of the bow. There they remained, swimming slowly with us for two hours until the fog cleared. Did they know that we couldn't see well enough to navigate from land bearings? Were they guiding us around Partridge Bank and the shoals of Smith Island? I knew that wherever they were, there was enough water depth for our boat. It was a very moving experience. Many times before my associates and I had felt that we were accepted in the orcas' midst, but this time it was they who had initiated the encounter, and we who were the ones being escorted. Only when the fog lifted did the whales disperse and proceed toward Haro Strait.

It is hard to imagine now, but 30 years ago it was generally thought by both laymen and scientists alike that killer whales hunting in packs were the most ruthless predators in the sea. They, and the large sharks, epitomized all that is fearful to us terrestrial beings as we awkwardly ventured onto or into the ocean. In scientific literature, killer whales' reputation as voracious hunters has preceded them since 1862, when D. F. Eschricht described the remains of 14 seals and 13 common porpoises in the stomach of one specimen found floating off Jutland in the North Sea. Eyewitness accounts of their coordinated and savage attacks on whales, dolphins, and seals leave little doubt that they are particularly fond of flesh and have no qualms about killing their cousin species to get it.

In the mid-1960s killer whales began to appear as the featured stars in aquaria and oceanaria. People could catch them alive, train them, hug them, and swim with them. While the public was drawn in part by the whales' fearsome reputation, the take-home image of killer whale was softened. In keeping with the gentle new image, many people now call them orca, the species name in the scientific binomial *Orcinus orca*. Much of the public has bought this "teddy-whale" image of orca, and many regret ever having used the appelation killer whale. But what do we really know about these amazing animals?

There had been two classic studies of killer whales done in this century by the time the orca star began to rise—one in Japan by

Masaharu Nishiwaki and Chikao Handa in 1958, and the other in Norway by Age Jonsgard and P. B. Lyshoel in 1970. Both studies relied on extensive orca samples taken by commercial whalers, primarily for predator control, and both mainly described the size of the whales caught, the sex ratio, length at sexual maturity, and aspects of their diet. Basically, they found that: killer whale males grow to 31 feet in length but average around 21 feet; females grow up to 27 feet long, are usually around 20 feet, and become sexually mature when they are about 16 feet. Newborns are about seven or eight feet long and weigh 400 pounds, but it was not known how long it took them to mature or how long they lived. Off Norway, killer whales primarily ate Atlanto-Scandian herring, and off Japan they ate squid, cod, flatfish, and marine mammals. From the carcasses of nearly 2,000 killer whales, little else came to light. Although the scientific literature contained numerous anecdotal observations, there had been no studies of living killer whales when the first one came into captivity.

In 1970, the Canadian government tasked Mike Bigg and Ian MacAskie of the Pacific Biological Station in Nanaimo, British Columbia, with finding the answers to questions about the abundance and distribution of killer whales off British Columbia. The study which they and photographer Graeme Ellis initiated has become a classic of this type and has resulted in a wealth of unexpected information about these whales in the Pacific Northwest. Most of what has been learned could never have been gleaned from studying carcasses or captive whales. By photographing every whale they could find between 1972 and 1975, these Canadian researchers were able to identify and alpha-numerically name 210 whales from 19 pods that occurred around Vancouver Island. They found that the composition of any given pod was the same each time they encountered it, and that the overall pattern of pod movements suggested two communities of "resident" whales—one occurring in Georgia Strait, Puget Sound, and around southern Vancouver Island; and the other occurring in Johnstone Strait, around northern Vancouver Island and up the mainland coast to Alaska's southeastern border. Additionally, there appeared to be some "transient" pods which episodically traveled through either area but never associated with the "residents."

The "transient" whales are morphologically distinguishable from "resident" whales. A "transient" whale's dorsal fin is generally more sharply pointed, and the "saddle" pattern extends far forward on the back and is generally "closed." The diet of "transients" includes marine mammals. Pod size rarely exceeds five individuals in "transients," whereas "residents" typically form pods of five to 20 whales.

Recent studies by John Ford, curator of marine mammals at the Vancouver Public Aquarium, show that the vocalizations of "transients" are entirely different from and less frequent than those of "residents": the two groups "speak" totally different dialects. Also, each "resident" pod appears to have its own dialect of calls used in communicating underwater. A specific dialect may help whales identify fellow members of their pod, and the relationships among dialects of different pods suggests a common ancestry.

Our encounter in the fog resulted from a study contracted by the National Marine Fisheries Service in Seattle in 1976 to verify whether only the British Columbia whales came into Puget Sound, or whether there were others. Since then, together with Bigg and other colleagues on both sides of the border, this study has continued uninterrupted. Funding from a variety of sources, and an immense amount of volunteer effort, most recently from Earthwatch, have produced a staggering amount of data which we are still analyzing.

In the Southern Resident Community of killer whales, for example, we have collectively photo-identified every living whale every year since 1976. Based upon our observations, our math-minded colleague, Peter Olesiuk, has calculated patterns of survival in the various age and sex categories. His method is analogous to the way a life insurance company calculates the survival probabilities of its subscribers. Olesiuk found that females have a mean life expectancy of 50.2 years and a maximum longevity of 80 to 90 years. Males, on the other hand, have a mean life expectancy of 29.2 years and a maximum longevity of about 50 to 60 years.

Obviously, with our photo-identification study only covering the past 18 years, we have not documented any whales reaching their maximum estimated longevity, but we do know that most of the whales were already mature, and some were probably very old, when the study began. Furthermore, we know from photographs in newspapers and books dating to 1960s that many of these whales were mature at that time. Hence, many survivors of that era are now at least 40 years old.

In the course of our study, we have observed many young whales as they grew up. Females typically give birth to their first offspring at about

13 to 15 years of age and then produce an average of about five calves during their estimated 25-year reproductive lifespan. We have seen that several females have produced calves at three-year intervals, which is probably near maximum productivity, given a gestation period lasting 17 months and nursing obligations for about a year.

We have discovered that offspring continue to have a strong social bond with their mother long after weaning and even after the young have offspring of their own. Looking back over the photo-identification history, we find grandmothers in nearly continuous association with their daughters and granddaughters. We are very near to the point of documenting great-granddaughters of living great-grandmothers in the population. This matrilineal "glue" that holds these animals together gives us many clues about pod formation and definition, as well as about their great longevity.

Matrilineal societies in mammalian populations are not all that unusual, but what is unusual (though not unique) about killer whales is that males, at least those in the Pacific Northwest "resident" communities, apparently do not disperse from their matriline either. It came as some surprise to us to find that virtually all of the males in a pod were "mama's boys," remaining by mother's side throughout her life (or at least for as long as we have been able to observe or surmise). When mother dies, the males may continue their association for a time with their sisters, but they occasionally die shortly after mother. Why this should be we do not know, but it seems to fit the disparity in estimated longevity between the sexes.

Given that the pod organization we observe does not fit our prior notions of a "harem" system (such as that in seals and sea lions and presumed to exist among whales), we have wondered just what is the mating strategy of killer whales. If all of the males' breeding occurred within their own matriline, the family tree would wilt—this would be poor breeding strategy. Likewise, if all of their breeding occurs within the pod ("kissing cousins"), the pod would eventually encounter genetic difficulties. Even if all of their breeding occurs within their community (which in the case of the southern "residents" numbers 88 individuals, of which only 59 are mature), there could be long-term genetic problems rendering such a mating system infeasible. What then is the mating structure which keeps this population viable? How does it avoid a genetic bottleneck?

———————————

Our observations do provide some clues. During late summer and autumn in the Pacific Northwest, we often see all of the resident pods of the southern community come together in what we call a "greeting ceremony." There is much sexual activity and very close contact among all members of the aggregation, young and old alike. In these gatherings, and at other times, we have observed the southern "resident" males being sexually and socially active within their pod and within their community —with females, other males, and juveniles; but we have never seen them intermingle or mate with "transients," or with whales from the northern community. We know from captive animals that individuals from each of these communities (and from communities around the world) can successfully interbreed, so it is apparently biologically possible to have one worldwide gene pool of *Orcinus orca*. But is that the case?

From color pattern variations, it has long been supposed that there are many geographic races of killer whales, but why should there be more than one race in a given geographic area? Wouldn't they compete for resources, and wouldn't one race ultimately win out? In recent years, there have been DNA fingerprinting studies done by William Amos and Rus Hoelzel with tissues from dead stranded "residents" and "transients," revealing them to be genetically quite different. Hoelzel has told me that there is sufficient separation between "residents" and "transients" to surmise that they have not interbred in the past 100,000 years. In contrast, the northern and southern community whales are genetically very similar, in spite of the fact that they do not apparently overlap in range or interbreed (at least in inshore waters). Do the "residents" represent an inshore tributary of some larger offshore gene pool? And do the "transients" represent another?

This past August, we obtained a spectacular new clue about what might be going on in the evolutionary strategy of Pacific Northwest killer whales. In one of our ocean surveys, we found and photographed a pod of at least 40 killer whales 25 miles west of Vancouver Island. When we processed the film, we discovered that every whale in the group was new to all of our catalogs of killer whales from California to Alaska, including the comprehensive catalog of British Columbia "residents" and "transients"! These new whales were in a large pod, like the "residents." They were also morphologically similar to "residents"—smoothly rounded fins and distinctly shaped "saddle" pigmentation—and they were apparently eating fish. They were well within the known offshore range of "resident" killer whales from both the northern and southern communities. This discovery brings us directly to one of the questions posed earlier: How do the small inshore populations avoid genetic problems?

My suspicion is that when either the northern or southern inshore "residents" depart local waters and head offshore, as they do from time to time, they may occasionally meet with these offshore "resident-like" whales. Perhaps they intermingle with them like we see in the "greeting ceremony," and perhaps they interbreed. If so, this would relieve the genetic difficulties of a small population and preserve the long-term continuity of a morphological type. It would also explain the genetic similarity of the northern and southern "resident" whales if both are members of the larger gene pool.

The offspring of such interbreeding would stay with their mothers. They would grow up in the maternal pod and remain with her community. To the outsider, the pod structure would remain the same; the only difference would be that by mixing with offshore "resident-like" whales, the gene pool would be enlarged. If there is no mixing between "resident" and "transient" whales, both groups would be perpetuated.

By extending this breeding strategy to other oceans, we might explain such phenomena as the geographically overlapping occurrence of such proposed species as the "yellow" piscivorous killer whales around the thin ice floes of Antarctica and the "white" carnivorous killer whales reported in nearby open water by Soviet researchers A. A. Berzin and V. L. Vladimirov.

In fact, the whole array of dozens of killer whale species and subspecies proposed from morphometric differences since Linnaeus' time may very well be due to a social fabric and biology that we are just beginning to perceive in the Pacific Northwest: the strong matrilineal bonds that persist throughout life for both sexes. Dispersal of individuals simply does not occur while mother is alive, and mother lives a very long time.

The result of this is that social contact with siblings and cousins is prolonged, and a pod is formed. Breeding occurs mainly within one's own community of pods, which may have a common ancestry. The entire community of killer whales comprises several generations of whales with lifespans more or less comparable to our own.

To adequately study these voracious predators is, forgive the pun, a life-consuming task. Studying whales is not like studying fruit flies, which produce several generations in a matter of weeks, or small

mammals, which may reproduce several times in a year. In fact, I sometimes feel that a mere 15 years after joining this study, the fog of mystery
surrounding the lives of killer whales is only just beginning to clear,
the way the fog lifted that morning near Smith Island when the whales
were our escorts.

BRUCE OBEE

# Gentle Giants

Trails of silt cloud the waters of Finnerty Cove, near Victoria, where a Pacific gray whale is foraging three or four metres below our boat. I'm impatient, watching bubbles break above the whale as it plows along the bottom, straining masses of tiny invertebrates through its baleen plates. Suddenly a barnacle-encrusted head bursts through the surface and a pungent plume gushes from its blowholes. I wince as the fishy fetor of freshly digested whale food drifts downwind and fans my face.

"See what it's eating," says biologist Pam Stacey. She reaches into the water and scoops a handful of wiggling shrimp-like things the whale has churned up from the bottom.

"Amphipods."

Prodigious as it may seem, this whale is only about three years old. In another five years it will weigh some 30 tonnes and measure 12 or 13 metres long. Even now it is well over twice the length of our four-metre boat: it could capsize us with a flip of its flukes.

The whale, however, appears undisturbed by our presence. It swims fluidly, making four or five shallow dives, blowing between each. Then it

BRUCE OBEE is a freelance writer who specializes in natural history and environmental topics. His books include *Guardians of the Whales: The Quest to Study Whales in the Wild*; *Coastal Wildlife of British Columbia*; *The Pacific Rim Explorer*; and *Wolf: Wild Hunter of North America*. "Gentle Giants" was originally published in *Canadian Geographic* in December 1990. Reprinted by permission of the author.

raises its enormous tail almost out of the water and rolls headlong into the depths, exposing a row of bumps, or knuckles, at the base of its back. Stacey snaps an identification photo for the Cascadia Research Collective, in Olympia, Wash., where information on West Coast whales is compiled.

A research associate with the Whale Museum at Friday Harbour, Wash., Stacey located this animal through the Whale Hotline—a toll-free system for people in Washington and British Columbia to report sightings of whales, porpoises or dolphins—dead or alive. Since it was established in 1976, the hotline has helped provide information on the seasonal distribution of marine mammals.

This whale at Finnerty Cove really should be travelling up the outer west coast of Vancouver Island. Between late February and early May about 21,000 Pacific (or California) grays migrate past the island to summer feeding grounds in the North Pacific and Arctic oceans. Eight or 10 usually stray into Juan de Fuca Strait and the Strait of Georgia, where they spend the summer, then join the southbound migration sometime between November and January. These whales are usually young and have been seen even amid the busy traffic in Vancouver Harbour and in the lower reaches of the Fraser River.

The incredible 16,000-kilometre return migration of the Pacific gray whale is the longest of any mammal on earth. It begins at breeding lagoons in Baja California, Mexico. Travelling alone or in groups of up to 16, the first migrants start to swim north in January, followed about eight weeks later by cows with calves. Though they may travel in groups, Pacific grays, unlike killer whales, do not form pods or close-knit families that stay together for life.

Often swimming close to shore, the whales are a prime attraction for naturalists. The halfway point in their migration is off Long Beach, in Vancouver Island's Pacific Rim National Park, where they arrive in their greatest numbers in late March and early April. Depending on conditions, as many as 200 a day can be seen passing the park at that time. They continue to hug the shoreline beyond Vancouver Island into the Gulf of Alaska and the Bering and Chukchi seas. They feed here until late summer when ice begins to force them out. In 1988, three Pacific gray whales lingered too long near Barrow, Alaska, and were imprisoned by advancing pack ice. The youngest whale died, but the other two were saved in a rescue operation televised around the world.

The Pacific gray whale's return from the brink of extinction is as remarkable as its migration. In the mid-1850s, the historic population of about 24,000 was hunted relentlessly in its Mexican calving lagoons. By the late 1870s, the whales had all but vanished. Their numbers grew again through the early 1900s and then they were decimated once more. It wasn't until 1946, with the formation of the International Whaling Commission, that the Pacific gray whale was protected.

By 1972, when Dr. Jim Darling began his gray whale research, the population had rebounded to about 11,000. Now considered Canada's foremost authority on this species, Darling is executive director of the West Coast Whale Research Foundation, which has a station in the village of Tofino near Long Beach.

It was at Long Beach that Darling, as a summer surfer, first encountered gray whales. He noticed their silty trails just beyond the surf line. But there was something unusual about these feeding whales. This was summer; the migration was over and they were supposed to be 4,000 kilometres north of there.

Darling told fellow biologist David Hatler of a gray whale with an orange scar on its back. Hatler said he had taken pictures of the same whale several summers earlier. Darling tracked down the scarred whale, photographed it, and began snapping pictures of other gray whales that appeared to take up summer residence in the waters off Pacific Rim. To scientists, the mottled gray and white markings on a whale's skin are as distinctive as fingerprints. By comparing photographs, Darling confirmed that the same whales often return year after year to stay for the summer.

By 1984, Darling had collected 5,000 photographs of gray whales off southwest Vancouver Island. He says that since 1970, 37 whales have been seen during more than one summer at Pacific Rim. One has been spotted for eight years, several others for seven years. Many return to the same locations at the same time each year, while others have been sighted at a number of places along the coast. Some remain at Wickaninnish Bay, in Pacific Rim, for more than 80 days at a time. The whales seen repeatedly are usually mature animals, while most of those that stay only one season are young.

The resident summer population off the west coast of Vancouver Island today is estimated at between 40 and 50 whales. They rejoin the southbound migration that peaks in the last half of December. There is only one short period between mid-January and early February when gray whales cannot be found off Vancouver Island.

The recovery of the gray whale has conveniently coincided with the development of Pacific Rim National Park, officially opened in 1971. As the gray whale population grows, so too does the number of tourists at Long Beach, and the villages of Tofino and Ucluelet at opposite ends of the park. Along with the sandy beaches, rain forests and rugged coastal scenery, gray whales have become a major component in the burgeoning tourist industry: last year a dozen or so charter boats took 30,000 people out to see whales. Whale-watching fares alone contribute nearly $1 million to the economy of an area populated by fewer than 3,000 people. Ucluelet now bills itself as the "Whale-watching Capital of the World," and the annual migration is celebrated during the Pacific Rim Whale Festival.

Dressed in winter woollens and rain suits, amateur naturalists gather on beaches and headlands, or aboard inflatable speedboats, converted herring skiffs and covered cruisers to look for whales. Even on calm days the sea here can be uncomfortably rough, with heavy swells from the open Pacific, wind-whipped whitecaps, and 30- or 40-knot gusts.

Aboard the 16-metre *Lady Selkirk*, I am one of 40 whale-watchers squinting into the drizzle, scanning the horizon for the distant spouts of surfacing whales. A foghorn moans in the mist as the little ship pitches and rolls past the lighthouse on Lennard Island, five kilometres south of Tofino.

"There's one!" comes a shout from the upper deck, and a voice through the P.A. system quickly announces: "Off the starboard bow, two o'clock." Instantly, everybody is on their feet, rummaging through bags for binoculars and cameras. Pressed against the rails, scanning the waves 50 metres away, the wait is endless. One minute, three minutes, four . . . suddenly the titanic beast explodes through the surface and a spout of vapour fires four metres into the air. Before a single shutter has clicked the whale is gone. But everyone has seen it now; everyone is eager for another glimpse.

Before the whale reappears, two others simultaneously break the surface off the port side. Air gushes from their lungs, forming heart-shaped spouts that are snatched away by the wind. A satisfied grin crosses the skipper's face and he launches into a practised spiel about the extraordinary comeback of the Pacific gray whale, one of the world's great wildlife success stories.

No one knows how many were left when the wholesale killing stopped and the population began to rebound, but it was certainly a fraction of traditional numbers. Gray whales were essentially ignored by early 19th-century whalers. Their baleen plates were too small to make corsets, their oil was less plentiful and inferior to that of other whales, and the meat was not especially good. Compared to offshore species such as sperm, fin, blue, right, humpback, sei and others, gray whales were hardly worth the effort. Unless they could be taken in large quantities.

That opportunity arose in the mid-1800s, when whalers discovered the Mexican calving lagoons. In these shallow, sheltered sanctuaries where cows quietly nursed their newborn, whales could be caught by the hundreds—and so the slaughter began. Such "lagoon whaling" had been going on at Baja California's Magdalena Bay for a decade before 1858 when Capt. Charles Scammon discovered the lagoon that now bears his name. He stumbled upon the greatest concentration of gray whales in the world.

Lagoon hunting was relatively easy, although gray whales soon earned the nicknames "hard head" or "devilfish" because of the way enraged females aggressively defended their young. Whalers used that trait to their advantage by harpooning a calf to lure the mother within "darting distance."

Even with harpoons and bomb lances, whalers were vulnerable in their wooden skiffs. "Repeated accidents have happened in which men have been instantly killed, or received mortal injury," Scammon wrote in his book, *The Marine Mammals of the Northwestern Coast of North America*.

Often these injuries were suffered without any whaling success. "In attacking 16 whales, two boats were entirely destroyed, while the others were staved 15 times; and out of 18 men who officered and manned them, six were badly jarred, one had both legs broken, another three ribs fractured, and still another was so much injured internally that he was unable to perform duty during the rest of the voyage," Scammon wrote. "All these serious casualties happened before a single whale was captured."

In spite of such confrontations, the whalers were the ultimate victors. So successful, in fact, were the hunts that whale sightings in the breeding lagoons soon became a rarity. The ships then abandoned the lagoons in favour of offshore whaling, leaving only shore-based whalers who set up gauntlets of small boats along the migration route. They shot migrating whales with swivel-mounted Greener's harpoon guns.

According to Scammon, other less-sophisticated whalers were also familiar with the gray whale's migratory habits. "Scarcely have the poor creatures quitted their southern homes before they are surprised by the Indians about the Strait of Juan de Fuca, Vancouver and Queen Charlotte's

Islands. Like enemies in ambush, they glide in canoes from island, bluff, or bay, rushing upon their prey with whoop and yell, launching their instruments of torture and, like hounds, worrying the last lifeblood from their vitals."

Whale hunts were immersed in ritual, and log books from early trading vessels suggest the Indians of Ahousat, 18 kilometres northwest of Tofino, customarily sacrificed a slave in honour of the first whale killed in a season. An anthropologist from the Smithsonian Institution describes Indians of the Pacific Rim area as "the most ardent whale hunters on the Vancouver Island coast."

They hunted from canoes, using harpoons with sealskin floats attached by long lines of sinew and cedar bark. The whale, taking refuge in the depths when struck, would fight against the buoyancy until exhausted. A lance would then be stabbed into the heart and, with the help of the floats, several canoes would tow the carcass ashore.

There is disagreement among researchers about the whale species taken by West Coast natives. Some say gray whales were the most important; others believe they hunted humpbacks. Each whale species has its own particular type of barnacles that affix themselves to the whale's skin. In Clayoquot Sound, which surrounds Tofino, barnacles from humpback whales, not grays, are more commonly unearthed from Indian middens, says Jim Darling.

Whether they took humpbacks or grays, the effect of Indian whaling on the overall Pacific gray whale population was insignificant compared to the devastation wrought by commercial whalers. By the time his book was published in 1874, Scammon, who along with other whalers was largely to blame for the gray whale's demise, seemed somewhat remorseful. "The mammoth bones of the California gray lie bleaching on the shores of those silvery waters, and are scattered along the broken coasts, from Siberia to the Gulf of California; and 'ere long it may be questioned whether this mammal will not be numbered among the extinct species of the Pacific."

When petroleum replaced whale oil in the early 1900s, there were perhaps only 2,000 gray whales left. The coastal stations shut down and they were forgotten. The whales' numbers grew virtually unchecked until 1914, when they were rediscovered and modern factory ships sailed onto the scene. World War I halted some whaling, but soon after, the butchery was revived with vigour: Norwegian, Soviet, Japanese and American whale ships took gray whales all along the North American coast. By 1937, when Canada, the United States and Mexico agreed to protect them, the future of the species was precarious. The Japanese and Russians continued to hunt them: one Soviet factory ship alone, the *Aleut,* killed 471 grays between 1938 and 1947.

With the formation of the International Whaling Commission in 1946, the Pacific gray, unlike more lucrative species, was given protection by 17 countries. Russian whalers continue to take about 200 gray whales a year for aboriginal Soviets. There was only a handful of whaling stations on the British Columbia coast, and between 1905 and 1967 few, if any, of the 24,000 whales processed in the province were grays. Canada's last Pacific whaling station, at Coal Harbour on northwest Vancouver Island, had been closed for five years when Canada officially ended whaling in 1972. Ten years later Canada dropped out of the IWC.

Last May, members of the IWC's scientific subcommittee met in Seattle for a gray whale conference. Researchers are attempting to assess the current population and its mortality and birth rates. A separate population in the Asian Pacific is thought to be extinct now, and countries such as Japan are interested in hunting gray whales on the North American coast. The scientific subcommittee provides data on which the IWC sets whaling quotas.

Gray whales are protected in Canada's 370-kilometre offshore economic zone under the Cetacean Protective Regulations, part of the Fisheries Act. Only Inuit, under ministerial permit, may hunt them. Legislation has its limits, however, and the Pacific gray whale, like all wildlife, faces other threats. In British Columbia, its most fearsome natural enemy is the killer whale, whose tooth rakes are borne by many gray whales. Gray whales are known to flee when killer-whale recordings are played in the water.

Unlike fish-eating whales, Pacific grays may not be as closely affected by overfishing or other changes in the fisheries. Their ability to adapt to available foods—herring eggs, amphipods, mysids and other plankton—may be a factor in their impressive comeback, says Jim Darling. They are mainly bottom feeders and protection of the seabed is needed to ensure their preservation. However, in early January last year, an oil spill from the U.S. barge *Nestucca,* which had been rammed by its own tug two weeks earlier 200 kilometres south of Vancouver Island, fouled the beaches of Pacific Rim. Only three months later, oil from the grounded *Exxon Valdez* contaminated another part of the gray whale's migration route in Alaska's Prince William Sound. So far there have been no indicators of the effect of these spills on the whales.

In Ahous Bay on Vargas Island, eight kilometres west of Tofino, Darling and I scan the ocean for the telltale spouts of surfacing whales. The beaches here, and at Cow Bay on nearby Flores Island, are like the surf-battered sandy shores that lure half a million visitors a year to Long Beach. This is a prime feeding area for gray whales.

There are no whales here today: they are likely farther south, says Darling, where I had seen them from the *Lady Selkirk* earlier in the migration. There is probably still oil from the *Nestucca* spill on the sea bottom below us, however. Darling conducted a survey of feeding areas after the spill for the Department of Fisheries and Oceans and found that 14 sediment samples from five sites contained hydrocarbons, oil and grease. "Those were just random samples," Darling emphasizes, "and we found oil in every one."

A gray whale feeds by scraping along sandy sea floors, sucking in silt and sand laden with bottom-dwelling crustaceans, tubeworms, amphipods, and other invertebrates. With the force of its massive tongue it expels the sand through baleen plates, trapping its food in a web of bristles.

There are too many unanswered questions to judge the effects of the oil on gray whales. What hydrocarbon levels naturally occur in these sediments? How do they influence the feed? How much oil can a whale tolerate in its food?

Researchers also are looking at the potential effects of whale-watching. As competition increases, there is concern about harassment of whales by charter-boat operators eager to satisfy their customers. So far no serious mishaps have occurred in Canada, but in Baja California, whales have reacted adversely to trespassers in their domain. In 1982, a gray whale upset a small whale-watching boat in Mexico's Scammon Lagoon, drowning two people. In several other incidents near the calving lagoons, a kayaker who ventured too close to a calf was shaken up when rammed by a mother whale, and a hovering helicopter carrying sightseers lost power when drenched by an angry whale. Fortunately it was close enough to make shore safely.

The Canadian government has informal whale-watching guidelines that suggest aircraft stay 450 metres above the water and that boats keep a distance of at least 100 metres. Last spring, Fisheries and Oceans officials met with charter-boat operators at Pacific Rim to discuss whale-watching protocol. New guidelines may be drafted and formal whale-watching legislation recommended.

"Most of the operators try their damnedest not to disturb the animals," says Darling, "but it's a question of volume." During summer a solitary feeding whale may be approached day after day by four or five tour boats, a plane or two, dozens of kayakers and private boaters. "We know that mammals react to stress and that over a long period it can affect their health," says Darling. Yet, he points out that there is currently no indication that whale-watching is harmful to gray whales.

Some whales, in fact, appear to enjoy being the centre of attention. Each summer, one or two "friendlies" inhabit the seas off Pacific Rim. They snuggle up to tour boats, as if craving the affectionate touch of a human hand.

"I think the benefits far, far outweigh the disturbance factor at this point," says Darling. "It's great that people are getting out and seeing whales in the wild."

Today, as in the last century, the Pacific gray whale has become the mainstay of a thriving industry. This time, however, neither its freedom nor survival as a species is threatened.

# Death
## at Sea and
## on Shore

~

BARRY LOPEZ

# A Presentation of Whales

On that section of the central Oregon coast on the evening of June 16, 1979, gentle winds were blowing onshore from the southwest. It was fifty-eight degrees. Under partly cloudy skies the sea was running with four-foot swells at eight-second intervals. Moderately rough. State police cadets Jim Clark and Steve Bennett stood at the precipitous edge of a foredune a few miles south of the town of Florence, peering skeptically into the dimness over a flat, gently sloping beach. Near the water's edge they could make out a line of dark shapes, and what they had taken for a practical joke, the exaggeration a few moments before of a man and a woman in a brown Dodge van with a broken headlight, now sank in for the truth.

Clark made a hasty, inaccurate count and plunged with Bennett down the back of the dune to their four-wheel-drive. Minutes before, they had heard the voice of Corporal Terry Crawford over the radio; they knew he was patrolling in Florence. Rather than call him, they drove the six miles into town and parked across the street from where he was issuing a citation to someone for excessive noise. When Crawford had

BARRY LOPEZ's many books include *Arctic Dreams*, which won the American Book Award in 1986, *Of Wolves and Men*, and several collections of fiction, most recently *Fieldnotes*. He has also received an Award in Literature from the American Academy and Institute of Arts and Letters, and the John Burroughs Medal for distinguished nature writing. "A Presentation of Whales" is from *Crossing Open Ground*. Copyright © 1980, 1988. Reprinted by permission of Sterling Lord Literistic.

finished, Clark went over and told him what they had seen. Crawford drove straight to the Florence State Police office and phoned his superiors in Newport, forty-eight miles up the coast. At that point the news went out over police radios: thirty-six large whales, stranded and apparently still alive, were on the beach a mile south of the mouth of the Siuslaw River.

There were, in fact, forty-one whales—twenty-eight females and thirteen males, at least one of them dying or already dead. There had never been a stranding quite like it. It was first assumed that they were gray whales, common along the coast, but they were sperm whales: *Physeter catodon*. Deep-ocean dwellers. They ranged in age from ten to fifty-six and in length from thirty to thirty-eight feet. They were apparently headed north when they beached around 7:30 P.M. on an ebbing high tide.

The information shot inland by phone, crossing the Coast Range to radio and television stations in the more-populous interior of Oregon, in a highly charged form: giant whales stranded on a public beach accessible by paved road on a Saturday night, still alive. Radio announcers urged listeners to head for the coast to "save the whales." In Eugene and Portland, Greenpeace volunteers, already alerted by the police, were busy throwing sheets and blankets into their cars. They would soak them in the ocean, to cool the whales.

The news moved as quickly through private homes and taverns on the central Oregon coast, passed by people monitoring the police bands. In addition to phoning Greenpeace—an international organization with a special interest in protecting marine mammals—the police contacted the Oregon State University Marine Science Center in South Beach near Newport, and the Oregon Institute of Marine Biology in Charleston, fifty-eight miles south of Florence. Bruce Mate, a marine mammalogist at the OSU Center, phoned members of the Northwest Regional [Stranding] Alert Network and people in Washington, D.C.

By midnight, the curious and the awed were crowded on the beach, cutting the night with flashlights. Drunks, ignoring the whales' sudden thrashing, were trying to walk up and down on their backs. A collie barked incessantly; flash cubes burst at the huge, dark forms. Two men inquired about reserving some of the teeth, for scrimshaw. A federal agent asked police to move people back, and the first mention of disease was in the air. Scientists arrived with specimen bags and rubber gloves and fishing knives. Greenpeace members, one dressed in a bright orange flight suit, came with a large banner. A man burdened with a television camera labored over the foredune after them. They wished to tie a rope to one whale's flukes, to drag it back into the ocean. The police began to congregate with the scientists, looking for a rationale to control the incident.

In the intensifying confusion, as troopers motioned onlookers back (to "restrain the common herd of unqualified mankind," wrote one man later in an angry letter to the editor), the thinking was that, somehow, the whales might be saved. Neal Langbehn, a federal protection officer with the National Marine Fisheries Service, denied permission to one scientist to begin removing teeth and taking blood samples. In his report later he would write: "It was my feeling that the whales should be given their best chance to survive."

This hope was soon deemed futile, as it had appeared to most of the scientists from the beginning—the animals were hemorrhaging under the crushing weight of their own flesh and were beginning to suffer irreversible damage from heat exhaustion. The scientific task became one of securing as much data as possible.

As dawn bloomed along the eastern sky, people who had driven recreational vehicles illegally over the dunes and onto the beach were issued citations and turned back. Troopers continued to warn people over bullhorns to please stand away from the whales. The Oregon Parks Department, whose responsibility the beach was, wanted no part of the growing confusion. The U.S. Forest Service, with jurisdiction over land in the Oregon Dunes National Recreation Area down to the foredune, was willing to help, but among all the agencies there was concern over limited budgets; there were questions, gently essayed, about the conflict of state and federal enforcement powers over the body parts of an endangered species. A belligerent few in the crowd shouted objections as the first syringes appeared, and yelled to scientists to produce permits that allowed them to interfere in the death of an endangered species.

Amid this chaos, the whales, sealed in their slick black neoprene skins, mewed and clicked. They slammed glistening flukes on the beach, jarring the muscles of human thighs like Jell-O at a distance of a hundred yards. They rolled their dark, purple-brown eyes at the scene and blinked.

They lay on the western shore of North America like forty-one derailed boxcars at dawn on a Sunday morning, and in the days that followed, the worst and the best of human behavior was shown among them.

The sperm whale, for many, is the most awesome creature of the open seas. Imagine a forty-five-year-old male fifty feet long, a slim, shiny black animal with a white jaw and marbled belly cutting the surface of green ocean water at twenty knots. Its flat forehead protects a sealed chamber of exceedingly fine oil; sunlight sparkles in rivulets running off folds in its corrugated back. At fifty tons it is the largest carnivore on earth. Its massive head, a third of its body length, is scarred with the beak, sucker, and claw marks of giant squid, snatched out of subterranean canyons a mile below, in a region without light, and brought writhing to the surface. Imagine a four-hundred-pound heart the size of a chest of drawers driving five gallons of blood at a stroke through its aorta: a meal of forty salmon moving slowly down twelve hundred feet of intestine; the blinding, acrid fragrance of a two-hundred-pound wad of gray ambergris lodged somewhere along the way; producing sounds more shrill than we can hear—like children shouting on a distant playground—and able to sort a cacophony of noise: electric crackling of shrimp, groaning of undersea quakes, roar of upwellings, whining of porpoise, hum of oceanic cables. With skin as sensitive as the inside of your wrist.

What makes them awesome is not so much these things, which are discoverable, but the mysteries that shroud them. They live at a remarkable distance from us and we have no *Pioneer II* to penetrate their world. Virtually all we know of sperm whales we have learned on the slaughter decks of oceangoing whalers and on the ways at shore stations. We do not even know how many there are; in December 1978, the Scientific Committee of the International Whaling Commission said it could not set a quota for a worldwide sperm whale kill—so little was known that any number written down would be ridiculous.*

The sperm whale, in all its range of behaviors—from the enraged white bull called Mocha Dick that stove whaling ships off the coast of Peru in 1810, to a nameless female giving birth to a fourteen-foot, one-ton calf in equatorial waters in the Pacific—remains distant. The general mystery is enhanced by specific mysteries: the sperm whale's brain is larger than the brain of any other creature that ever lived. Beyond the storage of incomprehensible amounts of information, we do not know what purpose such size serves. And we do not know what to make of its most distinctive anatomical feature, the spermaceti organ. An article in

---

* A quota of 5000 was nevertheless set. In June 1979, within days of the Florence stranding but apparently unrelated to it, the IWC dropped the 1980 world sperm whale quota to 2203 and set aside the Indian Ocean as a sanctuary. (By 1987 the quota was 0, though special exemptions permit some 200 sperm whales still to be taken worldwide.)

*Scientific American*, published several months before the stranding, suggests that the whale can control the density of its spermaceti oil, thereby altering its specific gravity to assist it in diving. It is argued also that the huge organ, located in the head, serves as a means of generating and focusing sound, but there is not yet any agreement on these speculations.

Of the many sperm whale strandings in recorded history, only three have been larger than the one in Oregon. The most recent was of fifty-six on the eastern Baja coast near Playa San Rafael on January 6, 1979. But the Florence stranding is perhaps the most remarkable. Trained scientists arrived almost immediately; the site was easily accessible, with even an airstrip close by. It was within an hour's drive of two major West Coast marine-science centers. And the stranding seemed to be of a whole social unit. That the animals were still alive meant live blood specimens could be taken. And by an uncanny coincidence, a convention of the American Society of Mammalogists was scheduled to convene June 18 at Oregon State University in Corvallis, less than a two-hour drive away. Marine experts from all over the country would be there. (As it turned out, some of them would not bother to come over; others would secure access to the beach only to take photographs; still others would show up in sports clothes—all they had—and plunge into the gore that by the afternoon of June 18 littered the beach.)

The state police calls to Greenpeace on the night of June 16 were attempts to reach informed people to direct a rescue. Michael Piper of Greenpeace, in Eugene, was the first to arrive with a small group at about 1:30 A.M., just after a low tide at 12:59 A.M.

"I ran right out of my shoes," Piper says. The thought that they would still be alive—clicking and murmuring, their eyes tracking human movement, lifting their flukes, whooshing warm air from their blowholes—had not penetrated. But as he ran into the surf to fill a bucket to splash water over their heads, the proportions of the stranding and the impending tragedy overwhelmed him.

"I knew, almost from the beginning, that we were not going to get them out of there, and that even if we did, their chances of survival were a million to one," Piper said.

Just before dawn, a second contingent of Greenpeace volunteers arrived from Portland. A Canadian, Michael Bailey, took charge and announced there was a chance with the incoming tide that one of the smaller animals could be floated off the beach and towed to sea (weights

ranged from an estimated three and a half to twenty-five tons). Bruce
Mate, who would become both scientific and press coordinator on the
beach (the latter to his regret), phoned the Port of Coos Bay to see if an
ocean-going tug or fishing vessel would be available to anchor offshore
and help—Bailey's crew would ferry lines through the surf with a Zodiac
boat. No one in Coos Bay was interested. A commercial helicopter service with a Skycrane capable of lifting nine tons also begged off. A call to
the Coast Guard produced a helicopter, but people there pronounced
any attempt to sky-tow a whale too dangerous.

The refusal of help combined with the apparent futility of the effort
precipitated a genuinely compassionate gesture: Bailey strode resolutely
into the freezing water and, with twenty-five or thirty others, amid flailing
flukes, got a rope around the tail of an animal that weighed perhaps three
or four tons. The waves knocked them down and the whale yanked them
over, but they came up sputtering, to pull again. With the buoyancy provided by the incoming tide they moved the animal about thirty feet. The
effort was heroic and ludicrous. As the rope began to cut into the whale's
flesh, as television cameramen and press photographers crowded in,
Michael Piper gave up his place on the rope in frustration and waded
ashore. Later he would remark that, for some, the whale was only the
means to a political end—a dramatization of the plight of whales as a
species. The distinction between the suffering individual, its internal
organs hemorrhaging, its flukes sliced by the rope, and the larger issue,
to save the species, confounded Piper.

A photograph of the Greenpeace volunteers pulling the whale showed
up nationally in newspapers the next day. A week later, a marine mammalogist wondered if any more damaging picture could have been circu-
lated. It would convince people something could have been done, when
in fact, he said, the whales were doomed as soon as they came ashore.

For many, transfixed on the beach by their own helplessness, the
value of the gesture transcended the fact.

By midmorning Piper was so disturbed, so embarrassed by the
drunks and by people wrangling to get up on the whales or in front of
photographers, that he left. As he drove off through the crowds (arriving
now by the hundreds, many in campers and motor homes), gray whales
were seen offshore, with several circling sperm whales. "The best thing
we could have done," Piper said, alluding to this, "was offer our presence, to be with them while they were alive, to show some compassion."

Irritated by a callous (to him) press that seemed to have only one

question—Why did they come ashore?—Piper had blurted out that the
whales may have come ashore "because they were tired of running" from
commercial whalers. Scientists scoffed at the remark, but Piper, recalling
it a week later, would not take it back. He said it was as logical as any
other explanation offered in those first few hours.

Uneasy philosophical disagreement divided people on the beach
from the beginning. Those for whom the stranding was a numinous event
were estranged by the clowning of those who regarded it as principally
entertainment. A few scientists irritated everyone with their preemptive,
self-important air. When they put chain saws to the lower jaws of dead
sperm whales lying only a few feet from whales not yet dead, there were
angry shouts of condemnation. When townspeople kept at bay—"This is
history, dammit," one man screamed at a state trooper, "and I want my
kids to see it!"—saw twenty reporters, each claiming an affiliation with
the same weekly newspaper, gain the closeness to the whales denied
them, there were shouts of cynical derision.

"The effect of all this," said Michael Gannon, director of a national
group called Oregonians Cooperating to Protect Whales, of the under-
current of elitism and outrage, "was that it interfered with the spiritual
and emotional ability of people to deal with the phenomenon. It was like
being at a funeral where you were not allowed to mourn."

Bob Warren, a patrolman with the U.S. Forest Service, said he was nearly
brought to tears by what faced him Sunday morning. "I had no conception of what a whale beaching would be like. I was apprehensive about it,
about all the tourists and the law-enforcement atmosphere. When I drove
up, the whole thing hit me in the stomach: I saw these *numbers*, these
damn orange numbers—41, 40, 39—spray-painted on these dying
animals. The media were coming on like the marines, in taxicabs, helicopters, low-flying aircraft. Biologists were saying, 'We've got to *euthanize*
them.' It made me sick."

By this time Sunday morning, perhaps five hundred people had gathered; the crowd would swell to more than two thousand before evening,
in spite of a drizzling rain. The state trooper who briefed Warren outlined
the major problems: traffic was backing up on the South Jetty Road
almost five miles to U.S. 101; the whales' teeth were "as valuable as gold"
and individuals with hammers and saws had been warned away already;
people were sticking their hands in the whales' mouths and were in danger of being killed by the pounding flukes; and there was a public-health

problem—the whales might have come ashore with a communicable disease. (According to several experts, the danger to public health was minor, but in the early confusion it served as an excuse to keep the crowd back so scientists could work. Ironically, the threat would assume a life of its own two days later and scientists would find themselves working frantically ahead of single-minded state burial crews.)

One of the first things Warren and others did was to rope off the whales with orange ribbon and lath stakes, establishing a line beyond which the public was no longer permitted. Someone thoughtful among them ran the ribbon close enough to one whale to allow people to peer into the dark eyes, to see scars left by struggling squid, lamprey eels, and sharp boulders on the ocean floor, the patches of diatoms growing on the skin, the marbling streaking back symmetrically from the genital slit, the startlingly gentle white mouth ("What a really beautiful and chaste-looking mouth!" Melville wrote. "From floor to ceiling lined, or rather papered with a glistening white membrane, glossy as bridal satins"), to see the teeth, gleaming in the long, almost absurdly narrow jaw. In *The Year of the Whale*, Victor Scheffer describes the tooth as "creamy white, a cylinder lightly curved, a thing of art which fits delightfully in the palm of my hand."

The temptation to possess—a Polaroid of oneself standing over a whale, a plug of flesh removed with a penknife, a souvenir squid beak plucked deftly from an exposed intestine by a scientist—was almost palpable in the air.

"From the beginning," Warren continued, "I was operating on two levels: as a law-enforcement officer with a job, and as a person." He escorted people away from the whales, explaining as well as he could the threat of disease, wishing himself to reach out with them, to touch the animals. He recalls his rage watching people poke at a sensitive area under the whales' eyes to make them react, and calmly directing people to step back, to let the animals die in peace. Nothing could be done, he would say. How do you know? they would ask. He didn't.

Warren was awed by the sudden, whooshing breath that broke the silence around an animal perhaps once every fifteen minutes, and saddened by the pitiable way some of them were mired with their asymmetrical blowhole sanded in, dead. Near those still breathing he drove in lath stakes with the word LIVE written on them. The hopelessness of it, he said, and the rarity of the event were rendered absurd by his having to yell into a bullhorn, by the blood on the beach, the whales' blinking, the taunters hoisting beer cans to the police.

One of the things about being human, Warren reflected, is learning to see beyond the vulgar. Along with the jocose in the crowd, he said, there were hundreds who whispered to each other, as if in a grove of enormous trees. And faces that looked as though they were awaiting word of relatives presumed dead in an air crash. He remembers in particular a man in his forties, "dressed in polyesters," who stood with his daughter in a tidal pool inside the barrier, splashing cool water on a whale. Warren asked them to please step back. "Why?" the man asked. Someone in the crowd yelled an obscenity at Warren. Warren thought to himself: Why is there no room for the decency of this gesture?

The least understood and perhaps most disruptive incident on the beach on that first day was the attempt of veterinarians to kill the whales, first by injecting M-99, a morphine-base drug, then by ramming pipes into their pleural cavities to collapse their lungs, and finally by severing major arteries and letting them bleed to death. The techniques were crude, but no one knew enough sperm whale anatomy or physiology to make a clean job of it, and no one wanted to try some of the alternatives—from curare to dynamite—that would have made the job quicker. The ineptitude of the veterinarians caused them a private embarrassment to which they gave little public expression. Their frustration at their own inability to do anything to "help" the whales was exacerbated by nonscientists demanding from the sidelines that the animals be "put out of their misery." (The reasons for attempting euthanasia were poorly understood, philosophically and medically, and the issue nagged people long after the beach bore not a trace of the incident itself.)

As events unfolded on the beach, the first whale died shortly after the stranding, the last almost thirty-six hours later; suffocation and overheating were the primary causes. By waiting as long as they did to try to kill some of the animals and by allowing others to die in their own time, pathologists, toxicologists, parasitologists, geneticists, and others got tissues of poor quality to work with.* The disappointment was all the

---

* A subsequent report, presented at a marine-mammals conference in Seattle in October 1979, made it clear that the whales began to suffer the effects of heat stress almost immediately. The breakdown of protein structures in their tissues made discovery of a cause of death difficult; from the beginning, edema, capillary dilation, and hemorrhaging made their recovery unlikely. Ice, seawater pumps, and tents for shade rather than Zodiac boats and towlines were suggested if useful tissue was to be salvaged in the future from large whales.

deeper because never had so many scientists been in a position to gather so much information. (Even with this loss and an initial lack of suitable equipment—chemicals to preserve tissues, blood-analysis kits, bone saws, flensing knives—the small core of twenty or so scientists "increased human knowledge about sperm whales several hundred percent," according to Mate.)

The fact that almost anything learned was likely to be valuable was meager consolation to scientists hurt by charges that they were cold and brutal people, irreverently jerking fetuses from the dead. Among these scientists were people who sat alone in silence, who departed in anger, and who broke down and cried.

No one knows why whales strand. It is almost always toothed whales that do, rather than baleen whales, most commonly pilot whales, Atlantic white-sided dolphins, false killer whales, and sperm whales—none of which are ordinarily found close to shore. Frequently they strand on gently sloping beaches. Among the more tenable explanations: (1) extreme social cohesion, where one sick animal is relentlessly followed ashore by many healthy animals; (2) disease or parasitic infection that affects the animals' ability to navigate; (3) harassment, by predators and, deliberate or inadvertent, by humans; (4) a reversion to phylogenetically primitive escape behavior—get out of the water—precipitated by stress.

At a public meeting in Florence—arranged by the local librarian to explain to a public kept off the beach what had happened, and to which invited scientists did not come—other explanations were offered. Someone had noticed whales splashing in apparent confusion near a river dredge and thought the sound of its engines might have driven the whales crazy. Local fishermen said there had been an unusual, near-shore warm current on June 16, with a concentration of plankton so thick they had trouble penetrating it with their depth finders. Another suggestion was that the whales might have been temporarily deranged by poisons in diatoms concentrated in fish they were eating.

The seventy-five or so people at the meeting seemed irritated that there was no answer, as did local reporters looking for an end to the story. Had scientists been there it is unlikely they could have suggested one. The beach was a gently sloping one, but the Florence whales showed no evidence of parasitism or disease, and modern research makes it clear that no single explanation will suffice. For those who would blame the machinations of modern man, scientists would have pointed out that strandings have been recorded since the time of Aristotle's *Historia animalium*.

The first marine biologist to arrive on the beach, at 3:30 A.M. Sunday, was Michael Graybill, a young instructor from the Oregon Institute of Marine Biology. He was not as perplexed as other scientists would be; a few months before he had dismantled the rotting carcass of a fifty-six-foot sperm whale that had washed ashore thirty miles south of Florence.

Graybill counted the animals, identified them as sperm whales, noted that, oddly, there were no nursing calves or obviously young animals, and that they all seemed "undersized." He examined their skin and eyes, smelled their breath, looked for signs of oral and anal discharge, and began the task of sexing and measuring the animals.

Driving to the site, Graybill worried most about someone "bashing their teeth out" before he got there. He wasn't worried about communicable disease; he was "willing to gamble" on that. He regarded efforts to save the whales, however, an unnatural interference in their death. Later, he cynically observed "how much 'science' took place at the heads of sperm whales" where people were removing teeth; and he complained that if they really cared about the worldwide fate of whales, Greenpeace volunteers would have stayed to help scientists with postmortems. (Some did. Others left because they could not stand to watch the animals die.)

Beginning Sunday morning, scientists had their first chance to draw blood from live, unwounded sperm whales (they used comparatively tiny one-and-a-half-inch, 18-gauge hypodermic needles stuck in vessels near the surface of the skin on the flukes). With the help of a blue, organic tracer they estimated blood volume at five hundred gallons. In subsequent stages, blubber, eyes, teeth, testicles, ovaries, stomach contents, and specific tissues were removed—the teeth for aging, the eyes for corneal cells to discover genetic relationships within the group. Postmortems were performed on ten females; three near-term fetuses were removed. An attempt was made to photograph the animals systematically.

The atmosphere on the beach shifted perceptibly over the next six days. On Sunday, a cool, cloudy day during which it rained, as many as three thousand people may have been on the beach. Police finally closed the access road to the area to discourage more from coming. Attempts to euthanize the animals continued, the jaws of the dead were being sawed off, and, in the words of one observer, "there was a television crew with a backdrop of stranded whales every twenty feet on the foredune."

By Monday the crowds were larger, but, in the estimation of a Forest Service employee, "of a higher quality. The type of people who show up at an automobile accident were gone; these were people who really wanted to see whales. It was a four-and-a-half-mile walk in from the highway, and I talked with a woman who was seven months pregnant who made it and a man in a business suit and dress shoes who drove all the way down from Seattle."

Monday afternoon the crowds thinned. The beach had become a scene of postmortem gore sufficient to turn most people away. The outgoing tide had carried off gallons of blood and offal, drawing spiny dogfish sharks and smoothhound sharks into the breakers. As the animals died, scientists cut into them to relieve gaseous pressure—the resultant explosions could be heard half a mile away. A forty-pound chunk of liver whizzed by someone's back-turned shoulders; sixty feet of pearly-gray intestine unfurled with a snap against the sky. By evening the beach was covered with more than a hundred tons of intestines. Having to open the abdominal cavities so precipitately precluded, to the scientists' dismay, any chance of an uncontaminated examination.

By Tuesday the beach was closed to the public. The whale carcasses were being prepared for burning and burial, a task that would take four days, and reporters had given up asking why the stranding had happened to comment on the stench.

The man responsible for coordinating scientific work at the stranding, thirty-three-year-old Bruce Mate, is well regarded by his colleagues. Deborah Duffield, a geneticist from Portland State University, reiterated the feelings of several when she said of him: "The most unusual thing was that he got all of us with our different, sometimes competing, interests to work together. You can't comprehend what an extraordinary achievement that is in a situation like this."

On the beach Mate was also the principal source of information for the press. Though he was courteous to interviewers and careful not to criticize a sometimes impatient approach, one suspected he was disturbed by the role and uncertain what, if anything, he owed the non-scientific community.

In his small, cramped office at the Marine Science Center in South Beach, Mate agreed that everyone involved—scientists, environmentalists, the police, the state agencies, the public—took views that were occasionally in opposition and that these views were often proprietary. He thought it was the business of science to obtain data and physical specimens on the beach, thereby acquiring rights of "ownership," and yet he acknowledged misgivings about this because he and others involved are to some extent publicly funded scientists.

The task that faced him was deceptively simple: get as much information as possible off the beach before the burning crews, nervous about a public-health hazard and eager to end the incident, destroyed the animals. But what about the way science dominated the scene, getting the police, for example, to keep the crowd away so science could exercise its proprietary interest? "I don't know how to cope with the public's desire to come and see. Letting those few people onto the beach would have precluded our getting that much more information to give to a much larger, national audience."

What about charges that science operated in a cold-blooded and, in the case of trying to collapse the whales' lungs, ignorant way? "Coming among these whales, watching them die and in some cases helping them to die—needless suffering is almost incomprehensible to me . . ." Mate paused, studied the papers on his desk, unsatisfied, it seemed, with his tack: ". . . there are moral and ethical questions here. It's like dealing with terminal cancer."

No one, he seemed to suggest, liked how fast it had all happened.

Had he been worried about anything on the beach? "Yes! I was appalled at the way professional people were going about [postmortems] without gloves. I was afraid for the Greenpeace people in a potentially life-threatening situation in the surf." He was also afraid that it would all get away from him because of the unknowns. What, in fact, *did* one save when faced with such an enormous amount of bone and tissue? But he came away happy. "This was the greatest scientific shot anyone ever had with large whales." After a moment he added, "If it happened tomorrow, we would be four times better."

Sitting at his desk, nursing a pinched nerve in his back, surrounded by phone messages from the press, he seemed seasoned.

Mate's twenty-seven-year-old graduate assistant, Jim Harvey, arrived on the beach at dawn on Sunday. At the first sight of the whales from the top of the dunes, strung out nose to flukes in a line five or six hundred yards long, the waves of a high tide breaking over them, Harvey simply sat down, awestruck at their size and number. He felt deeply sad, too, but as he drew near he felt "a rush of exhilaration, because there was so much information to be gathered." He could not get over the feeling, as he worked, of the size of them. (One afternoon a scientist stood confounded in a whale's abdomen, asking a colleague next to him, "Where's the liver?")

Deborah Duffield said of her experience on the beach: "It hurt me more than watching human beings die. I couldn't cope with the pain, the futility. . . . I just turned into myself. It brought out the scientist in me." Another scientist spoke of his hostility toward the sullen crowd, of directing that anger at himself, of becoming cold and going to work.

For Harvey and others, there was one incident that broke scientific concentration and brought with it a feeling of impropriety. Several scientists had started to strip blubber from a dead whale. Suddenly the whale next to it began pounding the beach with its flukes. The pounding continued for fifteen minutes—lifting and slamming the flukes to the left, lifting and slamming the flukes to the right.

When the animal quieted, they resumed work.

"Scientists rarely get a chance to express their feelings," Harvey said. "I was interested in other people's views, and I wanted to share mine, which are biological. I noticed some people who sat quietly for a long time behind the barriers in religious stances. I very much wanted to know their views. So many of the people who came down here were so sympathetic and full of concern—I wished I had the time to talk to them all." Harvey remembered something vividly. On the first day he put his face near the blowhole of one of the whales: a cylinder of clean, warm, humid air almost a foot in diameter blew back his hair.

"My view on it," said Joe Davis of the Oregon Parks Department, "wasn't the scientific part. My thought on it now is how nice it would have been to have been somewhere else." His smile falls between wryness and regret.

When something remarkable happens and bureaucrats take it for only a nuisance, it is often stripped of whatever mystery it may hold. The awesome becomes common. Joe Davis, park manager at Honeyman Dunes State Park, adjacent to the stranding, was charged by the state with getting rid of the whales. He said he didn't take a moment to wonder at the mystery of it.

If ethical problems beset scientists, and mystical considerations occupied other onlookers, a set of concerns more prosaic confronted the police and the Oregon Parks Department. On Sunday night, June 17, police arrested a man in a camouflage suit caught breaking teeth out of a whale's jaw with a hammer and chisel. That night (and the next, and the next) people continued to play games with the police. The Parks Department, for its part, was faced with the disposal of five hundred tons of whale flesh that county environmental and health authorities said they couldn't burn—the solution to the problem at Playa San Rafael—and scientists said couldn't be buried. If buried, the carcasses would become hard envelopes of rotting flesh, the internal organs would liquefy and leach out onto the beach, and winter storms would uncover the whole mess.

This controversy, the public-health question, what to do about excessive numbers of press people, and concern over who was going to pay the bill (the Forest Service had donated tools, vehicles, and labor, but two bulldozers had had to be hired, at a hundred dollars and sixty dollars an hour) precipitated a meeting in Florence on Tuesday morning, June 19. A Forest Service employee, who asked not to be identified, thought the pressures that led to the meeting marked a difference between those who came to the beach out of compassion and genuine interest and those for whom it was "only a headache."

The principal issue, after an agreement was reached to burn the whales, then bury them, was who was going to pay. The state was reluctant; the scientists were impoverished. (It would be months before Mate would begin to recover $5,000 of his own money advanced to pay for equipment, transportation, and bulldozer time. "No one wants to fund work that's finished," Mate observed sardonically.) Commercial firms were averse to donating burning materials, or even transportation for them; G.P. Excavating of Florence did reduce rental fees on its bulldozers by about one-third and "broke even" after paying its operators.

The state finally took responsibility for the disposal and assumed the $25,000 cleanup bill, but it wanted to hear nothing about science's wish to salvage skeletons—it wanted the job finished.* Arrangements were made to bring in a crew of boys from the Young Adult Conservation Corps, and the Forest Service, always, it seemed, amenable, agreed to donate several barrels of Alumagel, a napalmlike substance.

---

* Three months later, on September 6, 1979, an eighty-five-foot female blue whale washed ashore in Northern California. Ensuing argument over responsibility for disposal prevented scientists from going near the whale until September 13, by which time it had been severely battered on the rocks and vandalized.

It was further decided to ban the public from the beach during the burning, for health and safety reasons. Only the disposal crews, scientists, police, and selected press would be admitted. The criterion for press admittance was possession of "a legitimate press card."

The role of the press at such events is somewhat predictable. They will repeatedly ask the same, obvious questions; they will often know little of the science involved; occasionally they will intimidate and harass in order to ascertain (or assign) blame. An upper-level Forest Service employee accused the press of asking "the most uninteresting and intimidating kinds of questions." A State Parks employee felt the press fostered dissension over who was going to pay for the disposal. He was also angry with newspaper people for ignoring "the human side," the fact that many state police troopers worked long hours of overtime, and that Forest Service employees performed a number of menial tasks in an emotionally charged environment of rotting flesh. "After a week of sixteen-hour days, your nerves are raw, you stink, you just want to get away from these continual questions."

In the press's defense, the people who objected most were those worried about criticism of their own performance and those deeply frustrated by the trivialization of the event. The press—probing, perhaps inexpertly—made people feel no more than their own misgivings.

The publisher of the local *Siuslaw News*, Paul Holman, said before it was over that the whale stranding had become a nuisance. When police closed the road to the beach, a man in a stateside truck began ferrying people the four and a half miles to the whales for a dollar each. And a dollar back. The local airport, as well as tourist centers offering seaplane rides, were doing a "land-office business" in flyovers. Gas station operators got tired of telling tourists how to get to the beach. The Florence City Hall was swamped with calls about the burning, one from a man who was afraid his horses would be killed by the fallout on his pasture. Dune-buggy enthusiasts were angry at whale people who for two days blocked access to their hill-climbing area.

Whatever its interest, the press was largely gone by Monday afternoon. As the burning and burying commenced, the number of interested scientists also thinned. By Wednesday there were only about thirty people left on the beach. Bob Adams, acting director of the Lane Regional Air Pollution Authority, was monitoring the smoke. Neal Langbehn of the National Marine Fisheries Service stood guard over a pile of plastic-wrapped sperm whale jaws. Michael Graybill led a team flensing out skulls. The state fretted over a way to keep the carcasses burning. (It would finally be done with thousands of automobile and truck tires, cordwood, diesel fuel, and Alumagel.) As Mate watched he considered the threshold of boredom in people, and mourned the loss, among other things, of forty-one sperm whale skeletons.

A journalist, one of the last two or three, asked somebody to take her picture while she stood with a small poodle in her arms in front of the burning pits.

As is often the case with such events, what is salvaged is as much due to goodwill as it is to expertise. The Forest Service was widely complimented for helping, and Stafford Owen, the acting area ranger at the agency's Oregon Dunes National Recreation Area during the incident, tried to say why: "Most of us aren't highly educated people. We have had to work at a variety of things all our lives—operating a chain saw, repairing a truck engine, running a farm. We had the skills these doctors and scientists needed."

A soft-spoken colleague, Gene Large, trying to elaborate but not to make too much of himself, said, "I don't think the scientists had as much knowledge [of large mammalian anatomy] as I did. When it came to it, I had to show some of them where the ribs were." After a moment, Large said, "Trying to cut those whales open with a chain saw was like trying to slaughter a beef with a pen knife. I didn't enjoy any part of it," Large said of the dismembering with chain saws and winches. "I think the older you get, the more sensitive you get." He mentioned an older friend who walked away from a dead, fifteen-foot, near-term fetus being lifted out of a gutted whale, and for a time wouldn't speak.

On Wednesday afternoon the whales were ignited in pits at the foot of the foredune. As they burned they were rendered, and when their oil caught fire they began to boil in it. The seething roar was muffled by a steady onshore breeze; the oily black smoke drifted southeast over the dunes, over English beach grass and pearly everlasting, sand verbena, and the purple flowers of beach pea, green leaves of sweet clover, and the bright yellow blooms of the monkey flower. It thinned until it disappeared against a weak-blue sky.

While fire cracked the blubber of one-eyed, jawless carcasses, a bulldozer the size of a two-car garage grunted in a trench being dug to the north for the last of them. These were still sprawled at the water's edge.

Up close, the black, blistered skin, bearing scars of knives and gouging fingernails, looked like the shriveled surface of a pond evaporated beneath a summer sun. Their gray-blue innards lay about on the sand like bags of discarded laundry. Their purple tongues were wedged in retreat in their throats. Spermaceti oil dripped from holes in their heads, solidifying in the wind to stand in translucent stalagmites twenty inches high. Around them were tidal pools opaque with coagulated blood and, beyond, a pink surf.

As far as I know, no novelist, no historian, no moral philosopher, no scholar of Melville, no rabbi, no painter, no theologian had been on the beach. No one had thought to call them or to fly them in. At the end they would not have been allowed past the barricades.

The whales made a sound, someone had said, like the sound a big fir makes breaking off the stump just as the saw is pulled away. A thin screech.

FARLEY MOWAT

# A Whale for the Killing

Although my attempts to gain insight into the lives of the Finners [finback whales] were bound to be frustratingly inadequate, because I could only encounter them at the interface between air and water, I occasionally had a stroke of luck. Lee Frankham, a friend who was the pilot of a Beaver airplane on floats and who sometimes came visiting and took us joyriding along the coast, was responsible for one such happy accident.

On a July day in 1964 we flew off with him to visit the abandoned settlement of Cape La Hune, Uncle Art's one-time home. It was a cloudless afternoon and the cold coastal waters were particularly pellucid and transparent. As we were crossing the broad mouth of White Bear Bay, Lee suddenly banked the Beaver and put her into a shallow dive. When he levelled out at less than a hundred feet, we were flying parallel to a family of six Fin Whales.

They were in line abreast and only a few feet below the surface. As seamen would say: they were making a passage under forced draft. Lee estimated they were doing all of twenty knots.

He throttled back almost to stall speed and we slowly circled them.

FARLEY MOWAT has written more than twenty-five books, including *Never Cry Wolf, People of the Deer,* and *The Desperate People.* His passion for wildlife and for the people of Canada's Far North make each of his books compelling. This essay is adapted from *A Whale for the Killing,* published in the United States in 1972 by Little, Brown. Reprinted by permission of the author.

From our unique vantage point, they were as clearly visible as if they had been in air, or we in water, and we could see minute details of their bodies and of their actions. Yet if it had not been that their swift progress underwater was relative to a light wind-popple on the surface, it would have been hard to believe they were progressing at all.

Their mighty tails and flukes which, unlike the tails of fishes, work vertically, swept lazily up and down with what appeared to be a completely effortless beat. Their great, paddle-like flippers—remnants of the forelimbs of their terrestrial ancestors—barely moved at all, for these organs serve mainly as stabilizers and as diving planes.

There was no visible turbulence in the water although the whales were moving at a rate of knots which few of man's submarines can equal when submerged. The overall effect was of six exquisitely streamlined bodies hovering in the green sea and seeming to undulate just perceptibly, as if their bodies were composed of something more subtle and responsive than ordinary flesh and bones. There was a suggestion of sinuosity, of absolute fidelity, to some powerful but unheard aquatic rhythm.

They were supremely beautiful beings.

"It's like watching a fantastic ballet," was Claire's response. "Perfect control and harmony! They aren't *swimming* through the water . . . *they're dancing through it!*"

Dancing? It seemed a wildly imaginative concept for I knew these beasts weighed seventy or eighty tons apiece. And yet I cannot better Claire's description.

Man, being a terrestrial beast of rather rigid perceptivity, is limited in his ability to conceive of alien beings except in terrestrial terms. In attempting to convey something of the magnitude of the great whales, men have inevitably compared them with the largest dinosaurs that ever lived (the great whales are much larger), or with the largest surviving land animal, the elephant . . . "a herd of twelve African elephants could be contained inside the skin of one Blue Whale."

Even more misleading is the concept we have formed of the great whales from looking at them stranded on a beach or hauled up on the flensing plan at a whaling factory. Out of its own element (and stone dead in the bargain) one of the great whales becomes a monstrous lump of a thing: a shapeless and gigantic sack, loosely stuffed with meat and guts and fat, only remotely identifiable with the living, functioning entity it once was.

The living whale is something else. The all-too-brief period during which we watched the Fin family crossing White Bear Bay was a revelation. We were all three of us made sharply aware that these creatures were paragons of grace who had achieved a harmonious relationship to the world of waters such as man will never know in air or on the land, in nature or in art.

About ten minutes after we first saw them, the whales rose as one, surfaced, blew and inhaled several times, then sounded while still moving at full speed and without leaving more than a few faint ripples. Since they have excellent vision in air as well as in water, they may have seen our plane. In any event, when they sounded they went deep, shimmering and diminishing in our view as if they were sliding down a long, unseen chute leading to the privacy of the abyssal depths.

Since the last World War men have become very interested in how whales move so swiftly and smoothly in both the horizontal and vertical planes of their three-dimensional world. This interest has not been prompted by admiration or even by true scientific curiosity, but rather by the desire of human warriors to build better submarines with which more effectively to destroy one another. This curiosity, perverted though it be, has led to some fascinating discoveries about the whale as a machine; and everything science has discovered has strengthened the conclusion that whales are among the most highly perfected forms of life ever to dwell upon this planet.

One thing that sadly puzzled early investigators was the question of how a whale could achieve its great speeds with such a "rudimentary" power source as living muscle, and such a simple transmitter of power to water as a pair of flukes. Streamlining was obviously a part of the answer, but only a part. Most modern submarines are almost slavishly streamlined after whale pattern but, even so, and even when equipped with engines and propellers of maximum mechanical efficiency, they can only achieve speeds comparable to those of whales by expending many times the amount of energy. The secret seems to lie in the fact that the submarine is a rigid object and the whale is not. Experiments in test tanks with those little whales, the dolphins, show that the illusion Claire, Lee and I thought we were experiencing—that of seeing a sort of shimmering undulation in the dancing Fins—was no illusion at all.

Apparently the outer layers of a whale-skin, blubber, and the immediate underlying layers of connective tissue—have the capacity to simulate fluids in motion, almost as if they were themselves a liquid substance. This strange quality produces what hydrodynamic experts refer to as laminar flow, an effect which almost eliminates the normal turbulence produced by an object moving rapidly through water. Laminar flow has the effect (if one can imagine this) of lubricating the whale's body so there is almost no friction or drag. Although I am by no means certain the scientists fully understand what laminar flow is all about, they have certainly recognized its effectiveness. They have discovered, for example, that a dolphin of the same relative mass as a modern torpedo can attain torpedo speed with an expenditure of only one-tenth the energy.

A classic case illustrating the whale's efficiency is referred to by Ivan Sanderson in his fine book, *Follow the Whale*. An 800-horsepower catcher harpooned an 80-foot Blue Whale which then proceeded to tow the catcher, whose engine was running *full speed astern*, a distance of fifty miles at speeds up to eight knots! It was not brute power which made this feat possible. No, it was the almost unimaginable efficiency achieved by the whale's near-total adaptation to the aquatic medium.

We do not know the highest speeds attainable by whales. Some smaller species have been accurately clocked at 27 knots. The misnamed Killer Whale can evidently exceed 30 knots in short spurts, and Fin Whales have been seen to outrun Killers! However, unlike men, Fin Whales probably do not worship speed as an end in itself. For the most part they seem content just to loaf along, conserving energy, at a modest six to seven knots.

Although we are beginning to learn a little something about the mechanics of the whale as a living machine, we still know very little about the nature of whale society.

The toothed whales, which are more primitive than the baleen, seem to prefer extended family groupings rather like those of baboons and many monkeys. Such groups may include a hundred or more individuals. Polygamy, or at least random mating, seems to be the general rule among the toothed whales. All members of the group or tribe have mutual but generalized responsibilities toward one another. Mature males, or in some cases mature females, may assume leadership roles but all "hands" appear equally concerned with the well-being of the young. When a member of the group is injured, or endangered, all the adults within reach will rally to its assistance. There are many well-authenticated reports of toothed whales physically supporting a sick companion so that it can rise to the surface and breathe. And what is almost unique in the animal world, toothed whales of one species will sometimes come to the assistance of an individual of quite a *different* species.

Among the baleen whales, the social structure seems to be based on the closed family unit. I am convinced that each Fin Whale pod is actually a "nuclear" family consisting of a mated pair of adults, accompanied by the calf of the year plus one or several earlier and as yet unmated offspring. The Fin is not only monogamous, it evidently mates for life, and the bonds between a mated pair are extraordinarily close and tenacious.

Although Finners are strongly family oriented, they are also social in a broader sense. There are reports, dating back to the days when whales were still plentiful, of aggregations of as many as 300 Fins gathered together in one small portion of the sea. These were gatherings of family groups, rather than of individuals. Some whalers believed these gatherings took place two or three times a year and were in the nature of festivals at which unmated whales conducted their courtships in order to establish new family units.

The largest number of Finners seen at Burgeo, after the return of the species to the Newfoundland coast, gathered among the islands during the winter of 1964–65. There were five discrete pods numbering thirty or thirty-one individuals in total. Although some of the families might temporarily come together, and even remain together for a day or two, they would eventually separate again. Each family maintained its own cohesion and each had its own preferred fishing grounds.

The winter of 1964–65 saw the peak and the beginning of the decline of the re-occupation of the south Newfoundland seas by the several species of rorquals. Word of their return had spread all too rapidly until it came to the ears of the Norwegians, who, by that time, in company with the British, Japanese, Dutch and Russians, had swept the Antarctic waters almost clean.

While Claire and I were away in the winter of 1966–67, the whales' friends in Burgeo awaited the annual visit of the Finners with foreboding. It was common knowledge that 1966 had been a very good year for the [whalers] and that no great whales had been seen "in passage" by any of our local draggers throughout the autumn months. However, during the first week of December, Uncle Art was delighted to discover they had returned.

It was a sadly diminished band—a single family numbering five individuals.

Throughout most of December these five spent their time, as of old, in the runs among the islands; but during Christmas week their quiet occupancy was challenged by several big British Columbia herring seiners. These great steel vacuum cleaners began sucking up the herring with a restlessness that was terrifying to behold. Working so close to land that they several times swept away nets belonging to local fishermen, they roused the wrath of Burgeo; but the intruders did not care about the nets, the wrath, or about whales either. On one occasion Uncle Art reported seeing a seiner make what looked like a deliberate ramming run at a surfacing Finner. If it was deliberate, then it was also foolhardy, since a collision between ship and whale would have been disastrous to both.

The whales did not take to the newcomers. According to Onie and Uncle Art, they seemed uneasy in their presence. This is understandable since seiners and whale catchers are driven by diesel engines that must sound ominously alike.

A few days after the arrival of the seiners, the Fin family abandoned the island runs and shifted eastward to a little fiord called The Ha Ha and the nearby mouth of Bay De Loup, except when the seiners were absent delivering their catches to the reduction plant at Harbour Breton. It was on one such occasion, when only a single seiner was present, that Uncle Art and I stood on Messers Head and watched the whales demonstrate the superiority of their fishing techniques.

The whales were not alone in The Ha Ha. They shared it with several Burgeo fishermen working cod nets from open boats. When the whales moved in, these men were concerned for the safety of their nets. Two among them, the Hann brothers, Douglas and Kenneth—small, quiet, foxy-faced men from Muddy Hole—even considered moving their gear to some safer ground.

" 'Twarn't as we t'ought they'd tear up our gear a-purpose-like," Douglas Hann remembered, "but The Ha Ha is a right small place and not much water at the head of she. We t'ought, what with six fleets of nets scattered round, them whales was bound to run foul of some of them . . . couldn't help theirselves. Well, sorr, they never did. Sometimes when we'd be hauling a net they'd pass right under the boat close enough you could have scratched their backs with a gaff. First off, when they did that, we used to bang the oars on the side of the boat and yell to make them veer away; but after a time we sees they knowed what they was about, and was going to keep clear without no help from we.

"Still and all, 'twas scary enough betimes. One evening our engine give out. We had the big trap skiff and no tholepins for the oars so we had to scull her along. It were coming on duckish [i.e., dark] and we was alone in The Ha Ha and them whales begun coming up all round. They was only six fathom of water where we was to, and they was after the herring like big black bullets. We could hear the swoosh when they drove by, and foam would fair bile up where they took a big mouthful out of a herring school.

"I'd as soon have been home in me kitchen, I can tell you, but them whales is some smart navigators, for they never come nigh enough to do we any hurt. We was an hour poking our way to the pushthrough what leads into Aldridges Pond, and them whales stayed right along of we. Toward the end of it they give up fishing and just come along like they knowed we was into some kind of a kettle. Ken, he said maybe they was offering we a tow; but I suppose that's only foolishness."

What the Hanns told me of their experience reminded me of a story I had heard some years earlier from a very old man at Hermitage Bay, many miles to the eastward. As a youth this man had been employed at a whale factory in Gaultois, on the north shore of Hermitage Bay. His home was five miles across the full breadth of the bay, but on weekends he would row over to spend Sunday with his family.

One Saturday afternoon he was homeward bound when he saw a pod of Finners. There were three of them, and they were behaving in a peculiar fashion. Instead of briefly surfacing and then sounding again, they were cruising on the top. Their course converged with his, and as they drew close, my friend saw that they were swimming, as he put it, "shoulder to shoulder." The centre whale was blowing much more rapidly than the rest and its spray was pink in colour.

"'Twarn't hard to know what was the trouble," the old man remembered. "Yon middle whale had been harpooned and the iron had drawed and he'd got clear of the catcher boat. The bomb must have fired, but not deep enough for to kill he.

"I laid back on me oars, not wantin' to get too handy to them three, but they never minded I . . . just steamed slow as you please right past me boat, heading down the bay and out to sea. They was close enough so I could near swear the two outside whales was holding up the middle one. I t'inks they done it with their flippers. That's what I t'inks.

"When they was all clear, I rowed on home. Never t'ought no more about it. About the middle of the week a schooner puts in to Gaultois and the skipper was telling how he come across three whales outside Green Island. They was right on top of the water, he says, and never sounding at all, and making a slow passage to eastward. The skipper, he held over toward they, but when it looked like they was all going to go afoul of one another he had to alter course, for they had no mind to sound no matter what he did. When he passed alongside he saw the middle whale had a girt hole in his back.

"I made certain 'twas the same three I come across and 'twas agreed by all hands 'twas the same whale was harpooned by one of our boats that Saturday morning and got away. They two other whales took the sick one off someplace . . . some said 'twas to the whales' burying ground . . . but all I knows is they kept that sick one afloat somehow for five days, and close onto sixty miles."

GERARD GORMLEY

# Orcas of the Gulf

Mid-August. Over cobalt-blue water eighty miles south of Nantucket, Massachusetts, an albatross soared in the early morning light. Since sunrise the wind had been freshening out of the southwest, opposing the prevailing current and raising steep waves, but the weather was fair. Apart from a diagonal brushstroke of cirrus cloud far to the north, the sky was a flawless blue vault, the air so clear that the albatross could see waves crimping the horizon six miles away.

Pointing upwind when it wished to slow and examine the surface, swinging off the wind to speed up, the great bird followed a habitat interface marked by a change of sea color from cobalt to green. Now and again the bird swooped down to snatch food from a wave, then swung back into the wind and rose some fifty feet before resuming its zigzag course. Rarely did it need to beat its slender, ten-foot wings.

Twelve orcas came into view, swimming eastward over the continental shelf break. Like the albatross, they were following the habitat interface, but in the opposite direction. The pod's youngsters leapt from wave to wave. The adults maintained a more leisurely pace, boring through the eight-foot seas with fluid ease, their bodies straddling the troughs as they left one wave and penetrated the next.

---

GERARD GORMLEY's books include *A Dolphin Summer,* published in 1985, and *Orcas of the Gulf,* published by Sierra Club Books in 1990, from which this selection is taken. He is a winner of the John Burroughs Medal for distinguished nature writing. Reprinted by permission of Sierra Club Books.

The albatross turned and followed the orcas, but seeing no signs of feeding from which it might be able to scavenge, it soon swung back into the wind and moved out of sight.

The orca pod included two bulls, marked by their high dorsal fins and heavyset builds. Though not much longer than the cows, they were much stockier. One bull, a twenty-two-footer with scarcely a mark on his body, looked recently matured. The other was nearly thirty feet long and weighed eight tons. His back was laced with crisscross scars and pockmarks. Three bullet holes had perforated his dorsal fin, which was as tall as a man and came to a curly point. His sides bore puckered dents from tissue lost in accidents or fights. His teeth, the size and shape of half bananas, were darkened and worn. The gum tissue on the right side of his jaw was swollen as big as a seal's head. The two bulls seemed clearly related. Their dorsal fins were tipped with similar wavy hooks, and both bulls bore unusual gray chevrons on their left flippers.

Leading the pod was a twenty-four-foot cow at least as old as the ailing bull. She and he had identical gray patches behind their dorsal fins and similar white patterns on the undersides of their flukes. Her left flipper had a chevron similar to his, and her saddle patch and fluke patterns suggested kinship at least to the old bull, if not to both males. Her dorsal fin, a third as large as theirs, had no genetic tale to tell, but an old fisheries tag embedded in the base of her fin bore a 1919 date.

In addition to the old cow and two mature bulls, the pod included three other cows, two immature males, and four immature females, one of them a nine-foot suckling still showing the pointed snout and pink patches characteristic of first-year orcas. Soon her snout would round out and the pink would fade to ivory. By the time she was a year old, she would sport the same jet black and snowy white coloration as the adults.

Staying to one side of the pod, the old bull swam with his mouth partly open to cool his infected jaw. At one point he gnashed his teeth as if in pain, and the growth spewed bloody pus. A cow drew alongside him and uttered a lengthy pulsed phrase that sounded like a creaking door hinge. As she sonared the bull's swollen jaw and tried to investigate it with her tongue, he patted her with his flipper, then gently pushed her away.

White bellies flashing, two young males corkscrewed underneath the bull, then together shot out of the water ahead of the pod and bellywhopped. They wriggled and rolled against each other, dove, and popped up on opposite sides of the pod. As they bobbed in the wave crests, whistling to each other, the younger bull slipped a six-foot flipper under one of them and upended him. Buzzing like a chain saw, the juvenile chased the bull and hurdled him. With amazing agility the bull did a snap roll and snatched the youngster out of the air with his great paddlelike flippers, then hugging him against his chest, completed the roll and pulled him under. Apparently in need of air, the young male struggled desperately to get free. The bull held him underwater a while longer, then released him, rolled, and spanked him hard with his five-foot dorsal fin. The youngster rejoined his playmate, and they resumed their antics.

As the pod entered an area where great currents were colliding, the waves became steeper and lost all semblance of rhythm. Rather than waste energy fighting the craggy seas, the orcas began swimming in a series of shallow dives, each lasting about seven minutes. As they swam, they simultaneously called to each other and probed the sea with sharp pulses of sound. Their sonar clicks picked up a school of hake far below, but they did not give chase. Orcas typically prefer not to dive much deeper than 15 fathoms, though if necessary they can plunge many times that depth.

From all directions came a commotion of natural and mechanical sounds, but the orcas' sharp sonar clicks and strident communication calls stood out sharply from the background noise, so they had no interference problems. Still, they often remained silent for extended periods, the better to take prey by surprise, or simply to assess various sounds for their survival value. Just now, for example, they heard slow cataracts of mud and sand hiss down along the shelf break 90 fathoms below and knew that the tide was ebbing from the Gulf of Maine. From 170 fathoms below and to their right came a *boing*, followed by heavy snapping sounds that told them sperm whales were down there, hunting squid. Deeper still and farther out, a submarine purred through the blackness. Listening through acoustic windows located in various parts of their bodies, orcas are able to monitor sounds from all directions without having to change course.

Overhead drifted a stray from the sapphire blue Gulf Stream, a Portuguese man-of-war, its body an iridescent bubble in the sunlight, its deadly purple tentacles trailing so deep that several orcas had to avoid them. As the pod surfaced for air, seventy saddleback dolphins came skipping along from the south, then sensed the orcas and swung back out to sea. Shortly afterward, fifty pilot whales rose out of the darkness, spotted the orcas, and went deep again without even taking air. When orcas are not hunting in earnest, many animals tolerate them to come close, even swim among them, but those included in the orcas' diet know when to stay clear. And this was one of those times.

The orcas had just returned to swimming depth when the old cow applied full drag with flippers and flukes, coasted to a stop, and hovered head down, listening. The others followed her example. The keenly alert old cow had detected a faint sizzle of turbulence as two large bodies sped through the darkness far below the pod. Judging by the bottom sounds that framed the racing whispers, the unseen animals were inside the shelf break. That meant they could be no more than 90 fathoms deep. A quick estimate of angular velocity, based on past experience, told the orcas that the creatures below them were reaching speeds of forty knots. Such speed suggested bluefin tuna or some other warm-blooded sprinter equally good to eat. Still silent, the orcas listened and waited.

The faint hiss of cavitation faded, suggesting that the animals had plunged over the shelf break, but soon the sound returned, growing louder and louder. Moments later a ten-foot swordfish flashed out of the depths ahead of the pod, with a large mako in pursuit some five fathoms below. The broadbill rocketed through the waves and soared twenty feet into the air, its purple-blue back and silver-gray undersides glistening in the sunlight. A second later the mako, twelve feet of driving muscle sheathed in iridescent blue and snowy white, burst through the surface and bared its long curved teeth. It seemed certain to intercept the broad-bill in midair and rip out its belly, but just as the shark broke water, the swordfish executed a marvelous maneuver. Throwing off a great arch of sparkling spray, the fish jackknifed, pointed its sword downward and plunged like a living harpoon. The three-foot sword rammed into the mako's open mouth and burst through the back of its skull. With a heavy slap the two fish struck the water, then rolled over and over, the mako snapping off teeth as it tried to bite through the sword. The combined strength of the combatants severed the sword two feet from the tip, leaving the mako permanently impaled and unable to use its jaws effectively. Massive volumes of blood billowed darkly from its head. It tried to escape, but brain damaged, could only swim in circles.

The orcas approached. Seemingly oblivious to them, the broadbill rammed the mako with its splintered remnant of sword. As the broadbill circled to make another charge, the young bull orca darted in and sev-ered its tail, then the mako's. Neatly biting off thick steaks of firm flesh, the orcas consumed the broadbill and the mako, leaving only their heads to spiral into the depths, joined in death as they sank to the bottom. For all their great size, the mako and broadbill had yielded only a few hundred pounds of meat. Divided among eleven orcas (the suckling took little solid food as yet), that amounted to a mere snack for each.

A while later, again moving silently near the surface, the orcas surprised two eighty-foot blue whales that nearly swam right over them. Defecating in alarm, the whales took deep breaths, popped their nostrils shut, and sounded. By the time their flukes arched gracefully beneath the waves, the whales were making fifteen knots and were quickly working their way toward twenty. With scarcely a glance at the blue whales, the orcas continued on their way. Perhaps they were not quite hungry enough to take on such swift, powerful prey, for a well-fed blue whale that size weighs over a hundred tons.

The calf of that year, swimming safe and snug between her mother and the old bull, squealed and nuzzled her mother. The cow twisted her flippers, more winglike than the bull's broad paddles, and rolled onto her side. Still on the move, the calf pressed against her mother's belly and nursed. While the pod slowed to accommodate cow and calf, two juvenile females rubbed against the younger mature bull and excited him, then coquettishly avoided his advances. A juvenile male tried to nurse along with the calf and was rebuffed.

When the calf had drunk her fill, the pod resumed its original pace, about the speed of a brisk walk. The calf napped on the move, once again safely tucked between her mother and one of the bulls. For the better part of an hour the pod ambled along, staying generally over the shelf break.

From somewhere west of the pod came a cupped clap of sound. Still silent, the orcas spyhopped and scanned the area. They saw a minke clear the water and come down on its belly with a loud splash. The orcas headed that way.

Minutes later they came within sight of the minke, which was so busy feeding on mackerel stunned by its breaching that it did not sense the danger until too late. While most of the orcas spread out behind the whale, the younger bull circled wide ahead of it and doubled back. Frightened by the approaching pod, the minke sped up and tried to go deep, but the bull was waiting. With a broadside body block that could be heard for a mile, he slammed into the minke and slowed it down, then seized its sharply pointed snout in his jaws and held the whale in place.

Although the minke was twenty-five feet long, several feet longer than its attacker, it could not break the orca's grip. The minke went limp, then began to shudder and moan.

The rest of the orcas arrived, trailed by the senior bull, who merely looked on while one cow seized the minke's flukes and another sank her teeth into its genital slit and ripped open the skin. Then, while she gripped the flap of loose skin, the other cow and the young bull began to roll. They spun the minke like a piece of work being turned on a lathe, skinning it so neatly that it began to look like a freshly peeled fruit. As each long sheet of skin and subcutaneous fat was peeled away from the blubber, the orcas divided it among themselves, the senior bull getting first share. It took some twenty minutes to flay the minke, which through it all continued to shudder and moan. Surprisingly little blood was shed, but the surface all around became covered with a film of oil that formed rainbows and made water bead up on the orcas' backs. The youngest orcas watched the first part of the skinning process, then lost interest and began playing nearby.

The two adults who had been holding the minke shared the last sheet of skin between them, nibbled away the minke's lips, then forced open the whale's mouth and ripped out its tongue. Hemorrhaging massively, the minke went limp and appeared to lose consciousness. The orcas shared the tongue among themselves, leaving the rest of the minke, its blubber intact, to scavengers. Still bleeding heavily from the mouth, its flayed body glowing grotesquely orange against the dark depths, the minke sank slowly out of sight.

During the hour or so that the orcas fed on the minke, hundreds of sharks had been attracted to the scene. As some took exploratory bites on the sunken whale, the minke came to and made a feeble attempt to swim away, but then the sharks struck in force and brought its suffering to a bloody climax. Frothy pink bubbles rose and burst. Scraps of blubber floated to the surface. Scavenging jaegers mobbed the area, darting and swooping over the surface, fiercely contesting every morsel.

Slowly the sounds of ripping flesh became fainter and then inaudible as the orcas drifted back toward the shelf break. While the elders napped at the surface, the youngsters darted among them, chasing each other and anything else that came within range. The younger bull rolled belly-up and let the suckling calf ride on his belly. When he needed air, he rolled and gently dumped her to one side. She tried to swim atop his back and failing that, returned to her mother's flank. The bull moved close, affording the calf a snug space between himself and her mother.

When the shelf break was once again audible below them, the orcas resumed their eastward course, sonaring as they went. They soon began receiving strong echoes from a school of halibut that had ventured near the surface to feed. The orcas took air, went deep, and spread out. Without subjecting themselves to uncomfortable depths, they were able to dive below the halibut and herd them up against the surface, where the orcas easily outmaneuvered the frantic fish. The pod's two big bulls, despite their heavy builds and tall wobbly dorsal fins, staged an impressive show of speed and agility, turning tighter and tighter circles until their chosen halibut were caught.

Although the big bull had the look of a fading old scrapper who kept himself going on sheer grit, he was the first to catch a halibut. The catching proved easier than the eating, though. The hundred-pound flatfish was five feet long and half as wide, far too big to swallow whole, and the bull's infected jaw made it difficult for him to tear the flapping fish into pieces. The powerful halibut's struggles must have caused the bull great pain, for suddenly he flipped it over his back and struck it a mighty blow with his flukes. The halibut soared thirty feet into the air, hit the surface with a heavy slap, and lay there stunned. Four juvenile orcas shared it among themselves, then hurried to catch up with the others.

Moving sometimes in a cluster, other times in twos or threes, the orcas seemed to dislike doing anything the same way for very long. Now and then an adult surfaced and left a fish for a juvenile. All in all, though, pickings were lean for the next hour or so. As if swimming randomly until a meal presented itself, the orcas cast this way and that along the shelf break.

Outside the northeast shelf break lies a thirty-mile-wide belt of blue-green "slope" water, so called because it flows over the continental slope, where the bottom drops one mile in ten. Here cold currents from the Gulf of Maine and Nova Scotia are tempered by the Gulf Stream, keeping slope water temperatures near 50°F year around and making the region a favorite wintering place for many species of fish and mammals.

North of the pod's present position lie Nantucket Shoals. Ahead, in sunlit shallows above vast submarine mesas, are some of the world's richest fisheries. Over Georges Bank, Browns Bank, and several smaller inshore banks, giant bluefin tuna and other prime prey begin feeding in spring. By August of each year they have fattened themselves into prime condition. It is then, between July and September, that orcas are most frequently seen inside the Gulf of Maine. They are not seen in the gulf every year, though they may be there and simply go unreported.

The orcas are about to enter an area of great mixing. Cold tidal out-flow from the Gulf of Maine, discharged through Great South Channel between Cape Cod and Georges Bank, spills southward over the edge of the continental shelf and collides with prevailing deep-ocean currents and warm eddies from the Gulf Stream. This meeting stirs the sea to great depths, mixing cold and warm water with bottom nutrients and exposing the mixture to the energizing effects of sunlight. The resulting vitalization supports a tremendous abundance of life, while the diversity of habitats along the shelf break fosters a great diversity of life. This general rule—that habitat diversity seems to foster species diversity—is particularly true of habitat interfaces such as the shelf break. Where forest meets meadow, for example, you usually find a greater diversity of species than in forest or meadow alone.

The air remained clear and bright, the sea spangled with light. For miles around the sky was still cloudless, but far away a thunderhead grew tree-like on a dark trunk of rain.

As the orcas continued northeastward over the shelf break, they felt the prevailing westward current joined by a colder flow from the north. The upper waters began to swarm with sand lances, short-finned squid, and many species of fish that had gathered to prey on sand lances and each other. Picking off what squid and fish they could without exerting themselves, for energy would be wasted in pursuit of small prey, the orcas turned northward into Great South Channel. Within minutes the water temperature dropped from 65°F to 55°F.

The old bull opened his mouth wide and curled his tongue to chan-nel the cooler water against his abscessed jaw. He passed the old cow, who had stopped and was facing northeast, listening to something. The others doubled back and gathered around her. The old bull circled the pod and continued to cool his swollen jaw. The two immature males began butting each other and splashing noisily. With an outcry that sounded like the clang of a heavy iron gate, the old cow silenced them.

Several kittiwakes appeared out of the southwest and passed over-head, their wingbeats rapid, their flight path straight and purposeful. The old cow reared back with her head above the surface and watched the kittiwakes fly out of sight. Now a dozen greater shearwaters appeared over the southeast horizon, flying in the same general direction as the kittiwakes. From the south and not far behind the shearwaters came a flock of skuas. Three different species of birds seemed to be converging on a spot miles to the northeast. The old cow made a guttural sound akin to a gargle. The young bull repeated the sound, and together they led the pod northeastward. The ailing bull followed.

A five-mile swim brought them within sight of some thirty humpback whales, which were diving under schools of sand lances, then blowing great clouds of bubbles that drove the small fish to the surface and concealed the whales as they rose to swallow their prey. The roaring sound made as the whales released air underwater was similar to the old orca cow's guttural signal.

Kittiwakes, shearwaters, and skuas were feeding on fish spilled from whales' mouths at the surface. Just below the surface, a dozen giant bluefin tuna swam alongside the humpbacks to catch sand lances dribbling from the whales' mouths. Some of the humpbacks slapped the tuna away with their flippers.

One humpback detected the orcas and trumpeted a warning. The bluefin tuna fled the area at speeds approaching five knots. The humpbacks broke off their feeding and gathered in small groups at the surface. Nursing cows and their escorts protectively flanked calves that, though thirty feet long, were still nursing and quite dependent. The adult humpbacks' breathing became rapid and took on a wheezing sound.

The orcas dove and swam below the herd while the humpbacks remained at the surface, flippers and flukes curled inward to protect their underbellies. Shafts of sunlight, redirected by surface chop, probed the orcas' formation like flickering spotlights. Spiraling strings of bubbles formed by the sweep of humpback flippers and flukes sparkled in the light.

All at once the young orca bull sounded a chilling scream and flashed through the humpback herd, rushing one whale after another, passing so close to some that the tip of his dorsal fin grazed their bellies. As though swept up in the spirit of the hunt, most of the orcas followed the young bull's example. The water became clouded with the feces of frightened humpbacks.

Humpbacks are the slowest of the rorquals, toothless and seemingly defenseless, yet what promised to be a massive slaughter instead became a clash of titans. Bellowing and trumpeting like enraged elephants, the humpbacks lashed the sea white as they defended themselves against the streaking orcas. Flukes clapped like thunder. Flippers flashed like mammoth swords. And through this scene of awesome power the orcas—half the size of their prey—darted and weaved, screaming as they went, seeming to revel in the shrieking excitement as they whipped the humpbacks into a frenzy.

Meanwhile the old orca cow and bull, guarding the suckling calf, cruised well below the herd and gauged the humpbacks' reactions. It appeared that the orcas had hoped to stampede the humpbacks and pick off a straggler. If so, the strategy was failing, for the humpbacks were holding their positions.

Leaving the old bull to guard the calf, the senior cow recalled the attackers and signaled a change in tactics. Led by the old cow, the orcas began seizing humpbacks by the flukes, then darting clear as the various rorquals proved able to defend themselves. Moving in pairs through the herd, the orcas thus attacked one after another of the humpbacks. The rorquals suffered little more than deep scratches, for the orcas were merely testing their strength and mettle.

Then the orcas came upon six adult humpbacks gathered at the surface with heads together and bodies extended like the arms of a gigantic starfish. The circle enclosed by their heads sheltered three calves. In this formation the adults could breathe at will and avoid attack from above or ahead, while using flippers and flukes to protect their flanks and bellies. The orcas circled the formation and made feinting rushes, but the humpbacks lashed out with their flukes and repelled them.

Having completed one full circuit of the humpback herd, the old cow led her pod back about half a mile. There, at a signal from her, the orcas rushed a humpback calf flanked by its fifty-foot mother and her smaller male escort. The adult humpbacks began trumpeting and lashing the water white. It was remarkable how well the big whales maneuvered: they could swim forward or backward, wheel and turn within half their lengths, and whip their bodies into snap rolls that spun their fifteen-foot flippers like gigantic blades. Lashing out with their powerful flippers and flukes at any orcas that came within striking range, the two adult humpbacks kept the calf between them and defied their attackers.

Although the orcas outnumbered this humpback maternal group by ten to three (the ailing bull and suckling calf merely observed), five of the orcas were young and inexperienced. They tried to mob the calf, but with body blocks that sounded like big boats colliding, the adult humpbacks bumped them away and struck out at them. Colossal sheets of bubbles trailed from the humpbacks' one-ton flippers as they cut through the water in lethal edgewise chops. Even more dangerous were their flukes, which could strike above and below with crushing force or slash sideways with even greater speed and strength than the flippers. Although the orcas pressed the attack from all directions, they could not penetrate the humpbacks' defenses.

At a signal from the old cow, the orcas broke off the attack and left the area, but no sooner were they out of sight than they went deep and quietly circled back. When the humpbacks were once again visibly overhead, silhouetted against the surface glow, the orcas attacked silently out of the darkness.

The humpbacks sensed their approach, but too late. The young bull orca slammed into a calf and sank his teeth into its flank. An extraordinary clap of sound as the orca split open the young humpback's skin was followed by a gargantuan ripping noise as the bull spun and peeled away a foot-thick slab of blubber weighing at least a hundred pounds. The calf's blubber had separated from its underlying muscle tissue as cleanly as the peel from a thick-skinned orange.

Feces clouded the water, obscuring the orcas' vision as the humpback mother swung under her calf and lashed out at the attacking bull with flukes and flippers. The old orca cow sounded a loud danger call. Narrowly escaping injury, the young bull surfaced at a safe distance and settled down to eat. He was joined by the old bull and cow, with whom he readily shared his prize. The calf had been nursing for eight months and was in prime condition. Its blubber, which resembled stringy bacon, was apparently a great delicacy, for rather than wolfing it down, the orcas bit off ham-size chunks and seemed to savor each bite. While they ate, the rest of the pod attacked another trio of humpbacks.

Leaving the last portion of blubber for the ailing bull, the old cow and young bull went back for more.

Although not yet fully grown, the young bull was a formidable animal. He could streak through the sea at thirty knots, maneuver like a dolphin, and bite like a great white shark. As he matured, he would add another six feet and two or three tons and be a match for anything in the sea except perhaps a bull sperm whale. With maturity he would also acquire a bit more caution. Meanwhile, his cockiness sometimes got him into trouble, as was about to happen now.

Sounding a strident call, he darted ahead of the old cow and attacked an adult humpback that had become separated from the rest. The old cow and several others hurried over to help. While two cows seized the humpback's flippers and a third gripped its flukes, the young bull sank his teeth into the whale's genital slit and tried to rip open its belly. With a might born of desperation, the fifty-foot humpback freed its left flipper, which it swept downward in a vicious edgewise chop toward the young bull's back.

The old bull had finished the last of the blubber and was approaching the attack scene at the moment the humpback tore its flipper free. Seeing what was about to happen, the old bull accelerated from five to thirty knots within seconds and seized the humpback's flipper just before it struck the young bull. The old bull's momentum twisted the one-ton flipper safely clear, but the impact burst his abscess and dislodged two teeth already loosened by infection and bone damage. As he rolled clear and released his grip, sharp barnacles on the humpback's flipper lacerated his lips and tongue.

The big bull's charge threw the other orcas off balance, enabling the terrified humpback to break free and fight off its attackers long enough to reach a nearby group of other humpbacks. The orcas did not follow.

Bleeding heavily from his mouth, the old orca bull rested at the surface and gingerly flexed his jaw to make sure it was not broken. Then he used the tip of his tongue to probe his teeth. One was gone altogether. Another had been ripped halfway out of its socket and was sticking sideways into his mouth. Rolling and puffing in the swells, he prodded the loose tooth with his tongue and managed to push it out of his mouth. Blood now poured freely from both tooth sockets. Having no doubt put the worst of his pain behind him, after what may have been many months of suffering, he closed his eyes and rested. The young bull swam over and floated next to him.

The rest of the orcas made no further attempts to launch lethal attacks on the humpbacks. It may be more energy efficient to eat a fifty-ton whale than to chase down thousands of smaller animals, but even the most formidable predators must weigh efficiency against risk. Serious injury can mean death for any predator, and it appeared that the humpbacks in this herd were too strong and feisty for the orcas to make a kill.

Nonetheless, for an hour or more the orcas followed the herd, now and then separating some hapless humpback from a hundred or more pounds of its blubber. None of the rorquals was mortally injured, but many were left with wounds a foot deep and several feet across. The orcas fed primarily from the flanks, which the humpbacks had difficulty protecting. Little of the muscle tissue underlying the blubber was damaged. Some tried to force open the humpbacks' mouths to get at their tongues—which can weigh several tons apiece and are prized by orcas—but were unsuccessful.

At last the orcas left the humpbacks in peace and swam back to rejoin the bulls, who were now ten miles away, napping at the surface and calling occasionally to mark their position. The others gathered around them and went to sleep. Dozing in the current, they drifted back toward the shelf break.

Apparently too winded to dive, the humpbacks continued to wheeze and puff their way along the surface. Many left wakes greasy with oil and pink with blood. Some had lost hundreds of pounds of blubber. One would think that their suffering must be great, yet evidence indicates that a whale's blubber is fairly insensitive to pain. If so, the loss of a hundred-pound slab of blubber may be no worse an ordeal for a whale than is a badly skinned knee for a person.

After fifteen minutes or so, the humpbacks dove and headed northeastward.

A number of reliable observers have described orca attacks on minkes. In some cases, the orcas ate only the skin and subcutaneous fat layer. (This part of a seal, called *muk-tuk*, is relished by Inuit and polar bears.) Usually the orcas ate the tongue, as well. Sometimes all or most of the minke was eaten.

The minke attacked in this chapter suffered greatly, but this is not to suggest that orcas are particularly cruel. Lions often take hours to kill large prey, such as buffalo, and predation in general is a cruel business. As for orcas' habit of flaying whales, is it any more cruel than wild dogs eating the internal organs of a wildebeest while the hapless animal watches its own ordeal? And is either of these more cruel than a songbird dismembering a caterpillar and eating it alive? If we wince less at a caterpillar's demise, it is probably a matter of scale and whatever personal values we bring to these events.

The more sensitive among us may find comfort in the belief that prey animals go into shock and are spared the worst of their agony. We have no way of measuring another creature's pain, but the annals of surgery prior to the introduction of general anesthesia indicate that patients often screamed and struggled throughout lengthy operations. Many prey animals must suffer just as badly. For reasons unclear, nature has imposed cruel standards of suffering on its creatures. Imagine the pain wild animals like the old bull orca must endure when they develop severe infections or tumors.

Attacks like the preceding orca-humpback scene have been witnessed on three different occasions by Canadian biologist Hal Whitehead over Grand Banks, Newfoundland. The "starfish" defensive formation used by humpbacks was described to me by Douglas Beach, a biologist at the National Marine Fisheries Service in Gloucester, Massachusetts. About a third of the humpbacks seen in the Gulf of Maine bear parallel scars thought to be caused by the teeth of orcas.

By taking only a modicum of blubber from each whale, orcas are certainly conserving a resource, but it is unlikely that they do so purposely. More likely, they take what they can get with minimal risk. Orcas are not unique in their preference for tongue meat. Many terrestrial predators also regard the tongues of their prey as delicacies. Tongues and livers are often the first body parts eaten.

While resting on the move, orcas usually swim very slowly, covering only a few hundred yards on each long dive. Resting pods have been seen to enter tidal rips and be pushed backward for up to thirty minutes. Wild orcas appear to need only a few hours of sleep a day, most naps probably lasting ten to twenty minutes. Having no natural enemies, they may spend much of their waking time in a state of relaxed meditation, and thus need little in the way of sound sleep.

Assuming the narrative's events to be current, the 1919 fisheries tag (an artistic liberty) suggests that the old cow had lived for at least seventy years. Most reference books estimate life expectancy for *Orcinus orca* at thirty to thirty-five years, based on the counting of tooth layers and ovarian scars, but the validity and accuracy of these aging techniques have long been questioned.

Recent findings suggest that the life expectancy of *Orcinus orca* is equivalent to our own. In 1981 the International Whaling Commission's Scientific Committee concluded that the age of orca females at first pregnancy is at least seven to eight years, and that male orcas do not mature sexually until about sixteen years of age. It seems unlikely that males destined to live only thirty to thirty-five years would take half their lives to mature.

Michael A. Bigg, a research scientist with the Canadian Department of Fisheries and Oceans, who has closely studied the orcas of British Columbia since 1971, states that "the life span and ages of sexual maturity of the species are probably close to our own." Moclips (now known as the Whale Museum), a nonprofit research organization in Friday Harbor, Washington, has been studying the orcas of Puget Sound since 1976. From Moclips's studies and Dr. Bigg's research, it is estimated that female orcas in the wild can live up to one hundred years and that males can live from forty to sixty years.

All evidence considered, it appears that orca maturation and longevity correspond to our own. This, together with clannishness, may explain the species' low reproduction rate of four to five percent per year. In many parts of the world, men have been killing orcas faster than given communities can reproduce, and the animals may tend not to breed across community lines. In habitats where orcas have been heavily exploited, the species may be endangered.

Assuming that orcas of the western North Atlantic maintain extended families of the type found in British Columbia, the old cow in our story is probably the mother of both bulls, and most likely matriarch to the entire pod. In British Columbia, sixteen pods of orcas that live near shore year-round have been studied by scientists since 1971. These "resident" pods number about ten to fifteen animals each and appear to be genetically isolated extended families with lifelong membership for all, including adolescent and mature males. While going their separate ways for the most part, various pods stay in touch acoustically over considerable distances, and occasionally get together to socialize or hunt.

Similar temporary amalgamations of pods may take place in the Gulf of Maine. Pods seen there typically number ten animals or less, but as many as one hundred orcas were seen in one group near Cape Ann, Massachusetts, within the past decade. The second-largest group reliably reported in the Gulf of Maine was forty to fifty strong. It is possible that the habitat hosts an unusually large pod of some one hundred orcas, which may periodically break up into smaller hunting groups. Still, groups larger than ten to fifteen are rarely sighted, so it seems more likely that smaller pods occasionally join forces to form larger ones.

# A Splendid but Uncertain Company

W. S. MERWIN

# For a Coming Extinction

Gray whale
Now that we are sending you to The End
That great god
Tell him
That we who follow you invented forgiveness
And forgive nothing

I write as though you could understand
And I could say it
One must always pretend something
Among the dying
When you have left the seas nodding on their stalks
Empty of you
Tell him that we were made
On another day

W. S. MERWIN is one of America's foremost poets. His recent publications include *Travels*, which features several narrative poems about historic naturalists, and *The Lost Upland*, stories set in southwestern France. A longtime resident of the island of Maui, he is an active supporter of the campaign to save the Wao Kele O Puna rain forest from geothermal development. "For a Coming Extinction" is from *The Lice*, published in 1967. Reprinted by permission of the author.

The bewilderment will diminish like an echo
Winding along your inner mountains
Unheard by us
And find its way out
Leaving behind it the future
Dead
And ours

When you will not see again
The whale calves trying the light
Consider what you will find in the black garden
And its court
The sea cows the Great Auks the gorillas
The irreplaceable hosts ranged countless
And fore-ordaining as stars
Our sacrifices
Join your word to theirs
Tell him
That it is we who are important

FAITH McNULTY

# Gigi

Midway down the dry, rocky west coast of Baja California, there is a great, shallow lagoon known as Scammon Lagoon, after its discoverer, the same Captain Charles Scammon who described the humpbacks' "amorous antics." In 1857, the Captain had set forth from San Francisco to go whaling and "elephanting" (killing the huge, preposterous-looking, and helpless elephant seals that inhabited the rocks along the coast). Three hundred and fifty miles south of San Diego, off Sebastian Vizcaíno Bay, he steered his bark past rolling surf and through a narrow channel, and found himself in a vast, tranquil inland lake surrounded by desert and filled with great gray whales. He had discovered the grays' major breeding ground, where, as he reported in his memoirs, they "gathered in large numbers, passing and repassing into and out of the estuaries, or slowly raising their colossal forms midway above the surface, falling over their sides as if by accident and dashing the water into foam and spray about them."

The Captain sent out his whaleboats, and two large cows were easily killed. But the next morning, as a boat pursued a whale, the whale smashed it with its flukes, spilling the crew in all directions and injuring many of them. A relief boat was staved by another whale. The crew

FAITH McNULTY has written extensively on nature for *The New Yorker* and other magazines. She has also written books for children, including, most recently, *Snake in the House*. This essay was adapted from *The Great Whales*. Copyright © 1974 by Faith McNulty. Used by permission of Doubleday, a division of Bantam Doubleday Dell Publishing Group, Inc.

members were so demoralized by these attacks that when next they attempted to harpoon a whale most of them jumped overboard the moment it appeared beside them. One man dove, as he supposed, into the water, but landed on the flukes of the whale. Miraculously, he was not hurt. The Captain found his position peculiar: his vessel safe in smooth water, with countless whales nearby, but the men so panic-stricken that he couldn't man a boat. He had brought along a primitive type of explosive harpoon (or "bomb lance"), which he now decided to try out. With this weapon, his men safely killed all the whales the ship could handle and returned to San Francisco "so deeply laden that her scuppers were washed by the rippling tide."

Scammon's success soon brought other whalers down the coast. He described the scene in the lagoon the next season, when nine vessels and twenty or thirty whaleboats were there:

> The scene of slaughter was exceedingly picturesque and unusu-ally exciting, especially on a calm morning, when the mirage would transform not only the boats and their crews into fantas-tic imagery, but the whales, as they sent forth their towering spouts of aqueous vapor, frequently tinted with blood, would appear greatly distorted. . . . The boats . . . would be seen gliding over the molten-looking surface of the water, with a . . . colossal form of the whale appearing for an instant, like a spectre . . . while the report of the bomb-guns would sound like the sudden discharge of musketry; but one cannot fully realize, unless he be an eyewitness, the intense and boisterous excitement of the reck-less pursuit. . . . Numbers of [boats] will be fast to whales at the same time, and the stricken animals, in their efforts to escape, can be seen darting in every direction through the water, or breaching headlong clear of its surface, coming down with a splash that sends columns of foam in every direction. . . . The men in the boats shout and yell . . . it is one continually chang-ing aquatic battle scene.

During the eighteen-fifties, the hunting of gray whales extended along the coast of upper and lower California. "Every navigable lagoon of the region was discovered and explored, and the animals were hunted in every winding and intricate estuary. . . . In the seasons of 1858 and 1859, not only the bays and lagoons were teeming [with whalers], but the outside coast was lined with ships, from San Diego southward to Cape St. Lucas," wrote Captain Scammon. The Captain wondered if the killing hadn't been overdone:

> The large bays and lagoons, where these animals once congregated, brought forth and nurtured their young, are already nearly deserted. The mammoth bones . . . lie bleaching on the shores of those silvery waters, and are scattered along the broken coasts, from Siberia to the Gulf of California; and ere long it may be questioned whether this mammal will not be numbered among the extinct species of the Pacific.

The Captain's prophecy was twice almost fulfilled, but now there are estimated to be from eight to fourteen thousand gray whales—enough to make them a major tourist attraction. On their migratory journey, hundreds can be seen from the California shore, and people gather at vantage points or go out in small boats to watch them pass. In recent seasons, the San Diego Natural History Museum has chartered a large excursion fishing boat to take people three hundred and fifty miles down the coast to Scammon Lagoon for a closer look, and last year I was among those who made the trip. For two days, our boat—the *HM 85*, eighty-five feet long, with forty of us aboard, including the crew—sailed down the coast, stopping for brief, fascinating shore excursions at the rocky islets of San Benitos and San Martín, which are part of Mexico and are inhabited only by seasonal fishermen, elephant seals, sea lions, and birds. In the evenings, in the crowded cabin, I talked with Dr. William A. Burns, the museum director, about gray whales. Burns is not a biologist, but he is thoroughly acquainted with the subject. He is a former New Yorker—a squarely built man with warm blue eyes, great enthusiasm, and a large repertoire of entertaining stories. In discussing the whales, he gave credit for his information to the museum's whale specialist, Dr. Raymond M. Gilmore, whose title is Research Associate in Marine Mammals, and who has studied the gray whales extensively and made many trips to Scammon.

The California gray whale makes the longest migration of any mammal. The trip from its summer pasture in the northern seas to Baja California covers between four thousand and six thousand miles, depending on the route, and takes about three months of steady swimming. The gray whale cruises at four knots and covers from sixty to eighty nautical miles in twenty-four hours. It does not pause to eat, and probably sleeps little, if at all. Gray whales have been seen pegging along even on the darkest nights. How the whale navigates is not definitely known, but it is believed to use the position of the sun and, since it follows the coast for long stretches (the southward-migrating whales first come near shore in numbers off Oregon), underwater landmarks as well. Dr. Gilmore thinks that it is also guided by the remembered taste of sediment in the water that flows out of lagoons and estuaries.

It appears that this tremendous round trip of anywhere from eight to twelve thousand miles and the two months' stay in the lagoon—which is taken up with the strenuous activities of mating, and, for females, giving birth and producing milk—are fuelled by only four months of feeding in the northern waters in the summer. Most cetologists think the gray whale eats little or nothing on migration or in the lagoon, unless it accidentally runs into suitable small fish or squid. (Dr. Theodore Walker, a former associate at the Scripps Institution of Oceanography, has generated controversy by disputing this. He claims that gray whales shovel up food from the bottom of the lagoons, but Dr. Gilmore points out that every whale slaughtered on migration has had an empty stomach and that northbound whales are thin, or "dry," as the whalers used to call it.) Whether or not the gray whales feed in winter, their feeding habits are unique. In shallow water, they plow up the soft, sandy bottom with their snouts to stir up small invertebrates that they filter out of the water with their baleen.

When the whales start south, they are on a tight schedule. Pregnant females are in the van of the migration, for babies born in the cold, rough water of the open sea might die. Mating, gestation, and birth are all neatly arranged so that they happen in the right place and at the right time. The gestation period is thirteen months. After giving birth, a female spends eleven months nursing and resting. She mates during her next stay in the lagoon and carries the baby through the rich summer months, and it is born in the south the second winter after the previous birth. On the wintering grounds, then, half the mature females are giving birth or nursing and half are mating.

On our third morning, after an early breakfast, we rounded a buoy at the entrance to Scammon Lagoon. Ahead of us were high white sand dunes. On the right, breakers extended half a mile offshore. I admired Captain Scammon's nerve at taking his bark into these waters, and I wondered if this was where he had seen whales playing in the surf, as he described them in his memoirs:

> About the shoals at the mouth of one of the lagoons, in 1860, we saw large numbers of the monsters. It was at the low stage of the tide, and the shoal places were plainly marked by the constantly foaming breakers. To our surprise we saw many of the whales going through the surf where the depth of water was barely sufficient to float them. . . . One in particular lay for a half hour in the breakers, playing, as seals often do . . . turning from side to side with half-extended fins . . . at times making a playful spring with its bending flukes, throwing its body clear of the water, coming down with a heavy splash . . . with the heavy swell the animal would roll over in a listless manner, to all appearance enjoying the sport intensely.

I wished that I could witness intense enjoyment in a whale, but our captain did not take us close to the breakers. As we entered the channel, the dark-green seas became violently choppy and we were warned by the crew to hang on tight. Black-backed gulls flapped along beside us. Then I saw ahead a white plume rise from the surface of the water, hang, and vanish. Shortly after that, we overtook a whale surging along, its broad back awash and gleaming; it was heading purposefully for the entrance to the lagoon, as we were. Ten minutes later, we were out of the chop and inside the lagoon. There was sudden calm. On one side of us were sculptured mountains of white sand; on the other, rippling water reached to the horizon. The main lagoon is a long, irregular crescent varying from five to ten miles in width and extending into the desert for almost thirty miles. There are many shallows, islands, and sand flats. Here and there, small tributary lagoons branch off. All around is one of the world's most desolate deserts—the Vizcaíno, which matches the Sahara for dryness. There is only one natural source of fresh water within hundreds of square miles—Ojo de Liebre, or Jack Rabbit Spring, where there was once a small settlement. The shores surrounding us were roadless and totally uninhabited.

A rusty fishing boat, at anchor, now came into view. It was serving as a base ship for outboard-engine skiffs we would use for following whales in the lagoon. We anchored. The skiffs were brought alongside, and the tourists, wearing orange life jackets, climbed into them. I found a seat beside Dr. Burns. The sailor at the tiller of our boat steered us toward the center of the lagoon, where several whales had spouted, and we buzzed over the water. I regretted the motor, for I would rather have drifted and waited for whales to appear, but Dr. Burns explained that chasing the whales in this fashion gave the tourists a better chance of getting pictures, and that was what most of them wanted.

Within five minutes, we were coming up on a whale. First, its head appeared. I saw the long slit of its mouth, the small eyes, and a pattern of barnacles. It exhaled, with a sound like a steam pants presser, and then its huge back rolled out, ridged toward the tail with a series of small knobs, like the back of a prehistoric beast. We were so close that I felt my heart lurch. Being on the same level with a whale was quite different from viewing one from the deck of a big boat. The whale rose, blew, sank, rose again, blew another sighing, steamy breath, and disappeared with a wave of its flukes, leaving a swirling slick on the surface. The flukes, Dr. Burns said, are about ten feet across, weigh several hundred pounds, and can deliver a blow like that of a rubber sledgehammer. A couple of years ago, a diver swimming off La Jolla met a whale underwater and made the mistake of touching its tail as it glided by. The startled whale gave a mighty swish of its flukes, grazing the diver and knocking his mask off while the barnacles on its skin cut a gash in his forehead. He was lucky to survive. The flukes are a formidable means of defense for the whale, and Captain Scammon reported that sometimes angry mother whales also overturned boats by "rooting" them with their snouts, like pigs overturning a trough.

For the next hour, we motored here and there, seeing whales now close, now far off. Dr. Burns said he had heard it estimated that there were two or three thousand of them within the lagoon at this time. (Meanwhile, other groups of grays were wintering in other lagoons.) Every minute or so, a spout rose somewhere. We often saw whales performing what are called "spy hops"—sticking their heads eight or ten feet out of the water and hanging there for a few seconds, apparently intent on seeing what is going on. The most startling displays were the whales' extraordinary breaches, usually performed by males. A forty-foot whale on end towers as high as a three-story building. This incredible length shoots out of the water at terrific speed, hangs in the air, and falls amid fountains of spray. The whales may breach out of sheer exuberance, or the breaching may be primarily a display of strength by males, or possibly slapping against the water allays an itch from barnacles; occasionally mothers and calves also breach.

A number of times, we came upon mothers and young swimming side by side, the baby whale rising and falling in a rhythm that exactly matched that of its parent. These calves were a few weeks old. A newborn gray is from twelve to seventeen feet long and weighs from fifteen hundred to three thousand pounds. Captain Scammon wrote that as birth time arrived the pregnant whales collected in the remote reaches of the lagoon and "huddled together so thickly that it was difficult for a boat to cross the waters without coming in contact with them." He also wrote of the whales' strong maternal feelings: "This species of whale manifests the greatest affection for its young, and seeks the sheltered estuaries lying under a tropical sun, as if to warm its offspring." He described how a whale struck with a harpoon would attempt to escape by running along the bottom, and noted that if a mother was harpooned and lost sight of her calf she would instantly "stop and 'sweep' around in search." He added, "If the boat comes in contact with her, it is quite sure to be staved." In the case of the wounding of a calf, he wrote, "the parent animal, in her frenzy, will chase the boats, and . . . overturn them with her head, or dash them in pieces with a stroke of her ponderous flukes." Whalers sometimes deliberately shot a calf and towed it into shallow water because the mother would follow and could be more easily killed there.

We came across several sleeping whales, lying awash like logs. Having slept so little on migration, the gray whales catch up in the lagoons. We saw a sleeping mother whose calf was apparently trying to wake her by splashing and nudging as we approached. She seemed to wake with a start, and both of them dived out of sight.

What caused the greatest sensation in our skiff was coming across whales courting. This activity often involves not two animals but a trio. Since half the females are pregnant or nursing, only half are in breeding condition, so there are two males to every available female. The exact role of the second male—whether he is a bystander or a participant, perhaps assisting by lying across the female to stabilize her—is debated by cetologists. Whatever is happening, the three of them make a tremendous flurry in the water, rising, falling, splashing, and revolving, with giant flippers waving above the surface. We came on several such scenes, but nothing was explicit until, quite close to our boat, a whale revolved in the water, turning belly up on the surface, and there was a brief but distinct glimpse of its long, pink, erect penis. Our boatload was divided between the happy photographers who had caught this memorable view and the chagrined photographers who had missed it. Dr. Burns was jubilant, since both winners and losers had had a fair chance, and the trip was now undeniably a success.

When we got back to the *HM 85*, two people who were living aboard the rusty anchored fishing boat had come over to visit. They were Peter Paul Ott, a wildlife painter and photographer from Laguna Beach, and his wife, Holly. They had been living on the boat for two months, and had found the beauty and the solitude marvelous. Ott described some of their experiences with whales. He said that when the boat was quiet, with the auxiliary engine for generating electricity turned off, the whales seemed to become curious, and made closer and closer passes. One evening after dark, he had heard a whale blow very close. A large baby whale and a huge mother were coming straight for the boat. Ott shone a light on them and saw the calf dive underneath, looking like a blimp outlined in phosphorescence. The calf emerged, rolled over on its side, and looked up at Ott with its ridiculously small eye. Ott tried to scratch its back, but couldn't reach it. He said that sleeping whales sometimes collided with the boat as they drifted with the tide, hitting with a dull thud. In the calm of the night, a whale's blow could be heard for miles, and a breach sounded like a cannon as it echoed among the dunes.

Ott's most distressing experience, he said, was with an orphaned and injured calf. He saw it swimming alone, listing to one side. It became stranded on a beach. With an oar, Ott was able to heave it back in the water. There were two large whales nearby, but they offered no help. The next day, the orphan was stranded again, higher on the beach, and there was nothing that Ott could do for it. It rolled its eyes, watching him, and winced as he touched it. Its skin was so delicate that it broke at the touch of a fingernail. Gulls settled on it and tore it. The whale waved its tail as the gulls pecked, but it made no cry. Ott concealed himself and watched. Coyotes came and circled. It was very gruesome, Ott said, and he could think of no way to help or to administer a coup de grâce. He was greatly relieved when the whale died.

Ott and his wife had explored some of the shore and found tremendous salt marshes, with thousands of birds, and an island that held twenty-five or thirty pairs of nesting ospreys—an extraordinary concentration of these increasingly rare birds. On the way back from an excursion in their fourteen-foot skiff, they accidentally ran into the midst of a pod of six whales, several within arm's reach of the boat at once. They found the moment both wonderful and terrifying; an accidental flip of a fluke could have overturned them and drowned the motor. Ott was well aware that the water teems with sharks. He had just caught a leopard shark twelve feet long.

When I woke the next morning, a soft gray haze hung over the lagoon, and the water was like a dark mirror. The whales seemed to be moving more slowly or resting with their whole length on the surface. The *HM 85* coasted deeper into the lagoon, across shallows where weeds grew. I went ashore with a small group and walked alone on a beach bordered by strange rocks and twisted, thorny desert shrubs. The solitude seemed boundless; Captain Scammon and his bomb lances and cooking pots had left no trace. It was perhaps the most beautiful meeting place of land and sea that I had ever seen. Once in a while, as I walked along the silent, endless beach, a whale would rise just offshore, and I would hear its soft, sighing breath. It was a companionable sound.

In the nineteen-fifties, Dr. Paul Dudley White, the heart specialist, in the course of attempts to measure the heartbeat of a gray whale, pursued several in Scammon Lagoon, trying to implant a harpoon carrying electro-cardiographic equipment. After various difficulties, he at last connected with a whale, but the resulting data were far from clear, and he gave up. In 1965, Dr. Robert Elsner, a physiologist from the Scripps Institution, and Dr. David Kenney, a veterinarian who was also a vice-president of a marine park in San Diego called Sea World, decided to try their luck. They hired a Japanese whale gunner and went to Scammon, where they harpooned a baby whale and lifted it to the deck in a net. When the heart recordings were finished, it seemed useless to put the little whale back in the water, since it could only die of its wound, so they lashed it to the deck of their boat and took it back to San Diego. The trip lasted three days, but the whale lived, and was put in a pool at Sea World. Dr. Kenney patched it up, and, in spite of a collapsed lung, the whale amazed its captors by surviving for almost two months.

This episode convinced Kenney that, with gentle handling, a baby whale could be captured and kept indefinitely. He was fascinated by the possibility of raising such animals in captivity, and the other Sea World directors agreed to the project. In March 1971, Kenney again went to Scammon Lagoon. After a number of chases in a small boat, he maneuvered a mother and her calf under the bow of the boat, slipped a noose around the calf, and hauled it to the beach. The mother left as darkness fell. In the morning, the calf was worked onto a stretcher and floated out to a larger vessel, where it was put in a converted fish well for the trip to San Diego. The calf, an eighteen-foot female, arrived in good health and was put in a large, round tank. She was weighed in a sling and tipped the scale at forty-three hundred pounds. Now Dr. Kenney tried to fabricate whale milk from its known ingredients. The resulting mixture had the consistency of cooling fudge and would not go through a feeding tube, so he improvised a concoction of heavy cream, ground squid and fish, cod-liver oil, yeast, vitamins, and water. The whale, who had been named Gigi, reluctantly partook of it. Kenney's laboratory-animal manager, a tall, kindly Nebraskan named Bud N. Donahoo, was in charge of the feedings, for which the water in the whale's tank was lowered. To get the tube into Gigi's esophagus, Donahoo had to thrust his arm into her mouth, parting the bristles of baleen that hung like curtains from her jaw. This was apparently somewhat painful at first, but after a while there was a permanent gap and no further pain. In her first two weeks in the tank, Gigi lost a hundred and fifty pounds. Then she began to gain and grow, at the rate of twenty-seven pounds and a third of an inch a day. She was moved to a larger tank. The only abnormal thing about Gigi was that she seemed exceptionally fond of sleeping, even for an infant. A dolphin was put in with her for company, and girl swimmers from Sea World's corps of performing Sea Maids were employed to swim beside her, poking at her to keep her awake. After a while, Gigi came to life and began to tear around the tank, jumping, flopping, rolling, and waving her flippers, like a normal whale.

An important factor in the successful captivity of Gigi was the relationship that developed between her and Donahoo. He thought of her as a lonely, confused being, imprisoned in her great sensitive bulk of flesh and isolated by lack of communication. He also realized that she was only a baby and must long for reassurance. He searched for some way to make contact with her. By accident, when he was cleaning the tank one day, he sprayed a hose on her flukes, and she lifted them to hold them in the spray. It was a clue that she might enjoy being rubbed. He began touching her gently. At first, she shuddered and twitched, but soon he was rubbing her from nose to tail, and she relaxed under his hands. His next problem was to find a means of communication. He talked to her constantly, but it didn't seem likely that she would understand words, so he decided on a system of pats as signals—one pat for attention, two pats to open her mouth, three firm pats for "No" or "Be quiet." The whale learned these commands. Now Donahoo was able to move her about in the tank, and this was a tremendous help in handling her. With the water lowered, he could stand by her head, signalling to her, and she would wiggle her great bulk to follow him.

Gigi's weaning took place when Donahoo felt her sucking on his hand while he was putting the tube in her throat. He put a squid in her mouth, and she swallowed it gratefully. Soon she was eating squid by the handful, and then sucking them up from the floor of the tank. This was a development that fascinated scientific observers, for never before had the mechanics of a gray whale eating been directly observed. The cetologist William E. Schevill, of Harvard, watched as she scooped in the squid—turning on her side, opening one side of her mouth and sucking like a giant vacuum cleaner, and then ramming her tongue forward to squirt out the water. Once weaned, Gigi learned to take food from the hands of people swimming beside her or to come to the side of the tank at the sight of a bucket. When Donahoo dropped the water level and approached her, she would come over to him eagerly, with her mouth open.

One of the things that greatly puzzled Donahoo was how Gigi could distinguish him from anyone else. When other handlers tried to do things with her—often in connection with the numerous scientific tests she was undergoing—she often raised such a ruckus that they were forced to stop and send for Donahoo. As soon as he arrived, no matter what he was wearing—and in a wet-suit identity is well hidden—Gigi calmed down. Donahoo never figured out how Gigi recognized him, but it seemed clear that he had become her parental figure. Mutual affection also sprang up between the whale and one of the Sea Maids, a girl named Sue Bailey, who was deft at feeding Gigi.

By the end of Gigi's first year in the tank at Sea World, she had grown to nearly seven tons and was twenty-seven feet long. Scientists from numerous institutions had made a great variety of physiological tests, and Dr. Kenney had filing cabinets full of new whale data. Her rate of growth, food consumption, blood composition, and respiratory function had been recorded. But, to Dr. Kenney's regret, the managers of Sea World, which by now was spending two hundred dollars a day just on her food, felt that the upkeep expense was prohibitive, and they decided that soon they would have to put her back in the sea, before she got too big to be moved. When I heard about this, and having visited Gigi's birthplace at Scammon Lagoon, I decided to go to Sea World to see her.

At the gate of the park, I was met by Bud Donahoo, a tall, athletic-looking man in his late thirties with kind blue eyes and a boyish face, and Sue Bailey, a pretty girl with long brown hair. They led me to a circular tank, fifty feet across. A huge gray cylinder rested at the bottom of the tank. "That's her favorite place—by the water inlet," Sue said. After a minute or two, Gigi slowly pumped her flukes, rose, and began to glide majestically in a slow circle on the surface, blowing leisurely spouts. I said I thought she was lovely, and Donahoo and Sue beamed. Gigi sank peacefully to the bottom and went to sleep.

I went back the next morning, at the suggestion of Donahoo, who had told me that the water in the tank would be lowered then and Sue would attempt to ride her. First, Sue, in a wet-suit, approached the whale, splashing water ahead of her as though to announce her coming. She splashed Gigi's head, and then put her hands on her back and rubbed her vigorously. Donahoo, carrying a bucket of squid, approached and also patted her. "She's talking!" she shouted up at me. "Can you hear it?" Water splashing loudly over the rim of an adjoining tank drowned out any sound from the whale, but, as I watched, her whole body swelled and heaved in response to Donahoo's caress. Her huge, rubbery person seemed to emanate feeling. Sue took a handful of squid and began stuffing them into Gigi's mouth, her arm disappearing to the elbow. As Donahoo and Sue went on rubbing and patting vigorously, and stuffing in squid, the huge cylinder of flesh vibrated with responsive animation.

Then Sue put her hands on Gigi's back and leaped astride. Gigi's tail fluttered, and, ponderously, she began to move. As they slowly circled the tank, Donahoo climbed out and joined me. "If Gigi didn't like being ridden, she'd roll Sue off any time she liked," he said. The whale and the girl went around and around, Sue sitting astride her like a mahout aboard an elephant, and the whale's flukes pumping rhythmically. Then Gigi came to a halt. Sue patted her head and she moved again. Donahoo said that she was responding to signals from Sue. Sue stopped her, dismounted, and resumed caressing Gigi around the head and stuffing her mouth with squid.

Donahoo said it amazed him how Gigi could discriminate between different kinds of food. Given twenty pounds of squid with a few mackerel mixed in, she would swallow the squid and spit out the mackerel. "She's usually a docile animal," he said. "But she can be aggressive. She bobs her head up and down and shakes her whole body from side to side when she's perturbed. She's knocked me across the tank many times. But

I can always calm her down. The signal to be quiet is three firm pats. She may start right up again, but then I quiet her again until she gets over whatever it is that's disturbing her." Next, Donahoo told me about talking to the whale. He said Gigi made deep interior noises that he couldn't describe. One day, early in their relationship, he tapped out a peculiar rhythm on her head and was astonished to hear the whale repeat the sequence. He tried another rhythm, and she repeated that, too. He concluded that Gigi was trying to talk to him. Thereafter, throughout her babyhood, he had daily conversations with her, tapping and getting answers. Now her answers had tapered off, perhaps in discouragement at getting no whale sounds back, but she still talked on occasion. "I believe that this animal can be communicated with by sound," Donahoo said. To his regret, none of the visiting scientists had been interested in the phenomenon, because they did not regard it as part of the whale's natural behavior. Donahoo told me that he had learned to distinguish at least four different sounds made by Gigi. When she uttered them, he said, the whole tank vibrated. "The vibrations hit your legs," he continued. "When she's happy, there's one big grunt. Her whole body swells up. Sometimes she makes other sounds before or after, but the happy sound is just one."

Sue had mounted again, and she and Gigi were again making stately circles. Then the whale gave a leisurely roll and Sue fell off. She remounted and was dumped again. Leaving Gigi, she climbed the ladder and joined us.

Plans for releasing Gigi were made by Dr. William Evans, a marine biologist at the Naval Undersea Center, in San Diego, who had been studying her. He felt that she would have the best chance of survival if she was released in spring, when the gray whales were migrating north to the feeding grounds. Even so, he suspected that release would be a shock to her; the sudden change to the darkness of the sea's depths, the noise of ships' propellers, and the need to find food would be "harrowing," he told a newspaper reporter. He worked out a way to attach an instrument package, which could store and transmit data, to her back, in order to keep track of her after her release. A few weeks ahead of time, large stitches of nylon thread were sewn through the blubber of her back, with loops sticking up to hold the equipment.

Before dawn on a cool March day, Gigi was wrapped in a sling and hoisted from the tank by a crane. She was put down on a sixteen-inch-thick foam-rubber mattress on a thirty-two-foot Navy flatbed truck and covered with wet blankets. Donahoo and Sue rode with her, patting and reassuring her. She breathed quickly, indicating apprehension, but gave no signs of serious distress. The truck drove six miles through dark city streets to a Navy pier, and there Gigi was transferred to a barge, which carried her four and a half miles out to sea. Then, a few minutes before ten, a crane lowered the sling into the water. As it touched the surface, Donahoo dived over the side and, when the sling was released, pulled the canvas clear. The whale gave a graceful wave of her flukes and swam free. Donahoo swam beside her for twenty or thirty yards, and then she dived. She surfaced two or three hundred yards away, made a wide sweep around the boat, as though orienting herself, and started north. There were other northbound whales in the area, and their spouts were visible a half mile away. For several days, Evans tracked her in a small research vessel, picking up signals from the transmitter on her back. This was more difficult than he had expected. The transmitter sent its signals by means of a two-foot-tall antenna, which operated only when it was out of water. Evans had failed to allow for the fact that yearling whales do not roll as far out of the water as adults do, and so the signals were relatively brief and infrequent. When Evans left Gigi, a Navy plane picked up her signal, and her northward progress was recorded. She covered eighty miles in the first four days. The instruments indicated that she was diving to maximum depths of two and three hundred feet. From the plane, observers saw signs in the water that she had found something to eat. At one point, to Evans' dismay, she lingered to play in a kelp bed and bent the antenna, reducing the range of the signals from twenty-five or thirty miles to five or ten. Nevertheless, her progress was followed by plane for more than two weeks longer. At that point, the funds allotted for the project were exhausted and the Navy ceased to follow her. And at the last report, early in May, she was with other gray whales north of Monterey. She had covered more than five hundred miles. The transmitter was designed to work for nine months, and there was a remote hope that a ship or plane would pick up her signals during the summer or on her return journey south, but this didn't occur.

In any event, for the first time in all the eons of human and whale existence a great whale had been in the power of human beings and had escaped with its life.

FARLEY MOWAT

# The Whale that Never Was

The grey whale of the Pacific coast of North America is today one of the best known of all whales. Its annual migration between the lagoons of Baja California and the Beaufort and Chukchi Seas takes it some 9,000 miles, for the most part within sight of land. Whale aficionados gather in their thousands on headlands and cliffs to watch with awe and admiration as the stately procession of great sea mammals makes its leisurely way past.

It was not always so.

When the Pacific tribe of the grey whale nation was discovered by American whalers in 1846, it had not previously suffered at the hands of modern man and its numbers were still legion. The whalers soon rectified that. During the next few decades, they slaughtered grey whales by the thousands, mostly in the lagoons along the Mexican coast where the females gathered in enormous schools to calve.

Because the lagoons were shallow and almost totally enclosed, the whalers had little need for harpoons and lances. Instead they relied mainly on cannons that fire explosive shells into the whales either from shore

FARLEY MOWAT is among Canada's most distinguished authors. His many books—often inspired by life under conditions of natural adversity in Canada's Far North—have been published in over twenty languages in more than forty countries. Among his best-known works are *People of the Deer* and *Never Cry Wolf*. "The Whale that Never Was" is from *Sea of Slaughter*, published in 1984 by Atlantic Monthly Press. Reprinted by permission of the author.

or from anchored whaling ships. There was no need to immediately secure the carcasses, as had to be done at sea, because almost every animal hit by a shell was doomed to die sooner or later either from loss of blood, damage to its internal organs, or massive infections—and, once dead, the body would remain available. Whaleboats had only to tour the lagoons at intervals, collecting the floating or stranded corpses and towing them to the tryworks. Here it was found that the victims were mostly female and either pregnant or else lactating, having recently given birth. The whalers did not bother the orphaned calves, which had no commercial value. They were left to die of starvation.

The massacre of grey whales in the lagoons was so thorough that, by 1895, the species was commercially extinct along the Pacific seaboard of North America. The plight of a sister tribe inhabiting Asiatic waters was little better. It was savaged by Korean whalers who had been quick to turn the technology developed by Western whalemen to their own advantage.

Nevertheless, some grey whales remained alive and, during the respite provided by the First World War, the species made a modest recovery. This did not escape the notice of whalers of the post-war period, now mostly using deep-sea whale catchers and factory ships. The slaughter began anew. By 1938, Norwegian, Japanese, and Korean catchers in the western Pacific had destroyed all but a handful of grey whales there. Norwegian and American catchers operating from U.S. and Canadian stations had not been quite so efficient, and as many as 2,000 whales may still have been alive at the beginning of World War II. After that war, grey whales had less value and the commercial attack on them in eastern Pacific waters began to wane. But science took up the slack. Between 1953 and 1969 Canada, the United States, and the Soviet Union licensed the killing of over 500 greys for scientific purposes. Three hundred sixteen were slaughtered to provide data for two scientists in the U.S. Fish and Wildlife Service so that they could produce a study grotesquely titled: *The Life History and Ecology of the Gray Whale.*

In the early 1970s the remnant Pacific grey whales were, belatedly as usual, granted protection by the International Whaling Commission. It was a short-lived respite. In 1978, under pressure from the Americans, Japanese, and Soviets, the surviving grey whales were stripped of their protected status.

Largely because of massive pressure exerted by great numbers of people who had seen a grey whale in life, this protection has since been returned to them, at least in eastern Pacific waters. If we have truly found enough compassion in us to spare the grey whale of North America's Pacific coast from extinction it will be some small measure of atonement for what we did to the sister tribe that once inhabited the waters off America's Atlantic coast.

Until quite recently, the existence of grey whales in the Atlantic in historic times was denied by many zoologists and some even now are reluctant to accept the evidence, not only that it was once an abundant species on both sides of that ocean, but that it flourished along North America's eastern coast until as late as the end of the seventeenth century. For these authorities, it remains the whale that never was.

In the mid-1800s some very large bones were found on the shores of a Swedish inlet. They were identified as being those of a whale, although of what species no one could tell because the grey whale was then totally unknown to science. Some considerable time later, when the Pacific grey came to the attention of naturalists, the correct correlation was made with the Swedish bones. Similar relics had meanwhile turned up in drained areas of the Zuider Zee, and it was established that grey whales must at one time have lived in European waters.

But how long ago? The experts concluded that, since nobody seemed to have any documentary evidence to show that such a whale had lived in European waters in historic times, it could only have been present in some remote prehistoric period. Consequently the bones were labelled "subfossils," implying an antiquity of several thousand years. Thus was the otta sotta, the favourite prey of Basque whalers until they exterminated it, relegated to historical oblivion. The same treatment has been meted out to the grey whale of the New World, despite the fact that there is more than enough evidence testifying to its presence and abundance in historic times.

To begin with, let us go back to 1611 when the Muscovy Company dispatched a vessel named *Mary Margaret* on a pioneering whaling voyage into the icy seas to the north of Europe. Because the English were tyros in the business, *Mary Margaret* shipped six skilled Basque harpoonists from St. Jean de Luz. In the master's account of the voyage, we are told that part of their task was to instruct the English "how to tell the better sorts of whales from the worser, wherebye in their striking they may choose the good and leave the bad."

The various sorts are listed under their Basque names, and the fourth in order of "goodness" is called otta sotta. It is described as being "of the same colour as the Trumpa [sperm] having finnes [baleen] in its mouth all white, but not above halfe a yard long; being thicker than the Trumpa but not so long. He yeeldes the best oyle but not above 30 hogs heads."

This description fits the grey whale and no other known species. Moreover, since all the other chief kinds of large whales are accurately described and specifically named, there can be no doubt as to this identification. Yet by this date the Atlantic grey whale had long been extinct in European waters. How then to account for the Basque description of it as a species still of importance to whalers of the time? St. Jean de Luz, from which the harpooners hailed, was the major French Basque whaling port of that period, and we know that its whalers had been "fishing" almost exclusively on the northeastern seaboard of the New World for the better part of a century. It follows that one of the "better sort" they hunted there must have been the otta sotta.

In later times, when New Englanders first learned to go awhaling, they called the earliest "fish" they took the scrag whale. The Honourable Paul Dudley, a naturalist and Chief Justice of Massachusetts in the 1740s, has left us the sole surviving description of this whale. "It is near a-kin to the Fin-back, but, instead of a Fin upon his Back, the ridge of the Afterpart of his back is scragged with a Dozen Knobs or Kuckles; he is near the Right Whale in figure [shape] . . . his bone [baleen] is white but won't split." Once again the description fits the otta sotta, and *only* the otta sotta.

That the scrag was widespread and well known along the eastern seaboard in early historic times is confirmed in my view by the presence on old charts of a number of features bearing the name. I have found forty-seven Scrag Islands, Scrag Rocks, Scrag Ledges, and Scrag Bays along the shores of Nova Scotia, the Gulf of Maine, and the American coastal states as far south as Georgia. Sag Harbor, once a famous whaling port and now a fashionable resort, was originally Scrag Harbor. The bestowing and the survival of so many examples of the name of a specific kind of whale is unique. It resulted from the fact that the grey whale was, and is, a shore-hugging animal and so would have been the whale most frequently observed, encountered, and, as we shall see, killed by early European settlers; and, before their arrival, by aboriginals.

The Algonkian people who lived there for uncounted generations called it *Nanticut*—the distant place, a name this sea-girt island outflung into the Atlantic near Cape Cod well deserved. Low-lying, windswept, and composed mostly of sand covered with a scanty soil upon which beach grasses and scrubby oaks and cedars grew, it seems an unprepossessing choice of a place to live. However, those who made it their home in ancient times did so not because of what the land had to offer but for the sustenance that came from the sea around it.

As the November Hunter's Moon began to wane, the people waited. Young men topped the high dunes on the northern shore to stare fixedly seaward into the scud of autumnal gales or into the brilliant glitter of occasional sunny days. In the village of bark-covered houses, men, women, and children took part in ceremonial dances and incantations intended to encourage and welcome the gift of life that they awaited.

One day, the watchers on the dunes beheld first one or two, then half a dozen, then a score of misty fountains rising from a sullen sea. These blew away like smoke, only to be renewed again and again until, by day's end, the whole seaward horizon was fretted with them. The southbound columns of the sea creature the Indians called *powdaree* had reached Nanticut at last.

For weeks to come, the long procession would stream by within sight of the island people. The marine mammoths surfaced, blew, rolled in the surging breakers on the shoals, and came close enough to the beaches so the watchers could see the sea-lice and barnacles mottling the dark, gleaming skin. But always, and inexorably, they kept their stately way toward the south.

They did not pass entirely unscathed. On the first fair-weather day following their appearance, clusters of canoes put off from the island beaches. Captain George Weymouth, explorer of the Maine coast in 1605, was an eye-witness of what then ensued.

"One special thing is their manner of killing the whale which they call powdare; and [they] will describe his form; and how he bloweth up the water; and that he is twelve fathoms long; that they go in company of their king with a multitude of their boats; and strike him with a bone made in a fashion of a harping iron, fastened to a rope; which they make great and strong of bark of trees; then all their boats come about him as he riseth above water, with their arrows they shoot him to death; when they have killed him and dragged him to shore they call all their chief lords together and sing a song of joy; and those chief lords, whom they call sagamores, divide the spoil and give to every man his share, which pieces are distributed [and] they hang them up about their houses [to dry] for provisions."

The natives of Nantucket Island, as it is now called, were not the only ones who took a major part of their winter food from the powdaree. Many coastal tribes along the 7,000- to 8,000-mile migration route of the whales evidently did likewise. But considering the fearful risks involved in tackling forty-ton whales from bark canoes, there is little likelihood that any settlement killed more than one or two animals each season. One would have provided meat and fat enough, preserved by smoking and rendering, to feed two or three score people all winter through.

Leaving Nanticut behind, the river of grey whales, for such I believe the powdaree to be, forged slowly southward, moving perhaps thirty or forty miles a day and always staying close to the coast. By the end of December the head of the column might have been in the vicinity of the Florida Keys, but where it went from there is anybody's guess.

We do know that the by-then-very-pregnant cows would have been seeking shallow, warm waters spacious enough to allow free movement, but protected from storm seas. Such saltwater enclosures are to be found on the east Florida coast, but are especially abundant along the east, north, and western rim of the Gulf of Mexico, offering the whales an environment as hospitable as the Baja California lagoons. I conclude that this is where most of the powdaree calved and nursed their young.

In early February, the pods began to head northward toward the lush summer plankton grazing grounds. By mid-April, they would have been passing Nanticut again. Early May probably saw the head of the ponderous procession approaching the south coast of Newfoundland, then splitting into two streams, the one entering the Gulf of St. Lawrence through Cabot Strait and the Strait of Canso, the other veering eastward and then northward over the Grand Banks.

Where the northeast-bound powdaree went thereafter is also a mystery. If there followed a pattern similar to that of their Pacific cousins, they would have continued down the coast of Labrador seeking shallow northern seas where the small, bottom-loving crustaceans that comprised their chief food multiplied in their billions. Their chosen pastures may have included the shoal regions of Hudson Bay (Foxe Basin in particular), as well as the banks off southern Iceland. While there is no concrete evidence attesting to their use of Hudson Bay, there *are* seventeenth-century reports of otta sotta in Icelandic waters.

Initially Basque whalers in the gulf probably took small toll of the otta sotta. Although its blubber produced train of premium value, it yielded only about a third as much as could be rendered from a sarda [black right whale] and, as we shall see, even before the sarda had been devastated, the Basques had found an even more rewarding quarry in the bowhead whale. Nevertheless, the fact remains that the powdaree *did* vanish into limbo. Who sent it there?

The answer is to be found in a re-examination of the early history of Europeans in the eastern United States and in the elimination of errors that have become part of that history. All current accounts of what took place in New England during the early centuries correctly emphasize the importance of the whaling industry. However, they also state that the shore-based whaling that was the genesis of the industry was based on the black right whale—and this is simply wrong.

By the time the New Englanders began whaling in earnest in the mid-1600s the western sarda nation had already been so reduced that its survivors could not have sufficed to build an industry the size of the one that did emerge. It is also clear that the New England settlers were drawn into whaling by the abundance and availability of a whale that came so close inshore it could be attacked with success by people of limited seagoing pretensions and abilities. There is no doubt that these people learned whaling as the ancestors of the Basques had done, upon "fish" that came to them, rather than vice versa.

The first recorded attempt at shore whaling on the eastern coasts of what is now the United States was made by a Hollander named DeVries who, in 1632, brought two vessels and crews to the New Netherlands— the Dutch settlement on Long Island Sound. Whales were abundant in the sound and, within a few days of their arrival, DeVries' men had killed seven in the enclosed waters of South Bay. What kind of whales were they? All seven together yielded only about 150 hogsheads of oil, where- as a single sarda of only average size would have yielded at least eighty hogsheads. DeVries' whales could hardly have been sarda. The yield from them is, however, compatible with what would be expected from the grey whale. Their productivity was a disappointment to DeVries, who com- plained that "The whale fishery is very expensive when only such meagre fish are caught." The upshot was that he gave up the American experi- ment and the Dutch made no further attempts to exploit the New World whale fishery, preferring to concentrate their efforts on the rapidly unfolding and immensely lucrative Arctic bowhead fishery instead.

If the local whales were but small fry to the Dutch, they nevertheless sufficed to fire the cupidity of the English settlers. In 1658, twenty English families led by Thomas Macy "purchased" Nantucket Island from its Indian owners, optimistically hoping to farm its scanty soil. Either that same year or in the following spring, the settlers discovered a whale swimming about in their shallow harbour. They promptly set upon it, but with such blundering incompetence that it took them three days to kill it. Nevertheless, having crudely rendered its oil, they realized that they were onto a good thing.

Obediah Macy, one of Thomas's descendants, *tells* us in his *History of Nantucket* that this first whale was a scrag, and that it was the kind the island natives had long been used to hunting. In truth, it was the Indians who here, as elsewhere along the coast, taught the English how to catch these whales. Furthermore, through most of the succeeding century, native whalers were employed (dragooned might be a better term) to do most of the actual killing that fed a mushrooming proliferation of shore factories.

By 1660, scrag whales were being killed by shoremen along much of their migration route between Nova Scotia and Florida. During the northern migration of 1669, Samuel Mavericke alone took thirteen off the east end of Long Island and noted they were so abundant that several were seen right in the harbour every day. In 1687, seven small factories along the Southampton and Easthampton beaches of Long Island tried out 2,148 barrels of oil, while 4,000 barrels were made on Long Island in 1707. A forty-six-barrel whale was considered a good catch, while thirty-six-barrel whales were the norm. A black right of average size, it should be remembered, yielded up to 160 barrels.

By 1725, only three-quarters of a century after the diligent New Englanders had begun killing them, the last days of the powdaree had come. Although the English were not solely responsible for their destruction—French Basques whaling in the Gulf of St. Lawrence in the summer season undoubtedly killed their share as substitutes for the now all-but-vanished sarda—it was the New Englanders who doomed the powdaree.

In so doing, they found themselves forced to abandon their dependence on inshore whaling and to take to "ye deepes," as the *Boston News-Letter* of March 20, 1727, reported: "We hear from the Towne of the Cape [Cod] that the Whale-fishery amongst them having failed much this Winter, as it has done for several winters past, but having found a way of going to Sea upon that Business . . . they are now fitting out several Vessels to sail with all Expedition upon that dangerous design this Spring." These "several Vessels" were forerunners of the enormous and horrendously predatory Yankee deep-sea whaling fleet that would eventually scour all the oceans of the world in merciless pursuit of whales of many species.

Although the execution of the grey whale took place along much of the Atlantic seaboard of what is now the United States, by far the bloodiest destruction was committed in the Cape Cod and Long Island district, where extensive shoals lying athwart the whales' migration route made them especially vulnerable to boat whalers. Consequently, this region is fully entitled to its claim to being the cradle of the American whaling industry. It is also entitled to renown as the place that gave the impetus to the first major extinction to be perpetrated by Western man in North America . . . the first of many such.

PAULA BOCK

# Whale Watcher

Beep-BEEP-beep-BEEP-beep-BEEEEEP.

It figures these days that the first sign of killer whales is not the Pooooffff! Pooooffff! of *Orcinus orca* gently clearing cetacean snot from its blowhole, but rather, the electronic yelp of a black plastic pager. There! Triangulated on the liquid-crystal display, exact coordinates as reported by an on-shore spotter with a mighty powerful scope. There! Whales! Frolicking in the seasick mouth of the Strait of Juan de Fuca, headed west, toward the Pacific Ocean. Whales.

Not just any whales, but the 94 orcas who summer off the San Juan Islands. These are J, K, and L pods, and they may all look alike to the casual observer, but, of course, each is special to its mother. And to Friday Harbor whale biologist Ken Balcomb. He knows each by name, personality, physique, lineage. That 84-year-old great-grandmother breaching and slapping her tail is K7. There's L57's dorsal fin soaring above the water like the Matterhorn, and L12, whose saddlepatch looks like a huge comma leaking milk.

Balcomb has studied these whales for almost 20 years. He knows who hangs out with whom, who is sick, who gave birth, who is going

PAULA BOCK is a staff writer for *Pacific,* the Sunday magazine of the *Seattle Times.* She covers a range of subjects about the Northwest, including Amerasian refugees, community law enforcement, and Seattle's old Chinatown. "Whale Watcher" is her first article about whales. Reprinted from the *Seattle Times' Pacific* Magazine, October 23, 1994, by permission of the publisher.

through a growth spurt, who belongs to which mother. Orcas in these highly social resident pods stay with their mothers for life; Balcomb has family portraits. Every year, he and other researchers compile fresh mug shots of each whale into a catalog, a scientific field guide that's a cross between family album and whale yearbook.

The yearbook is missing one whale. Her name is Lolita. She has a gray saddlepatch that looks, from above, like a heart. She is 30 years old, 8,000 pounds and half as long as a school bus.

She lives in a tank in Miami.

But Lolita is no "Free Willy." She is a real live orca who could well be the Rosetta Stone of marine mammalogy, unlocking mysteries about cetacean behavior and environmental biology that have eluded scientists for years. And Balcomb, a facts and figures scientist, is not a character in a magical box-office hit. This biologist-in-Birkenstocks is the stuff of *National Geographic* documentaries.

Balcomb wants to teach Lolita to hunt for salmon, swim long distances, dive 20 times deeper than her 20-foot-deep tank. Ultimately, if she is fit, he would reunite her with her pod in greater Puget Sound, where she was captured 24 years ago. He'd track her travels, hormone levels, vocalizations. But before that ever happens, the founder of the Center for Whale Research must carefully navigate between aquarium owners whose profits depend on keeping the whale and animal rights extremists whose karma depends on releasing her.

"The truth of the matter," says Manny Garcia, Lolita's Miami trainer of seven years, "is that you can make all of your points, but you can never change people's hearts."

Animal behavior is not nearly as bizarre as human behavior. And real life, these days, is much more complicated than a children's movie.

For some, when they are young, there comes a random event that changes life forever. A car crash, a lethal bee sting, a hamburger tainted with bad bacteria.

For Lolita, it was the capture.

She was, at that time, about 6 years old, 14 feet long and 2,000 pounds, a slim young thing with clean lines where glossy black met white.

"She was so beautiful, unmarked, just a mellow nice animal," says Jessie White, her veterinarian for nearly 20 years. White, now semi-retired on a Florida ranch with 338 birds and four Maltese dogs, has, in 40 years as an animal doctor, custom-fabricated an artificial flipper for a sea turtle and served as midwife for manatees. Another of White's claims to fame is that he is the only human to do a nose job on a whale, the nose in question belonging to Hugo, a strapping 5-ton, 23-foot orca for whom, 24 years ago, the veterinarian chose lovely Lolita as a mate.

"Here I am a young veterinarian taking off going 4,000 miles to get a young female for a young male in Miami. That's a whale of a pimp." White picked up Lolita at Seattle Marine Aquarium on the waterfront a few days after she was captured in Penn Cove.

Penn Cove, off Whidbey Island, is cuddled in the rain shadow of the Olympics. That hot August week in 1970 was so clear you could see Mount Baker. Nobody, of course, was looking. Not the lawn-chair tourists with their beer, or the reporters with notebooks flapping, or the state game department guys in the tan Bermuda shorts, or the hairy protesters with their signs. Certainly, not the whale hunters themselves, salty and sweaty in skin suits. Everyone was focused on the dozens of squealing orcas—60, 70, maybe even 80 of them—corralled inside three acres of purse seine nets. Outside the nets, whales from three pods boiled the water, screamed, clicked, slapped the surface with their flukes, scattering droplets in the prevailing southwest winds. A few whales spyhopped, hanging vertical in the water so they could see above the surface. Dry grass hills, stands of Douglas fir, a madrona log cabin on shore. And there. There. A floating dock shaped like a square U. Men acting like cowboys, shouting, slipping lassos over young whales' fins, towing the orcas behind motorboats to the docks by the Standard Oil tank farm and look, look! Lolita breached in a canvas sling, clumsily rising out of the water, swaying, onto a flatbed truck.

At night, sounds floated across the mussel-shaped inlet: silverware clinking in the Captain Whidbey Inn dining room; a whale hunter on the tavern phone to Brussels, yes we've got whales, young ones, healthy, $30,000, right, you interested? Outside, silent stars, splashing flukes, squeals spiraling like high-pitched question marks. The tavern cat arched and went berserk.

That week in Penn Cove, dozens of whales from J, K, and L pods were captured. Most, too big to transport, were set free with fresh nicks and tears that years later would turn out to be helpful markers in Balcomb's photo-identification project. Seven young whales were sold to aquariums and marine parks around the world. One orca, a 20-foot cow, got caught in the nets and drowned. Months later, during the November rains, three baby whales washed up on shore not far from Penn Cove, their bloated bellies slit and weighted with anchors. For six years, whale hunters Ted Griffin and Don Goldsberry admitted nothing. "It could have been us or again it couldn't," Goldsberry told a *Seattle Times* reporter. "There could have been . . . accidents." Those carcasses turned the tide.

Griffin and Goldsberry, once local heroes, fell from public grace. "We were wearing white hats and all of a sudden I'm wearing a black hat," Goldsberry said in a 1976 KING-TV documentary in which he confessed to sinking the dead whales to avoid bad publicity. "My ex-partner and I care more about these animals . . . have done more for these animals than all the environmentalists put together. We've showed the public what they are like. They are a beautiful animal."

Killer whales, which are actually big dolphins, evolved about 25 million years ago. They have had a bad rap at least since first century A.D., when Roman scholar Pliny the Elder called orcas "an enormous mass of flesh armed with savage teeth . . . an enemy of other whales" that would "charge and pierce" females and their calves like "warships ramming." The top predators hunted in packs, bullying seals off ice floes, feasting on the tender tongues of sperm whales, leaving behind bloody blubber. The Navy gave orcas its highest plus-four danger rating and warned divers to get out of the water should they encounter the monsters. Local fishermen, just three decades ago, routinely blasted bullets into the black-and-white beasts because the resident orcas ate so much of the salmon catch.

The reputation of *Orcinus orca* changed in 1965 after Griffin triumphantly brought Namu, a killer whale from British Columbia, to his Seattle Marine Aquarium on Pier 56. Griffin loved the whale. He rode the whale. Namu sold tickets. The orca starred on T-shirts, baseball caps, mugs, sew-on patches and, eventually, in a book and movie by Griffin. The 21½-foot whale died after a year in captivity. But not before capturing the community's affection.

Griffin and Goldsberry went into the business of whale hunting, and for a dozen years after Namu's capture, the coasts of Washington state and British Columbia were virtually the only places in the world where live orcas were harvested for aquariums. In all, 308 orcas were captured, 11 died in the struggle, 240 escaped or were released. Fifty-seven killer whales were sold to seaquariums where, within a year, 20 of them died. The remaining Shamus and Corkys and Benkeis were accessible, huggable, lovable. Today, 33 million people a year visit the 24 orcas remaining in American marine parks.

"Seeing them in aquariums individualized these creatures, you see. They weren't just whales in the abstract," says Victor Scheffer, a retired biologist with the U.S. Fish and Wildlife Service who, at 87, is known as the dean of marine mammalogy. "At the same time, it also brought a backlash: Gee whiz, are we justified in holding them in captivity?"

The idea that whales could have rights evolved alongside the women's movement, the civil-rights struggle and Earth Day, Scheffer writes in *The Shaping of Environmentalism in America*. "There was a national self-examination, a kind of cultural revolution almost as important as the Industrial Revolution . . . It was a sobering moment. We realized we had been mistreating the earth and its resources."

Laws were changed. By 1972, Washington state required a $1,000 permit to capture orcas. Then the federal Marine Mammal Protection Act kicked in, further restricting killer whale captures. In 1977, after a string of protests and a major lawsuit involving Goldsberry and Sea World, the Pacific Northwest became, in effect, a killer-whale sanctuary.

After that, Iceland and Japan got into the multibillion-dollar industry, and recently, Russia, hungry for quick cash, began advertising killer whales from the Bering Sea—$1 million for an orca fresh off the boat; $2 million, trained. So far, no takers.

How the world has changed in a few decades. But not for Lolita. Through it all, she has performed two shows a day, 365 days a year, for 24 years, plus an occasional catered party under splashy lights. IiiIIIITTTtt'sss SHOWTIME! The patent-leather whale jumps 15 feet in the air with a handsome neoprene-clad trainer perched on her pectoral fins. She belly-flops back into her tank, splashing a toddler in Lion King sneakers who screams in delight. Sometimes, during leaps, Lolita glimpses the Miami skyline in the crack between flaking concrete bleachers and corrugated metal roof. At night, the whale looks up at stars in a sky polluted by pink-orange street lamps. She cannot see the ocean, though she may sense the warm waters of Biscayne Bay only a few hundred yards away. Her tank is clean and well-kept. It is four whales long and one whale deep, too shallow for Lolita to dive. You could swim across it in about 15 strokes. She shares it with four Pacific white-sided dolphins, who harass her when she's ovulating, and a battle-worn Risso's dolphin who resembles a graffiti-scarred subway train.

During the time Lolita has lived in that tank, trainers have come and gone, governments have fallen, a generation of kids was raised to love killer whales. Lolita is stuck, but she is loved. She gets free medical and dental, 180 pounds of restaurant-quality fish a day and tongue massages from her trainers. Her dorsal fin does not droop, her skin glistens. She feels to the touch like an enormous hard-boiled egg, peeled. Hugo, her whale friend with the nose-job, died in 1980, leaving Lolita alone in Miami. Her family is in the Pacific Northwest. Nobody knows whether she is happy.

Of the seven whales captured that hot August week in Penn Cove, Lolita is the only survivor.

Before you visit long-lost relatives, let alone move in, you call. And so, as Balcomb sees it, the first step to reuniting Lolita with her pod is a whale-to-whale phone call. This is not as crazy as it sounds.

Sound, in fact, is at the heart of the experiment. Orcas picture their world through sound, which, through water, can travel as far as from California to Japan. Whales echo-locate by bouncing clicks off objects. They can talk to each other from 30 miles away, their voices resembling birds chattering in a jungle canopy. Pods have distinct dialects, which is something like saying people in northern China speak Mandarin and those in southern China, Cantonese. In audio lingo, the primary acoustic energy for Pacific Northwest killer whales is between one and six kHz (kilohertz), with high frequencies shooting above 30 kHz. In plain language, nobody really knows how orcas talk or what they are saying. Balcomb wants to find out.

Why? Why do humans want to know this stuff about animals?

The 53-year-old scientist is bent over a wheelbarrow, scrubbing a beaked whale skull that smells thick and oily. His right eye twitches because he spends so much time one-eyed, peering through cameras and telescopes. His beard and hair are wavy and wild and flecked with white, like sea kelp. His watch calculates the tides. Earthwatch volunteers, who help with research and fund his work, wander barefoot around the property, which has an outhouse, apple trees, tepee, creaky computers and a sweeping view of whale runs in the Haro Strait.

Remember the sub-sub librarian in *Moby Dick*? Balcomb asks. The sub-sub, in an obscure appendix in the back of Melville's novel, is "a mere painstaking burrower and grubworm of a poor devil" who snivels around searching for higgledy-piggledy whale facts in the sub-sub basements of libraries and street-stalls of the earth, "picking up whatever random allusion to whales he could anyways find in any book whatsoever, sacred or profane."

The whole of human history, Balcomb says, is about gathering higgledy-piggledy facts. Everything we know, like how to make bronze or tune a car, is based on something pre-learned by somebody else. Balcomb, like Melville's sub-sub librarian, is motivated by acquisition of knowledge.

He could have turned out different. He was raised in tract housing during an era when the goal was to get a bike, then a car, then a wife, then a house and a job to make money so your kids could have the same. He was a Navy pilot for seven years in a hierarchy that says pilots are the best in the Navy, the Navy is the best branch of the military, Americans are the best humans, humans are the best living creature in the world. But all along, he studied whales. "As we began to learn more about these whales, Bing! the light goes off. We're pretty arrogant. We're animals." Suddenly, nobody was better than anyone else. Humans could not lord it over other species. Money, power—that all got thrown overboard. The only thing left was curiosity.

"Maybe this is another sideshow," Balcomb says of the Lolita experiment. "A big scientific sideshow. It's not morally superior to throwing whales in a swimming tank and charging people to see them." Still, there is stuff he must find out.

The acoustic experiment would be sort of like E.T. phoning home using a satellite hookup and hydrophones. Lolita in her tank at one end. At the other end, her pod swimming in the wilds of Haro Strait. Will she respond to them? Physically? Verbally? What types of sounds will she make? How will they react? Keiko, the movie-star whale who played the title role in the movie *Free Willy* got an erection when he heard recordings of other killer whales. Lolita vocalized excitedly while listening to orca tapes, even though the whales weren't speaking her dialect. Balcomb wants to see what Lolita does, what she says, when she hears the voices of her own pod feeding or foraging or resting or doing aerial acrobatics or being sexy. Will her hormone levels rise? Adrenaline? How about heart rate and respiration and brain-wave patterns?

By electronically manipulating the phone hookup, Balcomb hopes to learn whether orcas communicate in bursts of information or in a steady stream, whether chopping out high frequencies or very low ones will make a difference in what whales hear.

Yet the biggest question, when it comes to whales and phones, is about social bonds. Whether Lolita will recognize her family, whether they will remember her. "What the heck is she going to say to momma and brother on a live hookup?" Balcomb wonders. "What are they going to say back—where the hell are you? And where have you been all this time?"

Imagine the reunion. No, wait. First, think about a year of intense rehabilitation for Lolita. Before she ever left Miami, she'd have a complete physical, including tests for parasites and other diseases, to guard against transmitting sickness to whales in the wild. If she passes, it would be on to a year of training in a netted-off cove on San Juan Island. She would learn to swim long distances, to dive, to hunt for fish, to recall to a special whistle.

Eventually, Balcomb wants to bolt a transmitter to her dorsal fin that would record her blood levels and heart rate, vocalizations, speed when she's swimming, depth when she searches for bottom fish—gigabytes of information. What happens to Lolita's body when she dives? What does she say when she's eating? Where does she go with her pod? Do the fish she eats and the places she feeds change her chemistry? Will her levels of DDT, PCBs, heavy metals, mercury, selenium and other contaminants rise? Killer whales are top predators. Here in the Pacific Northwest, they eat fish, primarily salmon. We eat salmon. If pollution has infected their diet, it has likely infected the entire food chain in greater Puget Sound.

This fall, scientists at the Pacific Biological Station in Nanaimo, B.C., plan to biopsy resident pods to study their DNA. The tests could show whether Lolita is from J, K, or L pod, who is her mother, who is her great-grandmother, her aunt, her cousin. Female killer whales in the wild live into their 50s; it's likely a few Pacific Northwest orcas are octogenarians. They will remember Lolita, Balcomb believes.

Now. Imagine the reunion. It would be May of whatever year. Her pod would come into the Haro Strait, following the annual spring salmon migration. They'd hear each other from a long way off. "It'll stir something in her memory," Balcomb says of Lolita. "I'd be willing to bet the deed they'll be vocal, do aerial acrobatics, hang outside the net. We'd be prepared to open the gate. If there's a lot of excitement and carrying on, we'd let her go. If she's fearful and doesn't react, we wouldn't push it. We'd be prepared to care for her for the rest of her life in the cove."

That's Balcomb's dream experiment. It is risky. Lolita could die if she doesn't eat or runs into boats.

"I don't think it's absurd, but it's something we don't have a lot of experience with," says Ann Terbush, chief of the division that issues reintroduction permits for the National Marine Fisheries Service. "It would seem like a real uphill battle to deal with an animal that had been in captivity that long."

The release should not be used as an emotional placebo for humans at the ultimate sacrifice of the whale, warns Lolita's current veterinarian, Greg Bossart, an assistant professor of pathology at the University of Miami Medical School. "So we feel good about the release, but when you look at the statistics, the statistics are not that great."

Actually, what's not great is the dearth of statistics. We know this: A pilot whale, after eight years at Marineland, survived many years in the wild. Several dolphins were successfully released after years in captivity. When it comes to orcas, only a few have been released after long captivity, and those cases have had sloppy follow-up. Two killer whales, Charlie Chin and Pointed-nose Cow, escaped from a seapen in Pedder Bay, B.C., after seven months and have been photo-documented with their pod every year since. But that's just one example. Really, nobody knows Lolita's chances.

"Everything is pretty when they talk about a release," says Garcia, Lolita's trainer. "The reality is it's not going to be pretty. It's death. Life is rough out there. It's like saying, 'OK, grandma, we're going to kick you out.'

"How can someone who lives thousands of miles away, who doesn't know the animal, tell me she's unhappy? That she'd want to go back to the wild? I was with the animal five days a week for seven years. He doesn't know her."

It sounds crazy—a whale-to-whale phone call, the expectation that an orca who has been hand-fed for 24 years, who once freaked out when a live grouper swam in her tank, would learn to hunt for her own food. But no crazier, Balcomb says, than lifting a young whale from Penn Cove waters and flying her across the country to live for 24 years in a refrigerated saltwater swimming pool.

The Lolita thing is warming up in Miami. *Ocean Drive,* an upscale fashion and entertainment magazine with big-name advertisers, is running $10,000 "Free Lolita/Boycott Miami Seaquarium" double-page spreads sandwiched between ads for Bacardi, Hermes, Ralph Lauren. "We've never taken a stand on anything except choosing who our cover model was every month," says publisher Jerry Powers, who was inspired after seeing *Free Willy* last year. "We're not a cause publication. We felt this was a good way to start." Advertisers love it. Powers' campaign to free

Lolita will soon crank up to $7,000-a-month billboards on Interstate 95. Whatever it takes, whatever it costs, he says, "We have the money."

Balcomb has offered Seaquarium $250,000 to do the acoustic experiment, $1 million for the release. He could come up with more; there are donors.

The situation has become sufficiently heated that it is now easier to get an interview with U.S. Secretary of State Warren Christopher than with Seaquarium owner Arthur Hertz. Lolita is the star attraction at his marine park, a facility open since 1955 that now employs 250 people and grosses more than $10 million a year. This has not been a good few years for Seaquarium, what with Hurricane Andrew and the tourist shootings and legal deadlock with tony Key Biscayne neighbors over a $70-million expansion plan. Last year, 650,000 tourists visited the park, half the crowd of three decades ago.

Hertz has not officially nixed Balcomb's experiment, but he hasn't said yes, either. Right now, he's just not talking. Who do those whale people think they are, anyway? Where are they when sick whales strand themselves on the beach at 4 in the morning? Or when baby manatees get chewed up by boat propellers and need 24-hour bottle-feeding? Do they come waving fists of cash then? Seaquarium spends $1 million a year rehabilitating and releasing injured and stranded marine mammals. Where do you think that money comes from? Gate receipts! And why do you think people will pay the $17.95 admission? Not to get their hand stamped—to see Lolita!

After all the field work with binoculars and 300mm camera lenses, the meganights on the computer analyzing data, the endless hunt for pre-1976 photographs of J, K, and L pods, Balcomb was afraid this would happen. "We're pegged as screaming extreme animal-rights humaniacs. As if we haven't given a thought to it. As if we just want to throw a whale back in the ocean.

"Way back in the beginning, I didn't want to get into any battles with Sea World or the government or Greenpeace. I was into data. Facts. Information. There were 68 whales in 1976, 71 in 1977, 94 now. Good fun stuff to know. Something you can prove. I had to stay aloof and I pretty much have until this Willy thing came along."

The Willy thing. After the movie came out, producers Dick and Lauren Shuler-Donner, residents on neighboring Orcas Island, asked Balcomb to help with a plan to rehabilitate and eventually free Keiko, the movie-star whale with a droopy dorsal fin who now languishes in a

Mexican marine park. (The latest is that Warner Bros., the movie company, will build a larger, cooler $10 million tank for Keiko in Newport, Ore.)

Balcomb wrote a proposal and flew to Mexico. The CEO of Reino Aventura, the Mexican marine park that owns Keiko, agreed to give Balcomb responsibility for the whale. Handshakes all around. This is all on videotape. But suddenly, before Balcomb even got back to Friday Harbor, everything was called off. For Time-Warner, a multinational corporation whose tentacles wind around marine parks, releasing Keiko to the wild would be like opening Pandora's tank.

Lolita, Balcomb realized then, was a far better candidate for release than Keiko. Her health was better than Keiko's, and, thankfully, she would not be hounded by the complications attending a movie-star whale. Best of all, unlike Keiko's Icelandic family, Lolita's pod is known, studied and right here, in the Pacific Northwest.

Balcomb sorts through 3,600 photo negatives and hundreds of entries in the 1994 orca log, wrapping up the whale yearbook for yet another year. Summer wasn't kind to J, K, and L pods; scarcity of fish. L42's not looking good, the blubber behind his blowhole all sunken like he's starved. His uncle, L10, with the tall bite-nicked dorsal, is starting to show skull. These whales need food. And K17, the 28-year-old with the Nike swoosh-stripe markings, well, K17 is missing. Yesterday he was swimming behind his mother looking kind of tired; today she is around, but he is gone. Where? Where are the fish? Why didn't the pods follow them? Why are the male orcas suffering most? So much stuff to figure out. Maybe this will be K17's last year in the pod's family portrait.

Summer is over. Soon, the whales will scallop past Balcomb's back porch on an extended autumn sojourn. Past the place where the hills roll down into a long flat line, past the golden grasses falling off into the sea. The whales will spend their winter in waters where people are not—Desolation Sound, the west coast of Vancouver Island, 300 miles out in the stormy Pacific Ocean.

Lolita, for yet another year, will winter in Miami.

JONATHAN WHITE

# Voices from the Sea

Until the 1960s, most knowledge about whales was compiled from autopsies of stranded or harpooned carcasses. Roger Payne changed all that. Following his instinct, and against the better judgment of his colleagues, Roger insisted on studying live whales in their natural environment. Although there is still a lot to learn about whales, Roger's studies of whale behavior, vocalizations, identification, and migratory patterns have made enormous contributions to the field, and his benign techniques are now used all over the world. Roger's special interest in underwater acoustics led him and a colleague, Scott McVay, to discover that humpback whales sing, a discovery that has profoundly affected scientific thinking and public awareness of whales.

Roger spent the first eighteen years of his life in New York City, where he nurtured a love for music. An accomplished cellist, he claims that his passion for music led him to all his other interests. As an undergraduate at Harvard University in 1956, Roger researched the directional sensitivity of the ears of bats. He went on to study the ability of owls to locate prey in total darkness and received his Ph.D. in animal behavior and neurophysiology from Cornell University in 1962. Roger's

JONATHAN WHITE is the founder and former president of the Resource Institute, a nonprofit organization based in Seattle that focuses on the culture and traditions of the Northwest. White's book *Talking on the Water,* a collection of conversations with Roger Payne and others, was published in 1994 by Sierra Club Books. Reprinted by permission of the publisher.

postdoctoral studies at Tufts University focused on the ears of noctuid moths, and particularly on how moths use their acute sense of hearing to avoid bats.

A recipient of numerous honorary memberships and awards, including a MacArthur Fellowship in 1984, Roger is now director of The Whale Conservation Institute in Massachusetts. Among its numerous projects in conservation, education, and research, the institute has been involved in the study of right whales in Argentina since 1970. It is the longest continuous study of individually identified whales in the world.

The following interview took place over the course of two summers in southeast Alaska. On both occasions, Roger was on board the schooner *Crusader* for humpback whale research in the waters of Frederick Sound. On an August evening we happened on a large pod of whales at the entrance to Seymour Canal. Roger was as excited as a five-year-old at Christmas. We shut down the engine and drifted all night, sharing watches and listening to the whales through hydrophones. As far as I know, Roger never slept. He was either lying on deck, headphones in his ears, watching the star-filled sky, or tinkering with the mess of sound equipment and wire that tumbled out of the pilot house and into the sea. The last image I remember was of Roger leaning over the starboard rail. In the red light of the instrument panel I could see him looking into the water, shaking his head and smiling.

*Jonathan White:* We've been observing humpback whales here in Frederick Sound during their summer feeding season. How is their behavior different here than when they're in Hawaii or off the coast of Mexico in the winter?

*Roger Payne:* Well, here they're feeding and sleeping. As soon as they've filled their bellies utterly, they go into sort of a torpor and sleep for a while. Hours later they awaken, hungry again, ready for the next meal.

Hawaii and Mexico are the breeding grounds of this particular population. In Hawaii, they're feeding little, if at all. They're very active socially with each other. The males are competing for females, and some of the females are busy taking care of newborn calves.

The other obvious thing is that the males sing virtually all the time in Hawaii. They also sing in Alaska, but it's very rare. You might hear a song every two weeks, and then not even a whole song, but just a song fragment.

*JW:* Why do you think that is?

*RP:* I suspect that singing is connected with breeding, for songs are most often heard on breeding grounds. I'm surprised they sing in Alaska at all. They may be practicing the song or retaining it in their memories, or keeping versions that have come from other areas in front of the ears of whales that are visiting from other regions. But we don't know, and so I can't really say for sure why it is that whales sing.

*JW:* When we put the hydrophones down and drifted with the whales the other night, I was astounded by the loudness and variety of their vocalizations. In contrast to the absolute silence of Frederick Sound, it sounded like an underwater party of old men, burping, laughing, falling off their chairs, magnified a hundred times. For me, it added another dimension to their world.

*RP:* I was totally blown away by what we heard the other night, too. We've always called those vocalizations social sounds, but we're not sure what they mean. I only call them social sounds to distinguish them from songs. Most of them appear to be a different vocabulary. I've never in my life heard so many different sounds as we heard the other night. Marvelous, riotous sounds. They changed my whole perception of how much noise humpbacks make up here. I must say these sounds take you in a compelling fashion into the concept that, my lord, maybe these animals are having some sort of conversation with each other. There were a lot of them around when we were listening—maybe twenty or thirty—so there were plenty of chances to hear comments from other whales.

*JW:* I couldn't listen without getting giddy—like that noise we heard just before a whale breached.

*RP:* Yeah, you mean the one that goes "dee-bomp, dee-bomp . . . bom . . . bom . . . bom . . . bom whee whee whee whee wheewheewhee!!!" [Roger imitates the pre-breaching sounds like a jazz scat singer: first the notes descend rhythmically, growing lower and slower; then they rapidly ascend, growing short and higher until they're more like a squeal.] And then finally we saw a breach. Yeah, that was fabulous.

*JW:* What is your current thinking about why humpback whales sing?

*RP:* I think songs are sung by a male in hopes of a female, in hopes of being more attractive than other males. And I suspect that the form of the song is shaped and selected by females; in other words, males learn to sing.what attracts females. That's my guess. There are all kinds of things the song could be. A good song might give a male a momentary advantage over other males, giving him more opportunities to mate with the female.

Another possibility is that songs are a means by which a female can get some idea of the general fitness of a male, by noting how long he is able to hold his breath. If the female is listening from shallow water, the male will be unable to hide the fact that he is returning to the surface for a breath of air. Owing to the acoustics of the sea, the sound will become faint as he approaches the surface. So, if she hears the song get faint, she knows he's going to the surface for a breath. She could, for example, tell how often a given male needs to breathe. This suggestion was first made by Jim Darling, a man who's been studying these humpbacks for a long time. I think he may be right.

Another theory about why whales sing suggests the males are competing with each other, that their songs are actually threats hurled at each other. The idea here is that they recognize each other's voices and know whether it's worth it to pick up the gauntlet, so to speak, and go through with a fight. It would save time during the breeding season if males didn't have to settle their differences. They'd recognize the sounds of other males, and think, "Oh, my God, that's Fred, there's no way in the world I can beat him, I think I'll just retire from the field."

A lot of other explanations have been proposed for songs. Whales might use them the way the Aborigines of Australia claim to use songs as a means of memorizing the details of a long journey. But that doesn't make sense for humpbacks, because whales that share the same winter breeding grounds return to several different feeding grounds in the summer. If the song was something a whale memorized to find its way to a particular point, it should vary according to the whale's particular destination. But that's not what happens. Instead, all the whales on the same wintering ground—no matter where they spend the summer—sing the same song.

There are other theories. One is that songs might contain a saga, the story of the humpback's existence. If that's the case, I would expect the conditions on which they were commenting to repeat after a while. But even though we have samples of songs that go back forty years, we still haven't heard any repetition.

*JW:* Their songs are sweet and sad. The psychologist James Hillman says the feeling we get around an animal may be evoked by the animal itself. When we see an eagle, for example, we feel respect or awe, but we don't feel warmth—at least not the same kind of warmth we feel around a whale. When I see a whale and hear its song, I feel a certain sadness. Hillman says that maybe this has something to do with what the whale is feeling, something that it is communicating.

*RP:* It's a fascinating idea, but I have no personal evidence for it. However, if whales don't have a language like ours, what are they doing with their enormous and fancy brains? I have wondered whether one of the things they are doing is communicating emotion directly. When humans communicate with words, it's usually an attempt to elicit an emotional response. If I were speaking to a woman with whom I have fallen in love, I would try to use my language to bring her to the same emotion. Poets speak affectively of love. This is the way humans use language, but I can imagine a different approach. Maybe whales have developed a way where they can simply evoke the emotion itself in another whale. Of course, that's only speculation. No one knows what whales use their large brains for.

Since they live in an acoustic world where they need sound as a means of "seeing" what's around them, whales might have especially sophisticated acoustic processing techniques. It has never been clearly demonstrated that large whales can echolocate, which is a means of learning about their surroundings by making sounds and listening for the echoes. But we do know that porpoises echolocate with exquisite precision, and porpoises and whales are members of the same order, Cetacea. If you or I snapped our fingers, we might get some idea of the dimensions of this room, but we wouldn't be able to detect the two brass pipes supporting this table, these benches, and so forth, at least not without a sophisticated analysis. That kind of analysis may be what porpoises do with their fancy brains.

But bats do pretty much the same thing with a brain the size of the tip of your smallest finger, while the brain of these dolphins is the size of a human brain. I think we're going to discover that whales and dolphins use their brains for something entirely different than humans do. That's why I'm intrigued by the thought of them using their intelligence to communicate emotions directly.

One of the theories put forward some years ago for how whales name things was tested with an experiment that was unfortunately flawed. The theory stated that the way a porpoise names a fish is simply by imitating the sound it receives when it hits the fish with an echolocation pulse. As I mentioned before, the porpoise detects the fish by making a sound and getting an echo off it. The characteristics of the echo form an acoustic image, not a visual one as we are accustomed to. The theory is that maybe this acoustic image is what the porpoise uses as the name of the fish, by imitating it later when it wishes to "say" the fish's name to another porpoise.

Humans are more visual than acoustic. If we wish to refer to an object like a car to someone whose language we don't speak, we might find a photograph and point to it. We communicate by creating visual images. Porpoises may do this same thing, only with sound.

JW: Marine mammals are sometimes very curious about people and their boats. For example, a pod of orcas approached our boat a few months ago off the coast of British Columbia while we were sailing. They came right up to us—just a matter of a few feet away—and then dove under the boat, surfacing again immediately off our bow. We were in a wide open channel and they could have gone anywhere. Just how interested do you think these animals are in us?

RP: I've watched a lot of right whales in the waters off Argentina, and I often get the impression that they're bored stiff. When anything new or different comes into the area, they eventually start messing around with it. In Argentina, you can't moor a boat in the area where right whales congregate without them messing with the anchor line and dragging it away.

We used to install tide gauges, which are sticks driven into the beach face, in order to measure the tidal differences. The whales would come and mess them up. There was a female who seemed to derive particular pleasure in breaking the gauges. She would come along with her calf, ease up to one of the stakes, and slowly lean on it, putting her head against it. You could see her start to apply pressure by moving her tail up and down broadly. The stick would lean more and more until it broke. She'd swim off as it fell to the bottom. Finally, we had to design our stakes with breakable joints so they could be repaired easily. That's what it took. Sometimes the whales would break as many as three or four stakes a day.

We used to use small boats to hold our *sonobuoys*, devices that broadcast the sounds picked up by hydrophones under the boat. We used to moor the boats holding the sonobuoys in different places around the bay. But we always had the same problem. Whales kept messing up their moorings, getting tangled up in the anchors and moving them away. We slowly realized it was deliberate. They were doing it intentionally, fooling around with the boats until something let go.

There's an interesting thing happening in the coastal waters of Baja California. It's called the "friendly gray whale phenomenon," where gray whales come so close to whale-watching boats that the tourists can reach out and pat them. If I remember right, the first time this happened was in 1978, when someone reached out with a broom and scratched a gray whale that was hanging around a tourist boat. The whale seemed to like it and leaned into the broom, presenting its other side to be scratched, and so on.

The following year there were two or three whales behaving this way, and something like six or eight the year after, until the news apparently spread among the whales that boats were safe and even offered pleasant contact. The whales proceeded to seek out boats filled with tourists, until there were hundreds of whales doing it. Now there are more whales seeking contact with boats than there are boatloads of people to pat them, and so the whales compete with each other for the attention of boats. In Baja, it's boatloads of tourists, not whales, that are the scarce resource.

The whale biologist Jim Darling, who lives on Vancouver Island, was once called by a policeman who said, "There's a crazy gray whale out there. We're going to have to destroy it." Jim asked, "What did it do?" And the policeman said, "It rammed my boat." "Did it roll over onto its back right after it rammed your boat?" Jim asked. "Well, yes," the policeman answered, "as a matter of fact it did." And Jim said, "Well, scratch its belly, that's what it wants."

These are the same gray whales whose species were originally named "devil fish" by the men who discovered their breeding grounds in Scammon's Lagoon. Even though Captain Scammon and his men made a rich haul of oil and blubber while hunting these whales in the late nineteenth century, the men thought they were very dangerous animals. When they tried to kill the whales, the whales fought back!

So I think that whales' reactions to boats and to people are those of great curiosity, and for a long time that curiosity proved to be painful or fatal, particularly in the case of large whales that were harpooned. One of the wonderful things that has happened in recent years is that more people are accepting the possibility that these animals are approaching us in a peaceful way. Maybe it's safe to be around them. People have swum up to them and actually touched them in some cases, though that is illegal in U.S. waters. Whenever that's been done intelligently, the results have been positive.

There's a good example of this in Dingle, a small fishing port in Ireland. The so-called Dingle dolphin swims up to humans and allows them to pat or touch him. He doesn't accept food at all. People have tried, but he won't accept. He fishes for himself. One of the people who trained him first is a young woman named Sheila Stokes. She was a legal assistant with no special knowledge of dolphins. She went around to fishing villages asking the fishermen if there was a dolphin in their area. Finally, in Dingle, a fisherman said "Oh yes, there's one. He lives by those rocks over there. We see him every day." So she and her boyfriend got a tiny boat—about eight feet long—and they went out and swam with that dolphin on forty-two separate days until on the forty-second day the dolphin finally allowed her to touch him.

Everybody has hailed this dolphin as being a wonderful, very tame, exceptional animal. Having visited it, it's my suspicion that he may be particularly hard to tame and unexceptional. What is exceptional is Sheila Stokes. She had the patience to swim for forty-two days near the dolphin without success. I mean, how did she feel swimming out there on the thirty-eighth day of failure? How about the thirty-ninth and fortieth, and then the forty-first? I suspect this dolphin is basically a scaredy-cat. But by having had somebody persistent enough to bring him into contact with humans, he now accepts us and spends most of his energy messing about with us. He obviously likes people—now.

JW: Do you think it's exploitive when people make a business out of this behavior?

RP: There is, of course, a major business in people interacting with dolphins or seeing them in captivity. Dolphinariums are an example. I feel that some of the tricks that people get dolphins to do are degrading and should be stopped. I don't believe in them. But other tricks that show the natural abilities of dolphins—jumping, for example—can be inspiring for those who have not seen dolphins in the wild. And until somebody can demonstrate that television has replaced reality—real first-hand experience—then my feeling is that those few dolphins in captivity are playing an important role as ambassadors. They are training humanity to have a different attitude toward not just dolphins but all wildlife. I believe that if you could explain to the dolphins what role they were playing, they might go along with it. If I were living in a world controlled by another species whose opinion of me was that I would make good fertilizer, good oil, and good meat for dogs and cats, I think I would willingly give part of my life to being an ambassador to change the opinion of their children toward me. Maybe I'm somewhat crazy, but that's how I would feel.

There has been a huge struggle over the question of California condors, as to whether they should be caught and raised in captivity until we can change our ways enough to guarantee them a space in the wild. Those who are opposed to the idea believe a condor sitting in a cage with its wings folded and unable to soar on the thermals of its native California coast is not really a condor. My feeling is people aren't thinking of it from the point of view of the condors. Let us suppose for a moment that our fears for how badly they suffer in captivity are wrong and, in fact, their suffering is a thousand times worse. And let us suppose that that suffering continues for not just five or ten generations, but for a hundred generations. At the end of that time, let's assume we are standing with a condor that is about to be released. We say to him, "Well, was it worth it, all those hideous years your ancestors suffered in captivity?" I'm guessing his reaction would be, "I'm sure my ancestors didn't enjoy it, but I'm out of here. I've got my eye on blue sky."

My feeling is *anything* beats extinction. *Anything!* When people damn zoos and aquariums, they forget that most people don't live in the country but in cities where they see rats, pigeons, cockroaches, mice, dogs, cats, and nothing more. I have never felt deeply inspired by these species—have you? Maybe cats, but not truly, deeply inspired, not the way I felt when I first walked into the New York aquarium and saw the indescribable grace of a snow-white beluga whale. I have never seen anything more beautiful. The power of that image—standing face to face with whoever is on the other side of the aquarium window—is unique.

Some firsthand experiences are incomparably valuable. Until somebody demonstrates that this is not the case with captive dolphins, I will worry that getting rid of zoos and aquariums is more negative than positive. The function of zoos and aquariums is important to the future of the species that inhabit them. For example, if the rivers containing dolphins become so polluted that the dolphins can no longer survive, their only hope will be a long period in captivity. During that time, we will have a chance to rehabilitate the rivers, eventually transplanting the dolphins back into healthy systems. But if we have shut down all the aquariums and cease all efforts to improve techniques for keeping dolphins safely in captivity, then all we will do is stand back and wring our hands as we watch the last river dolphins die.

You asked about the business of whale watching. It doesn't make any difference what I or anyone else says, nothing will ever mean as much to a person as seeing a whale close-at-hand in the wild. That is something you never forget. Seeing whales at close quarters is a very important experience for people to have in terms of positioning their attitudes in favor of the wild world.

Whale watching is attacked vehemently by some people. They say, "Stay away from whales, don't bother them, it's their world, it's not our world," and so on. It's a wonderful position philosophically, but it doesn't do much for the protection of whales and it doesn't do much for winning friends for whales in high places or for building lobbies. Effective lobbies are populated by people who have had firsthand experience with their subject. Even if you feel sure that whale watching is bad for whales, you have to realize there is no evidence that it has had a significant negative effect, and you have to explain why year after year the same whales return to the same areas and feed in the same ways.

In Hawaii, humpback whales are giving birth to calves as quickly as biologically possible. If humpbacks are suffering in Hawaiian waters, why are they coming back? The facts are simply inconsonant with the great destruction a lot of people think whale watching is doing. I think whale watching is performing an extremely valuable function in terms of attracting people's interest and attention to whales. That's a brutal fact. For example, there are more calves born to humpback whales in whale watch areas than are known to be born to these whales anywhere else.

JW: Whale watching is a rapidly growing business. I've watched it grow tremendously here in Alaska over the last five years. First, is the history of whale watching long enough to really know its effect on whale populations? Second, as the business increases, so does the potential for harassment. What about the long-term effects on the quality of life for whales?

*RP:* Those are wonderful points, Jonathan, and I hear you loud and clear. I too worry about the subtle long-term effects. Whale watching has been going on long enough in some places, like eastern Massachusetts, to detect its effect. The populations of whales in that area are increasing. The same individuals are coming back every year. The rate at which they're giving birth is as high as it can be. Those are important considerations.

You also mentioned quality of life. What is the diminution of the quality of life of a chickadee that lives in your backyard, eats artificial foods from your feeder, and is now, in fact, totally dependent on them? If you removed the bird feeders throughout New England, you'd probably halve the populations of chickadees, nuthatches, downy woodpeckers, titmice, and other species that come with them. My feeling is that all of us are experiencing a diminution in quality of life. There's no way of pretending that the great undiscovered, unexploited herds of game that once existed in North America are still here. My God, they're totally gone, absolutely destroyed by our distant ancestors who seem to have brought final destruction to a number of other species as well, including wooly mammoths and wooly rhinos.

There's no question that there is a certain diminution of the lives of whales. But how bad is it? Look at the alternative. The alternative is an active whaling industry, unopposed, as was the case under the Golden Gate Bridge in San Francisco until the mid-1960s. The Del Monte whaling station, just a little farther inland, was killing whales until 1971!

So it's all a trade-off. There's no way we can completely turn our backs on whales now. If we do, the thing that will get them in the end will be lack of caring—things like accidental entanglement in fishing gear and accumulation of toxins in the oceans. The other considerations are minor. If we build a group of people who love whales, who have learned to love them through close encounters in an aquarium or sitting in a whale watch boat, they will no longer shrug their shoulders and say, "Aah, that's too bad" when they hear that a hundred thousand dolphins die accidentally every year in fishing nets. Instead, they'll get mad, and maybe one in every ten thousand will be vociferous enough to lean on their representatives to the point where something actually happens to alleviate the situation.

In that sense, I think whales are better off than they've ever been, even though some of them are probably having their lives diminished in areas where there is too much contact with humans. But those areas are small compared to the vast herds of whales swimming in seas most of us will never see.

JW: What is it that so attracts people to dolphins and whales? I was out with them just the other day and thinking, "What is it in me that wants to get so close to these whales? Would I be making the same effort to get close to them if they were the size of salmon?"

RP: That's a wonderful question. Why would you make a greater effort to see a redwood than a dogwood? Dogwoods have flowers, redwoods don't. Whales and redwoods both make us feel small and I think that's an important experience for humans to have at the hands of nature. We need to recognize that we are not the stars of the show. We're just another pretty face, just one species among millions more. The star of the show is nature, and we just may be the most unsuccessful species that's ever appeared on Earth, threatening our own existence in fewer generations than any other species ever has. Our fancy brain, which is a lot of fun to own, is very dangerous. I can't think of anything we've discovered in nature that is as dangerous. Cobra venom, hell, that's nothing to worry about. Just stay out of reach of the cobra. But you can't stay out of reach of human beings.

The snowfields here in Alaska are polluted with outfall from factories located thousands of miles away. The flesh-eating mammals up here have accumulated these deadly compounds in their system. We can't get away from it any longer. As Pogo says, "We have met the enemy and he is us."

But when you encounter a large species like a redwood or a whale, it introduces awe into your life. And awe is a very rare but very important experience. It's what started the major religions. Experiencing awe in the hands of the wild can cause you to feel the same essential ecstasy. It's an experience you can't find by watching television.

JW: Why is awe so important for people to experience?

RP: I think awe is like a sign saying, "You have captured my attention." Awe awakens attention and respect. When you find something that takes hold of human beings and causes them to change their ways—I mean, what is that worth? A trillion dollars? A hundred trillion? All the money that exists? More than that?

I was talking with a politician in Maine, a woman for whom I have great respect, and I said to her that I was frustrated by [then] President Bush and his lack of interest in the environment. I asked her, "How would you get his attention? How would you get the president to focus on the environment?" Without a moment's hesitation she said, "Through his grandchildren. They're probably the only people he really trusts. They're the only people he speaks to who don't have another agenda." So what would it be worth to have one of the president's grandchildren go up to him and say, "Grandad, why is it you allow forests to be ruined for lumber that's shipped off to Japan? Why is the Tongass National Forest going overseas in freighters? Why do you do that?" What would that be worth? How many hours of how many conservationists' time would it count for if the president heard that question from somebody he didn't fear?

We cannot speak with nature, but our sense of awe in it allows it to speak to us. The few things that happen to people in their lives that really affect how they live and what they respect and how they go about the business of their day-to-day lives, those experiences probably occupy a total of, what, half a minute? One minute of a lifetime? Yet they're what really matter. All the rest is just the packing material in which your life gets shipped.

But let me come back to the question you asked about why whales affect us the way they do. I think part of it is because they're mammals, and we have a natural sympathy for creatures that approach life in a similar way that we do. People seem to sense in whales a different presence than they do in other large animals like, for example, a whale shark. Even though they're as big as a whale, whale sharks are cold-blooded, and we sense that they may not be very smart, and . . . well, they're just not the same as a whale.

I can't imagine a whale shark embracing its young the way we see mother right whales do. In that sense, whales are more like sea otters. Why are sea otters so unbelievably attractive to people? I suspect it's partly because they're so tactile, that they hold and cuddle and embrace their young. It's a very basic instinct. For instance, the thing that was so important to Sheila Stokes, the woman who trained the Dingle dolphin, was to embrace it. And she did. There's a large difference between just watching an animal and being able to embrace it—a huge difference.

People laugh and call conservationists tree-huggers. They laugh at someone who wants to hug a whale. But it's only their own embarrassment that causes them to laugh, and their laughter betrays their discomfort with people who are courageous enough to embrace what they love.

*JW:* What has been your closest encounter with a whale?

*RP:* One night just before leaving Argentina, my thirteen-year-old son and I took a long walk on the beach. As we did, we passed close to the water's edge where there was a mother whale and her calf. As she rolled, causing a great slow disturbance in the water, she raised her flipper into the air so it towered over us. It had the sense of a benediction. I mean, no pope could have waved in such a way as to give me a more complete sense of blessing. And what were we being blessed by? By life, I suppose. The feeling it gave me was unforgettable.

I've never had an experience with a whale that really scared me. I've felt scared in retrospect, but never at the time. I don't have any gee-whiz whale stories where it's me against them—you know, the standard macho nonsense. I've had whales nearly breach on my boat. The most recent incident of this was last year off the coast of Colombia. I had to swerve the boat to prevent the whale from landing on it. There's a woman who works in my laboratory who had a whale breach directly on top of her boat. Not a glancing blow, but a direct hit across the bow. The boat was totaled, but I haven't had that sort of experience.

*JW:* One of the reasons I'm so drawn to these animals is that they have qualities I respect. When I go to a party and I see someone laughing or being playful or listening carefully to someone else, I am drawn to them. I want to be close to them and I want them to like me as a friend. In some ways it's the same kind of thing that draws me to the whales. I want them to like me the way I want a friend to like me.

*RP:* That's wonderful. I share those feelings. One of the great disappointments in my life with whales happened in Argentina with a whale named Troff. Since we've been there, Troff's had five calves. She's a wonderfully successful, excellent mother. I've spent a lot of my life watching her because she's often right off our camp. On three occasions I've been on the water next to her, only to discover that she's terrified of my boat. She gets away from me as fast as she can. As far as I can tell, I cause her maximum panic whenever I get anywhere near her. That's been a great disappointment.

There's another Argentine right whale I feel close to, but it's the same with her. I remember the first time I saw her after she had been away a couple years. I'd been watching a whale off in the middle of the bay all afternoon and it was inching its way toward the coast. It seemed to take forever to come in close. And as I watched it I slowly realized, my God, it's Y-Spot. And tears came to my eyes. It was a very emotional thing. I thought she had died. It was this encounter that first taught us that the whales only come back to Argentina every three years. When I saw Y-Spot again, it was just incredible, like thinking a friend had been lost in a war, then encountering them again. But as far as I can tell, neither Y-Spot nor Troff thinks of me as a friend. It's deeply disappointing because I've spent a lot of time watching them, and I love them both.

JW: There's another level at which this desire to get close doesn't seem exclusively personal—I mean, when it's not just you and a particular animal, but both of you together as part of nature.

RP: I've never met anyone who spends time getting close to animals who isn't more of a person because of it. Just as the modern whaling industry brings out the worst in people, having the courage to love an animal brings out the very best in people. That's what courage is—the willingness to admit, even in the face of adversity or nonacceptance, that you love something. Blowing everything away that threatens you like Rambo isn't courage, it's cowardice. Admitting you love something, that's courage.

JW: I met a man in eastern Oregon who loves birds and spends a lot of time around them. We called him the birdman. At one point in our conversation he raised his hand and whistled and within four or five seconds a chickadee flew in and perched on his finger. He brought the bird up close to his face and fed it a seed from his palm. It was such a tender, honorable contact between them, a huge man and a tiny bird. It seems that many of us are seeking a personal connection—a sense of belonging or acceptance—through our encounters in the field.

RP: Everybody could gain something from having more contact with the natural world. It brings rewards unequaled by anything else they could find in the human world. A friend of mine, Bill Eddy, says, "When you live in a world that is created entirely by people, like a city, eventually you begin to confuse the creator with human beings. And the bible of that world, in which the virtues of the creator are extolled on every page, is the Sears Roebuck catalog."

If people are willing to give themselves the gift of some improvement in their life, there is nothing that can beat having a deep and prolonged contact with nature. There's nothing I know of that's likely to be more rewarding. I once had a chickadee perch on my finger and take a seed from my hand. I'll never forget it. Never. Any situation where you allow an animal to trust you, and you trust it, builds a faith in your ability and the truth of what that represents. I think nothing could be a greater gift.

# Organizations Concerned with the Protection of Whales

Advisory Committee on
    Protection of the Seas
57 Duke Street, Grosvenor Square
London W1M 5DH
England

American Association of Zoological
    Parks and Aquariums
Oglebay Park
Wheeling, WV 26003-1698

American Cetacean Society
P.O. Box 2639
San Pedro, CA 90731-0943

American Oceans Campaign
725 Arizona Avenue, Suite 102
Santa Monica, CA 90401

Animal Welfare Institute
Box 3650
Washington, DC 20007

Aquatic Conservation Network
540 Roosevelt Avenue
Ottawa, ON K2A 1Z8
Canada

Bahamas National Trust
P.O. Box N4105
Nassau, Bahamas

Canadian Department of Fisheries
    and Oceans
P.O. Box 5667
St. John's, NF A1C 5X1
Canada

Canadian Nature Federation
453 Sussex Drive
Ottawa, ON K1N 6Z4
Canada

Center for Environmental
    Information
46 Prince Street
Rochester, NY 14607-1016

Center for Marine Conservation
1725 De Sales Street NW,
    Suite 500
Washington, DC 20036

Commission for the Conservation
    of Antarctic Marine Living
    Resources
25 Old Wharf
Hobart, TAS 7000
Australia

Conservation Agency
6 Swinburne Street
Jamestown, RI 02835

Cousteau Society, Inc.
930 West 21st Street
Norfolk, VA 23517

Defenders of Wildlife
1101 14th Street NW, Suite 1400
Washington, DC 20005

Earth Island Institute
300 Broadway, Suite 28
San Francisco, CA 94133

Earth Preservation Fund
4011 Jackson Road
Ann Arbor, MI 48103

Earthtrust
25 Kaneohe Bay Drive
Kailua, HI 96734-1711

Earthwatch
Box 403N
680 Mt. Auburn Street
Watertown, MA 02272

Earthwatch Europe
Belsyre Court
57 Woodstock Road
Oxford 0X2 6HU
England

Elsa Nature Conservancy
Tsukuba-Gakuen, P.O. Box 2
Tsukuba 305, Ibraki
Japan

Environmental Action Foundation
6930 Carroll Avenue, Suite 600
Takoma Park, MD 20912

Environmental Defense Fund
257 Park Avenue South
New York, NY 10010

Friends of the Earth
1025 Vermont Avenue NW,
    Suite 300
Washington, DC 20005

Friends of the Earth
    International
Keizersgracht 176
1016 DW Amsterdam
The Netherlands

Fund for the Animals
200 West 57th Street
New York, NY 10019

Grand Manan Whale and Seabird
    Research Station
P.O. Box 9, North Head
Grand Manan, NB E0G 2M0
Canada

Greenpeace, USA
1436 U Street NW
Washington, DC 20009

The Humane Society of the
    United States
2100 L Street NW
Washington, DC 20037

International Oceanographic
    Foundation
4600 Rickenbacker Causeway
Virginia Key
Miami, FL 33149

International Union for
Conservation of Nature
and Natural Resources
28 Rue Mauverney
1196 Gland
Switzerland

International Whaling Commission
The Red House
135 Station Road, Histon
Cambridge CB4 4NP
England

The Marine Mammal Center
Marin Headlands
Golden Gate National
Recreation Area
Sausalito, CA 94965

National Audubon Society
700 Broadway
New York, NY 10003

National Coalition for Marine
Conservation
P.O. Box 23298
Savannah, GA 31403

National Museum of Natural
History
Casilla Correo 399
1100 Montevideo
Uruguay

Natural Resources Council
of America
801 Pennsylvania Avenue SE,
Suite 410
Washington, DC 20003

Natural Resources Defense
Council
40 West 20th Street
New York, NY 10011

National Wildlife Federation
1400 16th Street NW
Washington, DC 20036-2266

Nature Conservancy
1815 North Lynn Street
Arlington, VA 22209

New England Aquarium
Central Wharf
Boston, MA 02110

New York Zoological Society
Bronx Zoo
185th Street & Southern
Boulevard
Bronx, NY 10460

Pacific Whale Foundation
101 North Kihei Road, 2nd Floor
Kihei, HI 96753

Project Jonah
9 Trelawney Street
Eastwood, NSW 2153
Australia

Rachel Carson Council
8490 Jones Mill Road
Chevy Chase, MD 20815

Sierra Club
730 Polk Street
San Francisco, CA 94109

Sierra Club Legal Defense Fund
180 Montgomery Street,
    Suite 1400
San Francisco, CA 94104

The Tarlton Foundation
50 Francisco Street,
    Suite 103
San Francisco, CA 94133

Union Québécoise pour
    la conservation
    de la nature
160 76 Rue Est
Charlesbourg, PQ G1H 7H6
Canada

Whale Conservation Institute
191 Weston Road
Lincoln, MA 01773

Worldwatch Institute
1766 Massachusetts Avenue NW
Washington, DC 20036

World Wide Fund for Nature
Avenue du Mont-Blanc
1196 Gland
Switzerland

World Wildlife Fund
1250 24th Street NW, Suite 400
Washington, DC 20037

# Further Reading

Ackerman, Diane. *The Moon by Whale Light.* New York: Random House, 1991.

Allen, K. R. *Conservation and Management of Whales.* Seattle: University of Washington Press, 1980.

Andersen, H. T., ed. *The Biology of Marine Mammals.* New York: Academic Press, 1969.

Baker, A. N. *Whales and Dolphins of New Zealand and Australia.* Victoria: Victoria University Press, 1983.

Berzin, A. A. *The Sperm Whale.* Jerusalem: Israel Program for Scientific Translations, 1972.

Bigg, Michael A., et al. *Killer Whales.* Nanaimo, B.C.: Phantom Press, 1987.

Bockstoce, J. *Whales, Ice, and Men: The History of Whaling in the Western Arctic.* Seattle: University of Washington Press, 1986.

Bodfish, H. H. *Chasing the Bowhead.* Cambridge: Harvard University Press, 1936.

Boeri, David. *People of the Ice Whale.* San Diego: Harcourt Brace, 1985.

Bonner, N. *Whales.* London: Blandford Press, 1980.

Boschung, H. T., Jr., et al. *The Audubon Society Field Guide to North American Fishes, Whales and Dolphins.* New York: Knopf, 1983.

Brower, Kenneth, and W. R. Curtsinger. *Wake of the Whale.* New York: Friends of the Earth, 1979.

Burton, R. *The Life and Death of Whales.* New York: Universe Books, 1973.

Carrighar, Sally. *Icebound Summer.* New York: Knopf, 1953.

Coerr, Eleanor, and William E. Evans. *Gigi: A Baby Whale Borrowed for Science and Returned to the Sea.* New York: Putnam, 1980.

Coffey, D. J. *Dolphins, Whales and Porpoises.* New York: Macmillan, 1977.

Connor, Richard C., and Dawn M. Peterson. *The Lives of Whales and Dolphins.* New York: Holt, 1994.

Cook, J. A. *Pursuing the Whale: A Quarter-Century of Whaling in the Arctic.* Boston: Houghton Mifflin, 1926.

Cook, Joseph J., and William L. Wisner. *Killer Whale!* New York: Dodd, Mead, 1963.

Corrigan, Patricia. *Where the Whales Are.* Old Saybrook, Conn.: The Globe Pequot Press, 1991.

Cousteau, Jacques-Yves, and Philippe Diole. *The Whale: Mighty Monarch of the Sea.* New York: Doubleday, 1972.

Darling, James. *With the Whales.* Minocqua, Wis: North Word Press, 1990.

Ellis, Richard. *The Book of Whales.* New York: Knopf, 1980.

Evans, P. G. H. *The Natural History of Whales and Dolphins.* New York: Facts on File, 1987.

Ford, John K. B., G. Ellis, and K. C. Balcomb. *Killer Whales.* Seattle: University of Washington Press, 1994.

Francis, Daniel. *A History of World Whaling.* Markham, Ont.: Viking, 1990.

Fraser, F. C. *British Whales, Dolphins, and Porpoises: A Guide for the Indentification and Reporting of Stranded Whales.* London: British Museum, 1976.

Gaskin, D. E. *Ecology of Whales and Dolphins.* London: Heinemann, 1982.

————. *Whales, Dolphins and Seals: With Special Reference to the New Zealand Region.* London: Heinemann, 1972.

Gormley, Gerard. *Orcas of the Gulf.* Sàn Francisco: Sierra Club Books, 1990.

————. *A Dolphin Summer.* New York: Taplinger, 1985.

Griffin, Donald R. *Animal Thinking.* Cambridge: Harvard University Press, 1984.

————. *The Question of Animal Awareness.* Los Altos, Calif.: William Kaufman, 1981.

Griffin, Edward I. *Namu: Quest for the Killer Whale.* Seattle: Gryphon West Publishers, 1982.

Haley, Delphine, et al. *Marine Mammals of Eastern North Pacific and Arctic Waters.* Seattle: Pacific Search Press, 1978.

Hand, Douglas. *Gone Whaling: A Search for Orcas in Northwest Waters.* New York: Simon & Schuster, 1994.

Harrison, R. J. *Functional Anatomy of Marine Mammals.* 3 vols. London: Academic Press, 1972, 1974, 1977.

Harrison, R. J., and J. E. King. *Marine Mammals.* London: Hutchinson University Library, 1965.

Herman, Louis, ed. *Cetacean Behavior: Mechanism and Functions.* New York: Wiley, 1980.

Howell, A. B. *Aquatic Mammals: Their Adaptations to Life in the Water.* New York: Dover, 1970.

Hoyt, Erich. *A Whale Called Killer.* New York: Dutton, 1981.

Hunter, Robert. *Warriors of the Rainbow: A Chronicle of the Greenpeace Movement.* New York: Holt, 1979.

Jones, Mary Lou et al. *The Gray Whale.* New York: Academic Press, 1984.

Katona, Steven K., Valerie Rough, and David T. Richardson. *A Field Guide to the Whales, Porpoises and Seals of the Gulf of Maine and Eastern Canada.* New York: Scribner's, 1984.

Kirdevold, Barbara C., and Joan S. Lockard, eds. *Behavioral Biology of Killer Whales.* New York: Alan R. Liss, 1986.

Laws, R. M., ed. *Antarctic Ecology.* London: Academic Press, 1984.

Leatherwood, Stephen, R. R. Reeves, and L. Foster. *The Sierra Club Handbook of Whales and Dolphins.* San Francisco: Sierra Club Books, 1983.

Leatherwood, Stephen, et al. *Whales, Dolphins and Porpoises of the Eastern North Pacific and Adjacent Waters.* New York: Dover, 1988.

Lockley, R. M. *Whales, Dolphins, and Porpoises.* New York: W. W. Norton, 1979.

Lopez, Barry. *Arctic Dreams.* New York: Scribner's, 1986.

McIntrye, Joan, ed. *Mind in the Waters.* New York/San Francisco: Scribner's/Sierra Club, 1974.

McNally, Robert. *So Remorseless a Havoc.* Boston: Little Brown, 1981.

McNulty, Faith. *The Great Whales.* New York: Doubleday, 1974.

Matthews, L. Harrison. *The Natural History of the Whale.* New York: Columbia University Press, 1978.

———. *Penguins, Whalers, and Sealers.* New York: Universe Books, 1978.

———. *The Whale.* New York: Simon & Schuster, 1968.

Mayo, Charles, Carole Carlson, Phil Clapham, and Dave Mattila. *Humpback Whales of the Southern Gulf of Maine.* Provincetown, Mass.: Center for Coastal Studies, 1985.

Minasian, S. M., K. C. Balcomb III, and L. Foster. *The World's Whales.* New York: W. W. Norton and Smithsonian Books, 1984.

Mowat, Farley. *A Whale for the Killing.* New York: Little, Brown, 1972.

Murphy, R. C. *A Dead Whale or a Stove Boat.* Boston: Houghton Mifflin, 1967.

———. *Logbook for Grace.* New York: Macmillan, 1947.

Nayman, Jacqueline. *Whales, Dolphins and Man.* London: Hamlyn, 1974.

Nickerson, R. *Brother Whale: A Pacific Whalewatcher's Log.* San Francisco: Chronicle, 1977.

Norman, J. R., and F. C. Fraser. *Giant Fishes, Whales and Dolphins.* London: Putnam, 1937.

Norris, Kenneth S. *The Porpoise Watcher: A Naturalist's Experiences with Porpoises and Whales.* New York: W. W. Norton, 1974.

————, ed. *Whales, Dolphins, and Porpoises*. Berkeley: University of California Press, 1966.

Obee, Bruce, and Graeme Ellis. *Guardians of the Whales: The Quest to Study Whales in the Wild*. Seattle: Alaska Northwest Books, 1992.

Ommaney, F. D. *Lost Leviathan, Whales and Whaling*. New York: Dodd, Mead, 1971.

Payne, Roger, ed. *Communication and Behavior of Whales*. Boulder: Westview Press, 1983.

Purves, P. E., and G. E. Pilleri. *Echolocation in Whales and Dolphins*. New York: Academic Press, 1983.

Ridgway, S. H., ed. *Mammals of the Sea: Biology and Medicine*. Springfield, Ill.: Thomas, 1972.

Robinson, F. D. *Thinking Dolphins, Talking Whales*. Wellington, New Zealand: Reed, 1976.

Scammon, C. M. *The Marine Mammals of the North-Western Coast of North America, Described and Illustrated*. San Francisco: John Carmany, 1874; rpt., New York: Dover, 1968.

Scheffer, Victor B. *A Natural History of Marine Mammals*. New York: Scribner's, 1976.

————. *The Year of the Whale*. New York: Scribner's, 1969.

Schevill, W. E., ed. *The Whale Problem: A Status Report*. Cambridge: Harvard University Press, 1974.

Slijper, E. J. *Whales*. London: Hutchinson, 1979.

————. *Whales and Dolphins*. Ann Arbor: University of Michigan Press, 1976.

Small, G. L. *The Blue Whale*. New York: Columbia University Press, 1971.

Watson, L. *Sea Guide to Whales of the World*. New York: Dutton, 1981.

————. *Whales*. New York: Basic Books, 1962.

Whitehead, Hal. *Voyage to the Whales*. Port Mills, Vt.: Chelsea Green, 1990.

Whittell, Giles. *The Story of Three Whales*. Vancouver, B.C.: Douglas & McIntyre, 1988.

Winn, H. E., and B. L. Olla, eds. *Behavior of Marine Animals: Current Perspectives in Research*. Vol. 3, *Cetaceans*. New York: Plenum, 1979.

Winn, L. K., and H. E. Winn. *Wings in the Sea: The Humpback Whale*. Hanover, N.H.: University Press of New England, 1985.

————. *Whales*. New York: Basic Books, 1962.

# Index

*Numbers followed by* n *refer to footnotes.*

# About Frank Stewart

A resident of the Hawaiian Islands since 1966, Frank Stewart is a teacher and writer who makes his home on Oahu and on the slopes of Hawai`i's Maunu Kea volcano. His books include, most recently, *A Natural History of Nature Writing* and *A World Between Waves*. Stewart's nature writing has also appeared widely in magazines and has been anthologized in *A Thousand Leagues of Blue: The Sierra Club Book of the Pacific* and *Nature's New Voices*. A poet as well as an essayist, he is a winner of the prestigious Whiting Writers Award. He is professor of English at the University of Hawai`i in Honolulu and editor of *Manoa: A Pacific Journal of International Writing*.